Rebound 1995

1982

Abortion: Readings and Research

Paul Sachdev

Butterworths
Toronto

Abortion: Readings and Research
© 1981 Butterworth & Co. (Canada) Ltd.

Printed and bound in Canada

The Butterworth Group of Companies

Canada:
Butterworth & Co. (Canada) Ltd., Toronto and Vancouver

United Kingdom:
Butterworth & Co. (Publishers) Ltd., London

Australia:
Butterworths Pty. Ltd., Sydney

New Zealand:
Butterworths of New Zealand Ltd., Wellington

South Africa:
Butterworth & Co. (South Africa) Ltd., Durban

United States:
Butterworth (Publishers) Inc., Boston
Butterworth (Legal Publishers) Inc., Seattle
Mason Publishing Company, St. Paul

Canadian Cataloguing in Publication Data

Main entry under title:

Abortion: readings and research

ISBN 0-409-86517-6

1. Abortion. 2. Abortion — Canada. I. Sachdev, Paul.

HQ767.A26   363.4'6   C81-094550-9

Printed by Alger Press
Cover design by Julian Cleva

To My Parents
To Whom I Am Fondly Indebted

Contents

Contributors

David Andres, PhD
Department of Psychology, Concordia University, Montreal.

Charlene Berger, PhD
Department of Obstetrics and Gynecology, Montreal General Hospital and Department of Psychology, Concordia University, Montreal, Quebec.

Willard Cates, Jr., MD, MPH
Chief, Abortion Surveillance Branch, Family Planning Evaluation Division, Bureau of Epidemiology, Center for Disease Control, Atlanta, Georgia.

Sharon Chapman-Sheehan, BA, BSW, MSW
Supervisor, Kawartha-Haliburton Children's Aid Society, Peterborough, and Clinical Lecturer, Family of Health Services, McMaster University, Hamilton, Ontario.

Henry P. David, PhD
Director, Transnational Family Research Institute and Associate Clinical Professor (Psychology), Department of Psychiatry, University of Maryland Medical School, Baltimore.

M. Corinne Devlin, MD, FRCS (C), FACOG
Associate Professor, Department of Obstetrics and Gynecology, McMaster University and Director, Reproductive Regulation Clinic, Chedoke-McMaster Hospitals, Hamilton, Ontario.

Milton Diamond, PhD
Professor, School of Medicine, University of Hawaii, Honolulu, Hawaii.

Bernard M. Dickens, LLB, LLM, PhD, LLD
Faculty of Law and Centre of Criminology, University of Toronto.

Peter Gillett, MD
Department of Obstetrics and Gynecology, Montreal General Hospital, McGill University, Montreal.

Esther Greenglass, PhD
Associate Professor, Department of Psychology, York University, Downsview, Ontario.

Robert A. Kinch, MD, FRCS (C)
Professor and Chairman, Department of Obstetrics and Gynecology, McGill University, Montreal, Quebec.

Paul MacKenzie, MD
Department of Obstetrics and Gynecology, Queen's University, Kingston, Ontario.

Richard W. Osborn, PhD
Professor and Chairman, Department of Preventive Medicine and Biostatistics, Faculty of Medicine, University of Toronto, Toronto, Ontario.

Keith Ian Pearce, MD, MB, BS, MRCS, LRCP, FRCP (C), MRC Psych.
Professor and Head, Division of Psychiatry, Faculty of Medicine, University of Calagary and Director, Department of Psychiatry, Foothills Hospital, Calgary, Alberta.

Morton S. Rapp, MD
Associate Professor, Department of Psychiatry, Sunnybrook Hospital, Toronto, Ontario.

Hyman Rodman
Director, Family Research Centre, University of North Carolina, Greensboro, N.C.

Paul Sachdev, PhD
Associate Professor, School of Social Work, Memorial University of Newfoundland, St. John's, Newfoundland.

Nathan M. Simon, MD
Associate Clinical Professor, St. Louis University School of Medicine and Training and Supervising Analyst, St. Louis Psychoanalytic Institute, St. Louis, Mo.

Christopher Tietze, MD
Senior Consultant, The Population Council, New York, NY.

Alphonse de Valk
Principal, St. Joseph's University College, University of Alberta.

Mary K. Zimmerman, PhD
Assistant Professor, Department of Behavioural Sciences, University of Minnesota, Duluth.

Preface

No other public issue in modern times has generated such fierce controversy and polarization as abortion. The central difficulty in the controversy is the question of when human life begins. This has raised questions about the sanctity of life, the meaning of sexuality, legal policy, abortion indications and government's role. The controversy remains largely unresolved, while the debate pendulum swings between a partial liberal and a more liberal climate, depending upon the relative strength of the pro-life and pro-choice arguments at the time. Despite moral questions the demand for abortion has not abated. Today more than two-thirds of the world's population live in countries which permit legal abortions on various grounds. The experts agree that in view of the currently available volitional contraceptive means, abortion will continue to be used either as an alternative or as a supplement to contraception.

The accelerated demand for abortion among Canadian women has stimulated interest on the part of a variety of professional groups in seeking knowledge about or rendering services to abortion seekers. This book represents the first attempt to amalgamate the rich experience of Canadian scholars and to bring together in one sourcebook the widely scattered research efforts conducted in the Canadian context. American authors are included to provide not only a transnational perspective but also to address issues of paramount importance to professionals and general readers on both sides of the border. In this sense the value of the book is not limited to a Canadian audience since concerns and issues regarding the subject of abortion are similar in both countries.

All the papers with the exception of two have been written specifically for this volume. Their authors represent a wide assortment of professions including psychology, social work, demography, sociology, medicine, and psychiatry, and many of them enjoy national and international reputations. In soliciting the papers the authors were encouraged to follow the criteria that (a) the work should be primarily research-oriented so that the presentation maintains factual specificity and avoids emotional and moral overtones; (b) it should not emphasize a particular position or engage in a prescriptive approach, but present a balanced and holistic viewpoint so as to permit prudent reflection on the issues involved; (c) the papers by the U.S. authors should as far as possible refer to the

Canadian data so that the presentation provides a comparative analysis of the issues; and (d) only non-medical aspects should be discussed. This approach, it is hoped, will permit the reader to make interpretation and application of the conclusions based on credible data.

The volume is not comprehensive in content coverage. Yet it addresses a range of issues most pertinent to the interests of academics and an informed public. If the book proves useful to a variety of professionals and para-professionals such as physicians, social workers, psychiatrists, nurses, sociologists, psychologists, demographers, and hospital administrators in their research, teaching, administration or counselling pursuits then the author will have fulfilled his purpose.

The task of developing a reader is a collaborative venture, and I thoroughly enjoyed this professional alliance and a sense of bonding with my colleagues. I am grateful to each of the contributors. They were remarkably responsive to my comments and showed an extraordinary patience in implementing editorial suggestions. Certainly they deserve my special debt of gratitude, for it is their contributions which have provided this volume with its range of utility and appeal.

I owe a special debt of gratitude to Dr. Christopher Tietze, who not only contributed his thoughtful chapter on schedule, but also assisted me in my efforts to contact experts in the field. My colleague Dr. Frank R. Hawkins provided me with the benefit of his critical evaluation of my work.

Finally, I want to pay tribute to my wife, Sudarshan, who provided me with the benefit of her critical intelligence and immeasurable support.

Part 1
Abortion: An Overview

Introduction

The amendment to the Criminal Code of Canada on August 26, 1969 provides for a woman who wishes to seek legal termination of her pregnancy in a hospital, in situations assessed as threatening to her life or health. Despite incessant controversy, the demand for legal abortions has continued to rise since the passage of the revised abortion law. The papers included in this section examine the multiple social and political forces in Canada which in consort led to the emergence of abortion out of back alleys. The papers review the impact of legalized abortion on the unwanted/unplanned pregnancies among married and unmarried women.

Valk identifies in his paper the forces and circumstances which catalyzed changes in political and social attitudes toward greater acceptance of legalized abortion, and he stresses the key role the news media and editorials played in shaping the public opinion. The author observes that the abortion reform movement was much aided by the permissive social climate created by the birth control controversy and the trend toward greater sexual freedom in the early 1960s.

Canada's revised abortion law is equivocal on two crucial provisions, namely the health of the mother and the gestational age limit to abortion. Dickens provides an analytical interpretation of the law including the legal meaning of "health." He argues that since pregnancy is not inherently dangerous to health, there is no objective way of predicting its psychological ill effects to the woman in the event she is forced to continue it against her wish. The critical test of legality is, therefore, not the accuracy of prediction but whether the physician reached his medical decision in good faith. It is noteworthy that the law confers an absolute right on the woman, adult or minor, to consent to her abortion, and prohibits her spouse, biological father, or parents to either impose or veto the abortion for which she is legally eligible. The author contends that the amended law, in fact, adds no additional grounds and the pre-amended method of justifying abortion *ex post facto* remains in effect. Accordingly, lawful abortion can be performed without prior certification by a therapeutic abortion committee.

Rapp is concerned with the dilemma psychiatrists face in the Canadian abortion law. This dilemma stems, firstly, from the moral controversy which has prevented abortion from achieving the legitimacy and status of other psychiatric therapies; secondly, from their personal value stance on the issue; and thirdly, from the ambiguities and vagueness in the interpretation of the law, especially

4 ABORTION: READINGS AND RESEARCH

the word "health." This is further complicated by the tenuous nature of the consequences that might result if abortion is denied to the woman. Thus, the decision-making in abortion surgery, he observes, is not a rational process.

It is interesting to note that despite the widespread use of abortion, the incidence of births out-of-wedlock has not shown a decline, as is revealed in Mackenzie's comprehensive survey of the operation of Canada's abortion law. During the period between 1970 and 1979, the abortion rates increased from 3.0 per cent to 18.1 per cent of live births, for a total of 397,000 legal abortions performed on Canadian residents. In comparison to other countries, however, the Canadian abortion rates are lower than those for European countries with the exception of Scotland, and the United States. Young, primiparous, never-married women constitute the highest proportion among the abortion seekers. The author claims that the overall decline in Canada's birth rate is due to the increased use of contraception and sterilization by married women. Significantly, abortion mortality among Canadian women is extremely rare and medical complications following the procedure are lower than those associated with a term pregnancy.

The goal of effective fertility control can only be achieved through the dual methods of abortion and contraception. But most governments hope that sexually active couples do not rely on abortion as another method of contraception but view it as a backup measure should contraception fail. The Canadian legislatures amending the abortion laws expected that contraceptive instruction would eventually foster effective contraceptive behaviour among fertile couples, thereby reducing the demand for abortion. But as is shown by Tietze in his paper, the relationship between contraceptive use and abortion is not simple. Using international data he demonstrates that women who use contraception are more likely to have experienced abortions, and vice versa, in a society where both are equally accessible. The author observes that an extensive utilization of abortion may either precede or follow adoption of contraception, but a sustained reduction in birth rate is achieved only through reliance on effective contraception while using abortion as a back-up measure.

1

Abortion Politics: Canadian Style*

Alphonse de Valk

Among lawyers there is a saying: hard cases make poor laws. In 1962 there was a celebrated legal case, the case of the Van de Put family in Liege, Belgium. This case aroused interest throughout the world, including Canada. One week after having given birth to a baby girl born without arms as a result of taking the drug thalidomide, the mother agreed with her husband, her sister, her mother and the family doctor, to give the newborn baby barbiturates in a mixture of honey. Subsequently all five were charged with murder. There was much popular sentiment favouring the defendants and a demand for acquittal.

The defence was based on the assertion that the five defendants felt pity for a "hopelessly condemned and wretched human being who faced a prospective existence without a glimmer of human existence." In his summation the defence attorney stated:

> If you tell the accused that they are not guilty you will have found the human conclusion to this trial. If these people chose a solution which may be erroneous they have only to account to their own conscience. God, perhaps, has already forgiven them. You may disapprove of the stand they took, but you cannot condemn them.

The all-male jury found the defendants not guilty.[1]

Major newspapers throughout Europe and America seemed to consider this verdict just and equitable. One exception was the Vatican daily, the *Osservatore Romano*, which considered the verdict of "not guilty" a mistake and an unhappy omen.

Another cause célèbre which also received much publicity in 1962 was the case of Mrs. Finkbine of Arizona. Here, too, public opinion seemed to be on the side of the mother. Mrs. Finkbine, a Phoenix housewife and local television performer, believed her baby might be deformed as a consequence of her taking

---

*This article is published in pamphlet form by the Life Ethics Centre, St. Joseph's University College, University of Alberta, Edmonton, T6G 2J5.

the thalidomide drug. Upon being denied an abortion in Arizona, the then 30-year-old mother of four flew to Sweden for an abortion. Later on, the fetus was reported deformed.[2]

The thalidomide crisis of 1962 and 1963, with its hundreds of horribly deformed babies, was an indication of how deeply and rapidly the consensus about abortion was changing during the early 1960s. While it was short-lived it was, nevertheless, of lasting importance. First, it suddenly revealed that many people were quite prepared to allow and accept abortion. Second, it became clear that they were prepared to do so on the mere *possibility* of a baby being born seriously deformed.

From 1963 on, the rule of "hard cases make poor laws" was forgotten. American periodicals such as *Pageant*, the *Saturday Evening Post*, *Parents Magazine*, the *Atlantic Monthly*, *Redbook* and others, which of course were also widely read in English-speaking Canada, all pleaded for liberalized abortion laws. The subject was usually dealt with in a standard version, opening with a horror story of a bungled back-street abortion, followed by a statement of indignation at the absence of safe legal ways of doing abortions, and proceeding with quotes from eminent doctors in favour of making abortions legal. The article would then move on to a consideration of proposed law reforms and conclude with an illustration of a particular bill going through a state legislature. The illustration would suggest that members of only one Church opposed the new legislation, and that the attitude of this Church compared unfavourably with that of what were usually called the more "broadminded" and "progressive" religious bodies. Indeed, it was implied, the attitude of this Church could be explained only as an unacceptable attempt to impose the views of a minority upon the majority.[3]

In Canada the periodical most persistently in favour of legalizing abortions was the much-read women's magazine *Chatelaine* under the editorship of Doris Anderson. In August 1959 it was the first popular magazine to publish an article and editorial calling for a change in the legal prohibition of abortion. From the beginning of the 1960s until Anderson's retirement in the mid-1970s, the magazine spearheaded or championed a variety of attacks upon traditional sexual and family morality, usually in the name of liberating women from the shackles of the past. However, a further mention of abortion had to wait four years until the spring of 1963, when the already noted thalidomide crisis suddenly opened new possibilities for changing the law. This second article written by a United Church Minister, Rev. Ray Goodall, marked the beginning of a more general campaign in Canada for what instantly came to be called "liberalizing" the law.

In May 1963 *Chatelaine* was joined by the United Church *Observer*, a monthly with several hundred thousand subscribers, where Goodall repeated his plea for a new law. Already three years earlier, the General Council of the United Church, the single largest body of Protestants in the country, had approved abortion as an emergency measure while still condemning it in general as the destruction of life. As a church body where principles of faith and morals are decided by majority vote, the discussion had been one of the briefest, with someone moving, someone seconding and, after a few questions, the Council approving the emergency resolution without apparently anyone realizing what it was that they had done. From 1963 onwards the logic of that decision was to become apparent: having accepted the legitimacy of killing unborn life in principle in 1960, the Church's stand would shift from year to year until by 1970 it favoured free abortion on request. When, in the mid-1960s, an Anglican Task Force followed suit in approving abortion in principle (while, of course, professing opposition to abortion in general) it seemed to many that approval of abortion by Christians in general was only a question of time, that is to say, as soon as their outmoded morality had caught up with progress and enlightenment.

The most important champion of legal abortion in Canada was the Toronto daily paper, the *Globe and Mail*. Unlike other Canadian newspapers which more or less went along with the general trend towards more liberal and permissive laws, but whose editors had no strong or definitive views on the matter, the *Globe* hammered on the issue throughout the 1960s. Its views represent those of a fairly small but, in English-speaking Canada, very influential school of intellectual liberalism which appears to have as its basic standard the idea that all moral standards supported by religion are suspect.

The *Globe*'s earliest call for a change in the law came in an editorial of September 1961, following which it published a series of seven articles by prominent individuals representing law, medicine and the churches. Only one of the seven, the Catholic spokesman, rejected abortion outright. Following this preliminary attempt, the *Globe* began its campaign in earnest in 1963. From then on it published more editorials on the subject than all major Canadian newspapers combined. It kept at it until the law was changed in May 1969 and then resumed writing in favour of abortion on demand in 1970 once it discovered that, in spite of the new law, residual opposition remained effective. Like the Canadian Broadcasting Corporation, it was to lionize Dr. Henry Morgentaler in the early and mid-1970s as a champion of freedom against intellectual obscurantists and reactionary forces.

The reasons which the editorial writers of the *Globe and Mail* have given for their stand during these years have varied from editorial to editorial. At the beginning of the controversy, in 1961, the *Globe and Mail* claimed that in view of the number of illegal abortions, the existing law was being rejected, and that "a law which is rejected by the public is seldom a sound law."[4] Already at that time, it cautiously queried whether "women should be allowed to make their own moral decision," and whether churches should have the right to present their view of the moral issue to anyone other than their own adherents. At the beginning of 1963 the *Globe* declared that a law which no longer conformed to the practices of society could bring all law into contempt.[5] Abortion, it said a few months later, "raised the whole difficult problem" of the relationship between law and morality.

The *Globe* continued to publish editorials on abortion during the next few years. By the close of 1966 the paper had repeatedly asserted that abortion was a question of private morality and that law, therefore, should *not* be concerned with it. As an explanation as to why the law had made abortion its concern in the past, the paper offered religious beliefs which it now declared both outmoded and representative only of a minority.

During 1967 the *Globe and Mail* went further in two directions. First, the paper now maintained that abortion was not a question of morality at all, but only of medicine. Decisions for abortions, therefore, should be left in the hands of the medical profession, a view which, by then, coincided with that of the Canadian Medical Association. Secondly, the paper began to place more emphasis on the women's liberation philosophy.[6] In an October editorial, the *Globe* attempted to have it both ways, arguing at once that the decision whether or not an abortion should be performed "should legally reside with the medical profession," and also that every woman should be permitted to have an abortion as a matter of right.[7]

Also by the end of 1967 the *Globe and Mail* had become more impatient. While the House of Commons Standing Committee on Health and Welfare conducted its hearings on abortion (in the name of Canada's politicians), the *Globe* claimed that the elected representatives were being intimidated by "what they know is not the majority of the Canadian people."[8] The reference, once again, clearly was to Roman Catholics whose spokesmen, however, had said next to nothing on the subject up till then. But this silence, as that of Protestant bodies other than Anglicans and the United Church, was based on the assumption that the unacceptability of legalizing abortion was still as self-evident as it had always been. It was this hidden weight of tradition which increasingly vexed the *Globe*'s editorial writers. When in February 1968 the Roman Catholic Bishops finally reiterated their traditional opposition to abortion in a modest, low-key statement marked more by questions and suggestions for delay than by a forceful exposition of why legalizing abortion was intolerable, the *Globe* exploded with its most menacing editorial yet, starting with the line: "One wonders if once again the conscience of some Roman Catholic Canadians will be allowed to violate that of millions of other Canadians." The editorial concluded: "At stake here . . . is a certain high conception of liberal democracy."[9] Accidentally or conveniently, the *Globe* overlooked that the Bishops had made a point of explaining how their opposition to abortion was *not* the consequence of some religious foible peculiar to Roman Catholics but rather the consequence of an understanding of the common good which should be common to everybody.

Before summarizing the overall trend and arguments of those in favour of changing the law, let us note that the issue of "legalizing" abortion came at a time when other issues affecting sexual morality, law, and authority were in dispute, with a general thrust towards an ever more permissive society. Especially we must not forget that the issue of abortion, which in the early part of the 1960s was only just beginning to come to people's attention, was overshadowed by the much more hotly debated issues of legalizing contraceptives and widening grounds for divorce. The new divorce law was passed in the summer of 1967; contraceptives became legally available at the same time as abortions, that is, in the spring of 1969. In each case there had been a retreat by the Churches, with the Anglican, the United Church, and some other Protestant bodies coming to accept the changes as in conformity with Christianity itself, while Roman Catholics adjusted to the law not by accepting the changes as legitimate to Christians in themselves, but by applying the ancient theological view that *civil* law does not in all cases have to reflect (Christian) *moral* law. Thus the Catholic Bishops continued to oppose divorce and contraceptives for their own faithful, while ceasing to oppose a more permissive approach in the laws of the country. Naturally, this shift in thinking, too, had its adverse effects on an already much-confused situation.

In order to disentangle the often contradictory thinking in the development of the pro-legalization view, it is necessary to recognize three interconnected threads, each with its own subsidiary points, some of which developed simultaneously and in parallel fashion, with others succeeding and replacing, and sometimes contradicting, earlier or even parallel arguments. The three threads concern, first, the nature of abortion; second, the nature of law and its relationship to morality; and third, the nature of the opposition and its arguments.

Developments concerning the nature of abortion itself are perhaps best illustrated by the attitude of the Canadian Medical Association. In 1963 the CMA still adhered to its own resolution that "the induction or procuring of abortion involves the destruction of life. It is a violation both of moral law and of the Criminal Code of Canada, except where there is justification for its performance." The only justification at all accepted by doctors at that time was the, by then, already hypothetical question of a pregnancy imperilling the life of the mother. In other words, Western civilization in general did not condone abortion at all. That this is so is clearly demonstrated, for example, by the medical code of ethics expressed in the 2,500-year-old Hippocratic oath which forbade the administering of abortion-causing instruments or drugs. Another example: when after World War II the World Medical Association wanted to draw doctors' attention to the unacceptable dissolution of medical ethics during that war through medical experiments on prisoners, it asked all doctors to subscribe to the Declaration of Geneva issued in September 1948 which says in part: "I will maintain the utmost respect for human life from the time of *conception*, even under threat, and I will not use my medical knowledge contrary to the laws of humanity. . ." (italics added).

Yet from 1963 on the CMA reversed its stand completely. First, doubts were raised whether the law did or did not forbid abortion. This was followed by a demand that doctors doing presumably medically necessary abortions be protected from an unclear law. By May 1965 the Ontario Medical Association had gone on record in support of lawful abortions if performed "to preserve the life or physical or mental health" of the woman, and by 1967 the CMA was convinced that abortions should be a question of medicine alone. Following the change of law in 1969, the CMA favoured social reasons by 1971; adopted a resolution for abortion on demand in 1973; removed the 2,500-year-old reference against abortifacients in the Hippocratic oath in 1975; and then, in 1977, declared abortion referrals a compulsory moral obligation for doctors who were personally opposed to doing them. This latter resolution, however, proved too much and had to be withdrawn in 1978.

The second thread, that of the nature of law and its relationship to morality, was the special concern of the Canadian Bar Association and the politicians, most of whom were lawyers. It relates closely to the third thread concerning the nature of the opposition to legalized abortions. In brief, the CBA and the government both came to accept the *Globe and Mail*'s "certain high conception of liberal democracy." This, in turn, is based on the modern liberal and utilitarian philosophy which has developed out of the nineteenth-century intellectual liberalism of John Stuart Mill. This philosophy denies that religious morality should have any influence on civil law at all. In order to preserve society, it is said, people must share *some* principles. But those basic principles are minimal and entirely rational and utilitarian. Religious principles or religious ideals are classified as non-rational and therefore belong to private morality. Sexual morality and mores, too, will fall under private morality and private judgment because they are based on "variable tastes and conventions." Hence, civil legislation ought to be separated completely from religious principles or morality. When we check the arguments used in 1968 and 1969 we find that the most frequently quoted phrases and most commonly expressed sentiments were that "sin is not the same as crime" and that morality ought to have nothing to do with civil law.[10]

In the area of public debate the promotion of this philosophy required the adoption of a twofold approach which included the arguments, first, that opponents of legal abortions were *imposing* their views on others; and second, that these views were religious and, therefore, emotional, non-rational, private, and not deserving of a place in the Criminal Code.

The conviction that no one has the right to impose personal views on society played an important, perhaps even decisive, role in the passage of new abortion legislation. According to the Oxford dictionary, to impose means: ". . . take advantage of (person); practice and deception (upon)." "To impose views" clearly conveyed the meaning of forcing beliefs upon people by undue means.

From the early 1960s on, the word "impose" increasingly implied a denial of the right to influence legislation, a denial which was directed especially against the churches and against religious leaders. It was used first with respect to the controversies about contraceptives and divorce mentioned earlier, but by the summer of 1967 it was being used regularly with respect to abortions. For example, in August 1967 an editorial in *Chatelaine* claimed that if the government "bowed" to the request of the Roman Catholic Church to delay legislation on abortion while the church prepared a report, "one segment of society will have imposed its views on the whole society again." At the parliamentary abortion hearing of March 5, 1968, Mrs. MacInnis wanted to know from the Bishops' delegation why the church insisted on "imposing" its views upon the rest of society. In April, 1968 the Anglican monthly, the *Canadian Churchman* wrote:

> In the area of abortion, contraception and homosexuality the choice is government by the individual's conscience. If his church is opposed then he has a moral obligation to obey his church's rules but he has no right to impose these rules on people of other faiths or no faith at all. There is a clear distinction between moral and civil law.

At this time the *Globe and Mail*, too, came out with the same charge once more in its March 11, 1968 editorial mentioned earlier.

The effectiveness of charging opponents of legalizing abortions with unduly attempting to coerce all of society was, of course, based on the double assumption that the opponents' views were mere private opinions and, second, that there were no objective ethical standards applicable to everyone. Suffice it to say that those who held these two assumptions proved victorious when government spokesmen declared the Criminal Code to be "neutral" and hence unsuited to incorporate a continued prohibition of abortions.

To illustrate the element of confusion as well as the interrelationship of all three threads we have only to place the principal reasons presented by the *Globe* over the seven years from 1960 to 1967 side by side: the existing law was inadequate because it was being *broken; law* should not reflect (religious) *morality* (and certainly not the morality of a minority); only Roman Catholics opposed a change in the law; these Catholics had no *right* to do so; abortion was a question of *private* morality; abortion was not a question of morality at all but of *medicine*; doctors alone should decide whether *health* reasons require abortions; and, finally, every woman ought to be able to have an abortion as a matter of *right*. When we look beyond the *Globe* to other arguments we find such views — widely accepted for short periods of time — that abortion did not involve a separate life but was only concerned with a blob of tissue; again, the idea that the aborted tissue was not human; or the view that if it were human, it wouldn't be human in the sense of those already born.

Let us not proceed to relate how the law was changed, nor what positions were taken by other public, semi-public and private bodies, nor how the debate evolved in the House of Commons, all of which may be found elsewhere. We know that the law was finally changed in May 1969. We also know the change was worded in such a way as to permit virtual abortion on demand. From the parliamentary debates in 1969 it is clear that this development was contrary to the expressly stated purpose of the government which intended to permit abortion only under fairly restricted circumstances. It is only one of a number of unhappy consequences foreseen by opponents but not by the government. Let me simply quote from my account of those debates to illustrate once more the confusion which reigned at the time:

Taking the nine speakers as representative of the party as a whole, it is clear that the motivations for accepting new abortion legislation were extremely varied and often contradictory. It was almost a case of nine different people with nine different reasons. One member supported the legislation because he did not think that existing law permitted any abortions at all. Another member favoured it because, like the Minister of Justice, he thought that a law which already permitted abortions needed further clarification. A third did not believe a foetus was human and thought that it was merely a question of preserving a woman's health. A fourth speaker, however, was convinced that the unborn child was alive and human, but that society needed compromise. A fifth accepted the proposals only as a step forward on the road to abortion on demand, contradicting others who favoured the new law but who vigorously denied that abortion on demand was either desirable in itself or would result from the proposed legislation. A sixth gave criminal assault on a woman as his sole reason — without noticing that the Government specifically meant to exclude abortions for rape. Finally, several speakers who presumably had voted numerous bills into law against the wishes of others, asserted that in the matter of abortion, they did not have the right to impose their views upon society. . . .[11]

What about opponents of legalized abortions about whose arguments we have said nothing so far? Let us conclude with a few brief points and an indication of their general view.

Opponents deny that their opposition is due to some religious foible of their own. They assert, therefore, that abortion is not a private affair and that there *are* objective ethical standards applicable to everyone. Legalizing abortion is, in reality, the legalizing of acts of violence and hence is contrary both to human reason and to the common good of society. Moreover, in matters of life and death, the Criminal Code cannot be neutral; the Criminal code is simply a moral code which happens to be public rather than private. But it is a *moral* code and must of necessity represent somebody's morality. By legalizing abortion, opponents point out, society has overthrown principles which are fundamental to its own survival, principles guaranteeing the preservation of life innocent of any crime, and holding that acts of violence directed against that life must be rejected and opposed rather than condoned and approved as they are today.

Opponents make three points about the nature of abortion. First, an abortion is not a response to an illness or a disease. The use of medical language is the use of a language of deception. As Dr. Harley Smyth has pointed out:

It is, thus, possible to speak of killing a sperm or killing an ovum, but an abortion never "kills" a baby, or a foetus or any embryo. It is said, instead, to terminate a pregnancy. The operative procedure is listed as "therapeutic" though in fact, such a procedure satisfies no therapeutic criteria; it treats no disease, cures no symptom, and removes, in the vast majority of cases, no abnormal tissue. Moreover, the major indication for most of these procedures is said to be "reactive depression in pregnancy," which I suppose must represent one of the most serious of all prostitutions of psychiatric diagnostic language.[12]

Abortion is not a medical problem, though it is a medical procedure, a procedure which takes about fifteen or twenty minutes. The question is not whether medical doctors *can* do abortions. Rather, the question is whether they *ought* to do them. Thus the opinions of doctors who speak in their function as medical experts are no more than the opinions of technicians who happen to have the skill to do a particular job more or less competently. As everyone in this country knows, the real reasons for abortion are social, with all this implies in a society in which economic, cultural, and philosophical impulses are closely interwoven. In its motivation, therefore, abortion is not a medical matter, but a *moral* one.

Second, abortion involves the killing of human life. An examination of the opinions of Canadian members of parliament before 1969 shows that, at the time, not a few people seriously maintained that the unborn was not alive; others that it was merely a blob of tissue; others again that it was not human in the same sense as life already born. Dr. Morgentaler argued this as late as October, 1976 when in an interview with *Maclean's* magazine he declared that up to five months or so one cannot speak of a baby but "only of a project." Science, however, leaves no doubt that the unborn is alive from conception onwards. This life has an identity of its own and is separate from, though not, of course, independent of the mother. Indeed, at ten weeks the fetus is a miniature baby with all the proper organs: fingers, toes, etc. Through the marvellous technology we have today, this ten-week-old unborn baby has been photographed sucking its thumb.

Third, some people argue that the "humanness" or "humanity" of the unborn life is sufficiently different from that of persons born to permit killing it. But they have provided no scientific evidence to indicate how and in what way a ten-week-old, or an eight-month-old unborn baby is *substantially* different from a one-day-old or one-month-old baby which is also completely dependent upon its mother. Meanwhile, the argument has moved from denying that the fetus is alive or different, to denying that this question is at all important. What *is* important, so it is said, is to save the quality of life of those already born. When Mrs. MacInnis said something similar in 1967 in Parliament, though apparently more in the heat of argument than by deliberate intention, the remark made headlines in Canadian newspapers. Today this utilitarian philosophy, whereby some lives are held more important than others according to some undetermined standard of utility, seems to be increasingly acceptable.

Let me conclude by noting what the opponents of legalized abortion regard as the major evil: the introduction into our society of the principle of selective killing; the introduction and approval of the principle that the end justifies the means, that one may kill human lives innocent of any crime in order to save the lives of those already existing. This, they say, is the most important implication of legalizing abortion. Moreover, if today we permit the killing of those who are a burden because they are in an *early* stage of development and not yet born, then tomorrow we will permit the killing of those who are a burden because they are in a *late* stage of life and no longer of any use.

If this prophecy sounded far-fetched in 1969, it should be noted that ten years after the passage of the abortion amendment, that is in February 1979, the Canadian Association of Psychiatrists published a statement publicly protesting the practice now accepted in some Canadian hospitals of starving to death new-born babies with severe neurological defects, babies which might be saved through surgery.[13] Similarly, by 1980 several provincial legislatures already have been confronted by growing pressure to pass legislation for more open forms of legalized mercy killing and suicide, under the guise of "right-to-die" laws.

Opponents of legalized abortion argue that if it is politically possible to repeal the amendment it should be repealed in order to return to a sane tradition. They say that if the government permits or is forced to continue the present situation, legalized abortions will fester like a cancer in the body politic. They argue that legalizing abortion has resolved nothing; on the contrary, it has added new and graver problems which in their philosophical implications will create far more dangerous conflicts than the practical problem of how to stop illegal, backstreet abortions. For a society to have many illegal abortions, they say, is no doubt a very serious situation. It will be very difficult to stop them. But to *legalize* abortion is to legalize an act of violence, thus corrupting the law, and thereby ultimately corrupting society. It will prove far more difficult to stop that corruption than it will be to stop illegal abortions.

We do not know how many Canadians are opposed to abortion. We do know that opponents of legal abortions are neither restricted to Roman Catholics nor do they number a mere handful. Lutherans, Mennonites, Pentecostals, Greek Orthodox, Jewish Orthodox, Moslems, Evangelicals, Mormons, all oppose it, not to mention some agnostics and such Presbyterians, Anglicans and United Church members who disagree with the various Task Forces or Boards of Evangelism of their Churches. I conclude, therefore, that the Canadian debate about abortion is not yet finished.

Notes

[1]*Globe and Mail*, November 6, 9, 12, 1962.

[2]Her case was mentioned again in a much later article on (the few) abortions being done in Canadian hospitals. *Globe and Mail*, April 11, 1967.

[3]For an analysis of such articles, see F. Canavan, "History Repeats Itself," *America*, May 21, 1966, p. 738. The Church in question was, of course, the Roman Catholic Church.

[4]*Globe and Mail*, September 1, 1961, p. 6.

[5]"Two Problems to be Faced." Editorial, *Globe and Mail*, January 2, 1963.

[6]See, for instance, the article by Jean Howarth, "Abortion: A Matter of Conscience," *Globe and Mail*, May 25, 1967.

[7]*Globe and Mail*, "The Reform Must Be Real," October 6, 1967.

[8]*Ibid.* See also the editorial, "A Parliamentary Bearpit," October 14, 1967.

⁹The statement of the Bishops has been reprinted in *Contraception, Divorce, Abortion*, Ottawa: Canadian Catholic Conference, March 11, 1968.

¹⁰For a more extensive discussion of this issue, see my book *Morality and Law in Canadian Politics, the Abortion Controversy*, Montreal: Palm Publishers, 1974, Chapter 10. (This book is available from Life Ethics Centre, St. Joseph's University College, University of Alberta, Edmonton, Alta.)

¹¹*Ibid.*, p. 107.

¹²Harley S. Smyth, "Motive and Meaning in Medical Morals," *Chelsea Journal*, March-April 1977.

¹³C.P. "Psychiatrists Condemn Practice of Letting Retarded Babies Die," *Globe and Mail*, February 16, 1979, p. 13. "This increasingly common act in medical practice," the statement said, "is being vigorously promoted by able and influential advocates within our profession. . . ." The Board of Directors pointed out that the statement did not apply to situations where death is inevitable.

2

Legal Aspects of Abortion

Bernard M. Dickens

Understanding Canada's abortion law may be best approached through reference to its recent history. The 1969 amendments to section 251 of the Criminal Code (Appendix) and observations of the Supreme Court of Canada in the *Morgentaler* case (*Morgentaler* v. *The Queen* (1975), 53 D.L.R. (3d) (161) provide means to comprehend the circumstances in which abortion may now lawfully be undertaken.

The Meaning of "Abortion"

Before the law can be considered, however, legal and medical differences in use of the concept of "abortion" must be distinguished. The historic prohibitions of the Criminal Code apply to those who "procure . . . miscarriage" (section 251(1) and (2)). The word "abortion" was introduced only in 1969, regarding therapeutic abortion committees whose certificates provide exemption from the historic prohibitions. In medical terms, "abortion" is usually taken to mean giving birth to an embryo or fetus prior to 20 weeks of gestation, when an embryo or fetus weighs less than 500 grams. Some Canadian provincial laws or regulations consistently consider abortion as spontaneous or induced interruption of pregnancy before the twentieth week of gestation, and require a still birth to be registered upon delivery of non-living fetuses produced after the twentieth week or weighing over 500 grams. Some have concluded from this that the Canadian Criminal Code does not permit termination of pregnancy to be induced after the twentieth week of gestation.

This is not correct, however, since the Criminal Code has no gestational limit upon pregnancy termination, and its prohibition and exemption from prohibition are coterminous. The misinterpretation focuses upon what the amended Code allows, and ignores what the historic Code prohibits. The Criminal Code punishes procurement of miscarriage, subject to such procurement being lawful, notably when approved by therapeutic abortion committees. If the Code governing the practice defined it as limited to up to 20 weeks of gestation, this would limit the penal prohibition of abortion to that period, with later pregnancy terminations falling outside the prohibition. Since this is clearly not the meaning of the Code, the concepts of "abortion" and "miscarriage" must be taken as identical, governing terminations of pregnancy before commencement of the process of birth. This is consistent with ordinary dictionary meanings. The *Shorter Oxford Dictionary*, for instance, defines "miscarriage" as synonymous with "abortion," which is defined as "giving untimely birth to offspring; the procuring of premature delivery so as to destroy offspring."

The Law Before Amendment

In considering the effect of the 1969 amendments to the Criminal Code, the Supreme Court of Canada in the *Morgentaler* case considered the earlier law. Referring to the leading Commonwealth abortion decision (Cook and Dickens, 1979; Dickens and Cook, 1979), the English case of *R.* v. *Bourne* in 1938, Pigeon J. observed that, "When that case was decided, the law on abortion in England was much the same as our own law before the 1968–69 amendments" (p. 191). The *Bourne* case ([1939] 1 K.B. 687) held that abortion is lawful when performed in good faith to preserve a female's life or her physical or mental health (Dickens, 1966).

The legislation in England, like the pre-amendment legislation in Canada, expressed in its terms no grounds upon which abortion was lawful, but the courts recognized by case-law a necessity justification. This covered a female's abortion when "necessary to preserve her life" (Lamont J. in *Re McCready* (1909), 14 C.C.C. 481 (Sask. Sup. Ct.) p. 485), and when necessary to preserve her health. This included both physical and mental health, since the *Bourne* case concerned a female whose continued pregnancy created risk that she would become "a mental wreck."

Medical assessment and prognosis of the female's condition had to be made in good faith. Evidence of medical professional good faith consists, *inter alia*, of obtaining a second concurring professional opinion. Accordingly, a physician evidencing good faith, notably by having a second medical opinion, could find a female's life or health to be so threatened by continuation of pregnancy that an abortion procedure she seeks or consents to would be medically indicated. After the procedure is performed, its legality might be tested by criminal prosecution or, for instance, in disciplinary proceedings for medical professional misconduct.

The 1969 Amendments

Analysis of abortion laws in different jurisdictions discloses a number of general indications justifying the procedure (Cook and Dickens, 1978; Dickens and Cook, 1979). These are:

(i) Risk to life and grave risk to health (the strict necessity indication);

(ii) Risk to physical or mental health from continuation of pregnancy, meaning risk beyond that normally associated with pregnancy (the therapeutic indication);

(iii) Some degree of likely serious physical or mental impairment of a child if born (the fetal or eugenic indication);

(iv) Pregnancy by rape or incest (the juridical indication);

(v) The effect of childbirth upon the health and welfare of the female's existing children and family (the social, sociomedical or socioeconomic indication);

(vi) Jeopardy to the social position of the female or her family (the family indication);

(vii) Failure of a routinely employed contraceptive means (the contraceptive indication); and

(viii) Request.

Canadian abortion law before the 1969 amendment of the Criminal Code recognized only indications (i) and (ii), and the amendments added no new indications. The British Abortion Act 1967 was considered by Parliament in so far as it added to British law indications (iii) and (v), but such amendments were not adopted in Canada. Accordingly, the amended Criminal Code did not liberalize the legal grounds for terminating pregnancy. The sole legal grounds for a female's induced abortion remained that "continuation of the pregnancy . . . would or would be likely to endanger her life or health" (section 251(4)(c)).

The amendments address only the means of ensuring the legality of an abortion before it is performed. Under the earlier law, a physician acting in good faith could lawfully terminate pregnancy to save life or physical or mental health, acting preferably with a supporting medical opinion, but legality could be tested and confirmed only *ex post facto*. By the 1969 amendments, legality could be established beforehand, by certification of a therapeutic abortion committee. Because physicians have an understandable reluctance to face prosecution or professional disciplinary proceedings, even when they will be acquitted and exonerated, a means of prior clearance is likely to make legal abortion services more available. In this sense, the 1969 Criminal Code amendments may be described as liberalizing.

The pre-existing means of establishing legality continue to exist, when no certificate of a therapeutic abortion committee has been issued. In the first *Morgentaler* case in 1975, where no committee certification had been obtained, the Supreme Court found the defendant to have presented no express evidence of necessity to preserve health, so that he failed to establish the *Bourne*-type defence surviving under the new law. In Dr. Morgentaler's second and third trials (the third being a re-trial of the first case), he did show such necessity, however, and his acquittals were allowed to stand (Dickens, 1976). Accordingly, abortion may now be shown lawful in one of two ways, namely by prior committee certification under the amended Criminal Code, or by the *Bourne*-type necessity defence, established after the event.

A development of the *Bourne* defence exists, however, in that a physician may be expected to have recourse to a therapeutic abortion committee where one is reasonably available. Failure to have recourse to a committee offering reasonable access to an abortion service may reflect adversely upon the good faith of a physician who acts independently. The 1977 Report of the Badgley Committee (Report, 1977:141) showed, however, that under the committee system, abortion services are inequitably available in Canada, and that "the procedure provided in the Criminal Code . . . is in practice illusory for many Canadian women." Where no committee is reasonably accessible, such as when a female lives outside the catchment area of a hospital with a committee, and the nearest hospitals with committees decline to admit as abortion patients females living outside their catchment areas, or have restrictive quota limitations, a physician may lawfully act under the continuing old law to terminate pregnancy. Equally, when a committee has refused certification upon unstated grounds, or upon grounds a physician considers to leave his patient's life or health at risk, the physician may have legal grounds to proceed without certification. The Criminal Code expresses no emergency exception to its committee certification procedure for prior approval, but the *Morgentaler* case clearly shows that subsequent legal recognition of abortion is accommodated.

The "Health" Indication for Abortion

The relativity of the concept of "health" is shown regarding pregnancy, which is a natural condition affecting health status. Its progressively disabling characteristics can be invoked to show that a female who is not pregnant is at less risk to health than one of comparable physique and physical status who is. Equally, however, there are minimum-risk pregnancies and risk-laden pregnancies measurable by objective tests, irrespective of whether pregnancy is voluntary or involuntary. The psychological difference between voluntary and involuntary pregnancy may itself have a bearing, however, upon the danger of pregnancy to health, particularly mental health.

While pregnancy *per se* presents health risks, and continuation of pregnancy can be shown in the long term to be more hazardous to health than early abortion, for instance by vacuum aspiration, the mere fact of pregnancy cannot be taken to "endanger . . . life or health" for legal purposes so as to justify abortion, since it is not inherently dangerous.

There is no legal definition of "health." Canada subscribes to the Charter of the World Health Organization, the preamble to which states that: "Health is a state of complete physical, mental and social well-being and not merely the absence of disease or infirmity." Pregnancy cannot be taken in itself to endanger health in this sense, although in individual cases, particularly when it is involuntary, it well may. The frequency with which infertility and the unfulfilled wish to be pregnant reduces health, as so defined, tends however, to neutralize the contention that pregnancy *per se* endangers this standard of health.

A restrictive legal interpretation of danger to health requires it to be read as being in the same order as danger to life; the *ejusdem generis* rule of statutory construction limits danger to danger such as may threaten life. Historically, "health" includes mental health, but mental ill-health can be of an order to endanger life when an individual is suicidal; in the first *Morgentaler* case, for instance, the issue was raised that the woman might "do something foolish" (pp. 190, 214). Thus, even the mental health indication may be read in this restrictive way.

As against this, however, criminal legislation is to be construed in favour of defendants, here meaning procurers of miscarriages and women consenting to their own abortions. Accordingly, the terms of criminal prohibition must be read restrictively, and the terms of exception must be read more generously. Further, the critical test of legality is whether a physician reaches a medical assessment in good faith, and not whether the assessment is correct objectively or according to medical consensus. For criminal conviction, it must be shown beyond reasonable doubt that a physician was not acting in good faith.

The Report of the Badgley Committee showed how widely physicians acting in good faith disagree about the extent to which non-medical circumstances affect health. Moreover, while the source cannot be invoked in court to assist statutory interpretation, the Parliamentary Secretary to the Minister of Justice at the time of the *Morgentaler* case indicated how non-health matters may legally affect health assessments. Gilles Marceau observed that:

> The danger for the pregnant woman's life or health is the only criterion in this matter. If it is proven medically that financial, social or other circumstances endangered or would probably endanger the mother's life or health, a certificate may be given; but the decision must be based on reasons of real danger to life or health, and not on social or financial factors as such (119 Can. H. of C. Debates (April 22, 1975) at 5103).

A physician practising holistic medicine, or otherwise prepared in good faith to interpret a female's health status and health prognosis to be so affected by non-medical factors as to face real danger, may properly find in such factors medical indications for abortion, which would therefore be lawful. A woman's fear of genetic disease or of congenital injury in her fetus might affect her health in a way justifying abortion, for instance, even though Canadian law has no fetal or eugenic indication. A liberal understanding of "health" or of dangers to health is no less lawful than a conservative interpretation (Rozovsky, 1979:112). If a therapeutic abortion committee decides by a majority decision of not less than three physicians (section 251(4) and (6)) to certify abortion on such a basis, the procedure is lawful *ab initio*. If there is no certification, the procedure may be proven lawful *ex post facto*.

This may appear to be arbitrary, unpredictable, and placing emphasis upon the form and expression of medical certification rather than upon the substance of a female's condition and circumstances. This is legally inevitable, however, since the amendments to the Criminal Code concern not the grounds for abortion, but the procedure for prior approval. Further, since medical diagnosis and prognosis are uncertain, latitude for reasonable intraprofessional differences may be taken to be intended.

The Patient's Consent to Abortion

Although abortion is permitted only on therapeutic grounds, that is, where danger exists to a female's life or health, she is almost invariably able to decide freely to accept such danger and continue the pregnancy. This was generally implicit in the old law, and was reinforced in subsection (7) amending it in 1969. Section 251(7) of the Criminal Code now provides that:

> Nothing in subsection (4) [permitting committee certification] shall be construed as making unnecessary the obtaining of any authorization or consent that is or may be required, otherwise than under this Act, before any means are used for the purpose of carrying out an intention to procure the miscarriage of a female person.

In principle, therefore, the female's own consent must be obtained. Nevertheless, that consent may be implied where she is unconscious or otherwise incompetent to express her true wishes and her very life or permanent health are endangered (see the strict necessity indication above). Further, the necessity to save her life may in law justify abortion over her conscious and considered refusal, such as where her life is in grave jeopardy and a child is unlikely to be born alive. This appears to follow from section 221 of the Criminal Code, which governs deliberately causing death to an unborn child in the act of birth; under section 221(2), no offence is committed by "a person who, by means that, in good faith, he considers necessary to preserve the life of the mother of a child, causes the death of such child." The section makes no reference to the mother's consent, although its denial may reflect upon the actor's good faith. Equally, before the act of birth commences, when the offence of abortion may be committed, abortion may legally be procured in good faith when considered necessary to preserve the life of the mother, even if she opts for likely death. There is in Canada no lawful right to risk dying an imminent but avoidable death (Dickens, 1979:111).

Because abortion is legally indicated only where danger exists to life or health, a physician cannot make its performance upon a patient conditional upon her agreeing to other terms. A requirement of pre-payment may not in itself be unlawful, such as where a service is offered outside a provincial health plan, because this may be a precondition to creation of the physician-patient relationship. Where a physician-patient relation arises, however, a collateral condition of abortion that the female accepts, for instance sterilization, may be unlawful. Lacking her free consent, the collateral procedure may constitute a serious assault leading to criminal charges and a civil suit for heavy damages. Where sterilization is medically indicated, a physician should make clear that its performance is separate in principle from the abortion, even if proposed for the same time, and that a female will be given the abortion for which she is eligible even if she does not consent to be sterilized.

Third Parties' Consent to Abortion

A requirement of spousal consent is not obviously contained in section 251(7) (Dickens, 1979:47). In Ontario, section 65(2) of The Family Law Reform Act, 1978 expressly precludes it, since it provides that "a married person has and shall be accorded legal capacity for all purposes and in all respects as if such person were an unmarried person." Section 114 of Quebec's Health Services and Social Services Act comparably provides that "the consent of the consort shall not be required for the furnishing of services in [a health] establishment." The position is less clear regarding other provinces, but it must be remembered that a female's abortion is lawful only when "continuation of the pregnancy . . . would or would be likely to endanger her life or health" (section 251(4)(c)). The Criminal Code seems not to give a spouse the right to insist that his wife endure such danger by awarding him power to veto the abortion to which she consents. Indeed, on the contrary, section 197(1) provides that "Every one is under a legal duty . . . (b) as a married person, to provide necessaries of life to his spouse." By section 197(2), he commits an offence by failing without lawful excuse, the proof of which lies upon him, to perform that duty if "the failure to perform the duty endangers the life of the person to whom the duty is owed, or causes or is likely to cause the health of that person to be endangered permanently." In *R.* v. *Brooks* (1902), 5 C.C.C. 372 (B.C. Sup. Ct.) it was confirmed that "necessaries of life" may include medical aid. Accordingly, the Criminal Code may appear to require a husband to provide for a lawful therapeutic abortion service to which his wife consents, especially when the abortion has been certified by a therapeutic abortion committee, and afford him no veto power.

A biological father seems to have no greater veto power than a husband. Where the female is married, the law applies a very tenacious presumption that her husband is the father, but where he is considered not to be or where she is unmarried, a putative father cannot veto a life- or health-preserving, medically approved procedure to which she consents. Since, unlike the law on other jurisdictions such as the United States and Britain, Canadian law permits abortion only upon therapeutic grounds, a third party, whether a common-law partner, occasional lover or, for instance, a rapist, has no power to step between a consenting female and a legally empowered physician to prevent the therapy and compel the female to remain endangered.

The same applies in principle to parents of daughters of minor age (Dickens, 1979:93). Several provinces have deliberately set the age of surgical or of general medical consent below their age of majority; in Quebec, for instance, the age of medical autonomy is 14. Further, by the Common law principle of the Mature Minor, a person of below majority age or below the age of surgical or medical consent where this is lower, may give legally effective consent to surgical or medical treatment where the person is of adequate intellectual and emotional maturity to appreciate its nature and consequences. This is so where parental consent is lacking, and even where parental consent is expressly denied. Uncertainty whether a minor is adequately mature may be resolved by a physician taking a second medical or other appropriate opinion. Similarly, by the Emancipated Minor principle, minors wholly or partially cast adrift by parents and taking their own decisions in life, or in aspects of their lives, may be able to exercise medical independence of their parents, and legally decline to seek their wishes or to submit to their different wishes.

Where minor girls are neither mature nor emancipated, however, they are under parental control. Parental power is not absolute in law, but exists to permit parents to discharge their legal responsibilities. Section 197(1) of the Criminal Code (above) obliges every person ". . . as a parent, foster parent, guardian or head of a family, to provide necessaries of life for a child under the age of sixteen years." Similarly, the duty under section 197(2) binding spouses binds such persons too. Duties under the Criminal Code are reinforced under provincial child welfare or protection legislation (Dickens, 1978). Under The Child Welfare Act of Ontario, for instance, a person unlawfully leaves a child "in need of protection":

> where the person in whose charge the child is neglects or refuses to provide or obtain proper medical, surgical or other recognized remedial care or treatment necessary for the child's health or well-being, or refuses to permit such care or treatment to be supplied to the child when it is recommended by a legally qualified medical practitioner (section 19(1)(b) (ix)).

Parents are concerned, of course, with more than their children's health needs; their spiritual and, for instance, religious needs are also a proper concern. Nevertheless, where danger to a child's life or health is involved, the courts do not afford parental preference the same free range of choice a parent may exercise regarding his or her own body. The life, health and body of a child are not simply at a parent's legal disposal, to serve the parent's whim, philosophy or religion. A decision to refuse a child a legally justifiable therapeutic abortion may expose a parent to criminal proceedings, protection proceedings, and indeed proceedings taken by or on behalf of the child for breach of parental duty.

Equally, parents cannot necessarily compel daughters to have abortions to end health-endangering pregnancies which the daughters wish to continue. This is obvious where mature or emancipated minors are concerned, but even dependent and less mature girls may resist prudent but not life-saving or permanent health-preserving abortion. This is particularly so when the health indication is mental rather than physical. Parental consent is a necessary condition for abortion in such cases, but is not in itself a sufficient condition. A physician acting solely upon parental consent without the girl's own independent consent or unwritten assent, might in principle face criminal assault charges, a civil suit for battery, and professional disciplinary proceedings.

Unresolved Issues

It is trite and self-evident to observe that abortion is contentious, and at times divisive. Individual physicians, nurses and other health-care providers may oppose the practice on religious and ethical grounds, and hospitals eligible to constitute therapeutic abortion committees under Criminal Code provisions and provincial legislation or regulations may decline to do so. Accordingly they may refuse to admit as patients females seeking abortion services. Similarly, individual physicians may decline involvement with those seeking abortion services.

Neither hospitals nor physicians are so free, however, where existing patients are concerned. Unlike abortion legislation in other jurisdictions (Cook and Dickens, 1979; Dickens and Cook, 1979), Canadian law has no "conscience clause" permitting those opposed to abortion in principle to excuse themselves from involvement in non-emergency cases. A hospital with no therapeutic abortion committee in which a patient becomes eligible for and seeks therapeutic abortion faces a dilemma. It may not be able to require her to leave without facing liability for negligence and/or abandonment, cannot refuse her information of the therapeutic option, lest alternative treatment may lack her informed consent, and may be unable to obtain her free and genuine consent for treatment in continuation of the terminable pregnancy (Rozovsky, 1979:37). Abortion may be undertaken under the *Bourne* defence, of course, established *ex post facto*, but the hospital's dilemma arises not from its lack of legal power, but from its philosophical attitude to the procedure. Its choice may be between the forms of legal liability to its patient to which it becomes subject.

The individual physician opposed to abortion may discharge legal responsibility by referring the female to another physician or facility known not to be opposed. Some opponents of abortion consider this oppressive, and spiritually tantamount to procuring the procedure they oppose. Legal liability for abandonment is not ended, however, by their mere conformity to the Canadian Medical Association's Code of Ethics, which provides that:

> An ethical physician . . . (16) when his morality or religious conscience alone prevents him from recommending some form of therapy will so acquaint the patient (Marshall, 1979:15).

An earlier provision in the Code is that:

> An ethical physician . . . (9) will on the patient's request, assist him by supplying the information required to enable the patient to receive any benefits to which the patient may be entitled (Marshall, 1979:14).

A physician putting personal morality or conscience before the patient's therapeutic choice may also compromise the very first principle of ethical behaviour: "Consider first the well-being of the patient." Terminating the physician-patient relation by due notice may be an ethical and legal escape where the patient can find a suitable alternative physician, but the search may be subject to time constraints. In case of emergency, a physician's severance or refusal of a patient may be limited, furthermore, because of the exception in the general rule that: "An ethical physician . . . (12) shall, except in an emergency, have the right to refuse to accept a patient." Disregard of these ethical requirements is likely in practice to escape sanction under the Criminal Code and perhaps under principles of civil (that is, noncriminal) liability to pay compensation, but may leave the physician exposed upon the patient's complaint to a professional disciplinary charge of professional misconduct.

A further unresolved issue in abortion law relates to the definitional problem of when pregnancy commences. The issue is of particular importance with widespread use of intrauterine contraceptive devices (IUDs), and availability of means of menstrual regulation. Menstrual extraction may be undertaken before pregnancy is established, and an IUD may operate not to prevent fertilization but to obstruct implantation in the uterus of a fertilized ovum, which is a biological condition of its normal development. Abortion laws in some jurisdictions, such as New Zealand, make implantation the point of commencement of abortion liability, so that prompt post-coital insertion of an IUD and preimplantation menstrual extraction may fall outside the abortion law. In Canada the position is less clear.

Pre-coital insertion of an IUD appears to be contraception, even though it may cause expulsion of a fertilized ovum, but insertion after missed menstruation may constitute abortion if intended to prevent embryonic development. Similarly, menstrual regulation or extraction after missed menstruation may be abortion, whereas the same procedure after, for instance, rape, for the purpose of protecting against venereal disease, may not; indeed, diagnostic dilation and curettage of rape victims is not uncommon, even if this ends an early pregnancy.

The legal approach must consider two matters. First, although a female acting to procure her own miscarriage commits an offence only if she so acts "being pregnant" (section 251(2)), and must be shown to be pregnant to be convicted, any other person acting on her with like intent commits an offence "whether or not she is pregnant" (section 251(1)). Second, the essential issue is one of intent, and not one of effect. One who acts on a pregnant female intending another lawful purpose commits no abortion offence even though as a result pregnancy is foreseeably terminated (Rozovsky, 1979:111). Thus, tubal or ectopic pregnancies can be removed on routine therapeutic grounds without committee certification. Whether or not restoring the menstrual cycle after interruption may be abortion depends, however, upon all of the circumstances of the case, and the reflection they cast on the intentions and good faith of the parties involved.

In conclusion and less controversially, another means of lawful abortion for a Canadian national or resident may be stated. Abortion is not an extraterritorial crime, so that no offence is committed against Canadian abortion law by a national or resident female obtaining legal abortion out of the jurisdiction upon grounds or by means unlawful in Canada. The Report of the Badgley Committee (Report, 1977:80) showed that one in six females in Canada having an abortion does so in the United States. Further, assisting a female in Canada to obtain such a medical service out of the jurisdiction is no less legal than, for instance, arranging a gambling trip to Las Vegas.

Appendix

THE ABORTION LAW

Criminal Code, Revised Statutes of Canada 1970, Chapter c-34. Section 251.

251. (1) Every one who, with intent to procure the miscarriage of a female person, whether or not she is pregnant, uses any means for the purpose of carrying out his intention is guilty of an indictable offence and is liable to imprisonment for life.

(2) Every female person who, being pregnant, with intent to procure her own miscarriage, uses any means or permits any means to be used for the purpose of carrying out her intention is guilty of an indictable offence and is liable to imprisonment for two years.

(3) In this section, ''means'' includes

   (*a*) the administration of a drug or other noxious thing,

   (*b*) the use of an instrument, and

   (*c*) manipulation of any kind.

(4) Subsections (1) and (2) do not apply to

   (*a*) a qualified medical practitioner, other than a member of a therapeutic abortion committee for any hospital, who in good faith uses in an accredited or approved hospital any means for the purpose of carrying out his intention to procure the miscarriage of a female person, or

   (*b*) a female person who, being pregnant, permits a qualified medical practitioner to use in an accredited or approved hospital any means described in paragraph (*a*) for the purpose of carrying out her intention to procure her own miscarriage,

if, before the use of those means, the therapeutic abortion committee for that accredited or approved hospital, by a majority of the members of the committee and at a meeting of the committee at which the case of such female person has been reviewed,

   (*c*) has by certificate in writing stated that in its opinion the continuation of the pregnancy of such female person would or would be likely to endanger her life or health, and

   (*d*) has caused a copy of such certificate to be given to the qualified medical practitioner.

(5) The Minister of Health of a province may by order

(*a*) require a therapeutic abortion committee for any hospital in that province, or any member thereof, to furnish to him a copy of any certificate described in paragraph (4) (*c*) issued by that committee, together with such other information relating to the circumstances surrounding the issue of that certificate as he may require, or

(*b*) require a medical practitioner who, in that province, has procured the miscarriage of any female person named in a certificate described in paragraph (4) (*c*), to furnish to him a copy of that certificate, together with such other information relating to the procuring of the miscarriage as he may require.

(6) For the purposes of subsections (4) and (5) and this subsection

"accredited hospital" means a hospital accredited by the Canadian Council on Hospital Accreditation in which diagnostic services and medical, surgical and obstetrical treatment are provided;

"approved hospital" means a hospital in a province approved for the purposes of this section by the Minister of Health of that province;

"board" means the board of governors, management or directors, or the trustees, commission or other person or group of persons having the control and management of an accredited or approved hospital;

"Minister of Health" means

(*a*) in the Provinces of Ontario, Quebec, New Brunswick, Manitoba, Alberta, Newfoundland and Prince Edward Island, the Minister of Health,

(*b*) in the Province of British Columbia, the Minister of Health Services and Hospital Insurance,

(*c*) in the Provinces of Nova Scotia and Saskatchewan, the Minister of Public Health, and

(*d*) in the Yukon Territory and the Northwest Territories, the Minister of National Health and Welfare;

"qualified medical practitioner" means a person entitled to engage in the practice of medicine under the laws of the province in which the hospital referred to in subsection (4) is situated;

"therapeutic abortion committee" for any hospital means a committee, comprised of not less than three members each of whom is a qualified medical practitioner, appointed by the board of that hospital for the purpose of considering and determining questions relating to terminations of pregnancy within that hospital.

(7) Nothing in subsection (4) shall be construed as making unnecessary the obtaining of any authorization or consent that is or may be required, otherwise than under this Act, before any means are used for the purpose of carrying out an intention to procure the miscarriage of a female person.

References

Cook, Rebecca J. and Bernard M. Dickens. "A Decade of International Change in Abortion Law: 1967–77." *American Journal of Public Health* 68(7) (1978):637–643.

Cook, Rebecca J. and Bernard M. Dickens. "Abortion Laws in Commonwealth Countries." *International Digest of Health Legislation* 30 (1979):395–502, republished as *Abortion Laws in Commonwealth Countries*. Geneva: World Health Organization, 1979.

Dickens, Bernard M. *Abortion and the Law*. London: MacGibbon & Kee, 1966.

Dickens, Bernard M. "The Morgentaler Case: Criminal Process and Abortion Law." *Osgoode Hall Law Journal* 14(2) (1976):229–274.

Dickens, Bernard M. "Legal Responses to Child Abuse in Canada." *Canadian Journal of Family Law* 1(1) (1978):87–125.

Dickens, Bernard M. *Medico-Legal Aspects of Family Law*. Toronto: Butterworths, 1979.

Dickens, Bernard M. and Rebecca J. Cook. "The Development of Commonwealth Abortion Laws." *The International and Comparative Law Quarterly* 28 (1979):424–457.

Marshall, T. David. *The Physician and Canadian Law*. Toronto: The Carswell Co. Ltd. 2nd. ed., 1979.

Report of the Committee on the Operation of the Abortion Law (Chairman: Robin F. Badgley) Ottawa: Minister of Supply and Services, 1977.

Rozovsky, Lorne E. *Canadian Hospital Law*. 2nd ed. Ottawa: Canadian Hospital Association, 1979.

3

The Role of the Psychiatrist in Canadian Abortion Law

Morton S. Rapp

Introduction

This chapter touches on two controversial issues. The role of the psychiatrist in any endeavour may be ambiguous. The approach of any citizen to Canadian abortion law is an intellectual challenge and an emotional trap. At the intellectual level, abortion is embraced by humanistic, legal, religious, moral, philosophical, medical and psychological considerations. Thus, any attempt to discuss only one or two sides of this multifaceted topic is bound to fall short.

At the emotional level, abortion remains "a controversy with a life of its own" wherein "those most passionately embroiled in the struggle have defined the terms of the debate" (Hacker, 1979:16–22). Those persons holding the most extreme views on abortion generally have other axes to grind, and only rarely are they able to touch on the underlying attitudes which have led to their stated positions.

Despite these pitfalls, it is important for psychiatrists to examine their role in Canadian abortion law, because their role is central to its operation.

Some Paradoxes in Canadian Abortion Law

Badgley reports that abortion law is not working equitably in Canada (Report of the Committee on the Operation of the Abortion Law, 1977:17). If one examines the wording of that law, and if one considers the vagaries of human nature, it is surprising that the law is working at all.

Looking first at human nature, there are two extreme views on abortion. The first holds that abortion is a form of murder, with all the consequences that view implies. The second holds that failure to permit abortions is a social crime and medical negligence. A surprisingly large number of people subscribe to one or the other of these extreme views (or something very close to them). This includes individuals involved in health-care administration in its broadest sense, such as doctors, nurses, social workers, hospital administrators, and others. Given the opportunity, these people will interpret the law in accordance with their own biases. That is hardly a novel state of affairs.

What is novel, however, is that the law is worded in such a way that no one can be sure exactly what it means. Furthermore, unlike other laws which medical personnel must respect, abortion law must not only be implemented by persons with no legal training, it must also be interpreted by them. Thus, the intrusion of individual biases into abortion decisions are inevitable.

The law permits a woman an abortion if the continuation of the pregnancy "would, or would be likely to, endanger her life or health" (section 251.3(c)). Since physical dangers from pregnancy are few, if legislators were expecting the new law to result in a larger number of "legal" abortions, they must have been relying on the criterion of threat to the woman's mental health. But reliance on this criterion is full of problems.

First, there is no broad general agreement about the underlying health of any woman who seeks abortion. Romm for example, stated:

> The very fact that a woman cannot tolerate pregnancy, or is in intense conflict about it, or about giving birth to a child, is an indication that the prepregnant personality of this woman was immature and in that sense can be labelled as psychopathological (1967:209).

At another extreme, Watters (1976) sees abortion as a healthy option for the unwillingly pregnant woman. Between these extremes, there exists a spectrum of views held by various psychiatrists. The question this raises, however, is not which position is correct, but why legislators entrusted abortion decisions to a profession that was so manifestly divided on the very nature of an abortion wish.

Second, abortion law assumes considerable predictive capacity on the part of psychiatrists. However, there is no evidence that such predictive capacity exists.

Third, the definition of mental health varies from person to person. To many, it is the absence of definable psychiatric disease. To others, it involves the ability to engage in specific coping behaviours. For example, Freud characterized mental health as the ability to love and to work. To yet others, mental health is best expressed in World Health Organization terms, that health is not merely the absence of disease, but a positive state of physical and psychological well-being. It is clear that Canadian women entitled to abortion if the third definition is used, are not entitled to it if the first one is used, under the present law. However, the law allows psychiatrists to employ any definition they choose, because it does not specify which definition should be used.

Finally, the relationship between the availability of abortion and its effects on mental health, is inverse. Women with severe, fixed psychological problems do not seem to benefit much from abortion; but they rarely have it refused. Women with milder symptomatology do benefit from abortion, but these are the women who are less likely to be able to obtain one under Canadian law.

The Phenomenology of the Unwillingly Pregnant Woman

A woman who becomes pregnant without intending to do so becomes anxious. If the pregnancy cannot be terminated, she often develops signs of depression which are generally considered to be reliable indicators of psychiatric disease (Zung, 1965:63). If the pregnancy is terminated, the depression and anxiety lift dramatically (Priest, 1972:293–299), and there are no common psychological sequelae. On the other hand, if the pregnancy goes to term, the depression usually remits shortly after delivery, and the future mental state of the woman will depend on (among other things) her social circumstances. Pregnancy is a major biological event with additional psychological and social implications, and either its termination or completion is likely to have observable sequelae for some women (though not for all). Generally speaking, if the woman's wishes for the pregnancy (termination or completion) are carried out, the incidence of psychological sequelae is minimized. No credible study contradicts this rather commonplace observation.

In general then, the termination of pregnancy shortens a state of depression by about six months.

The Phenomenology of the Psychiatrist in Analogous Situations

If a psychiatrist is given the opportunity to shorten the duration of a state of suffering by six months, there are many other forms of action, comparable to abortion in their potential for side effects, which the psychiatrist ordinarily will use without hesitation. These include psychotherapy, pharmacotherapy, behaviour modification and electroconvulsive therapy. If he hesitates to employ (or allow) abortion as a remedy for depression, he must be doing so for special personal or philosophical reasons, which may bear no relationship to the patient's needs. Excluding these, then, it is not surprising that psychiatrists will agree to sit on abortion committees, or to refer patients to them. While Priest's comment that psychiatrists have become identified as permissive liberals (1972:293–299) is accurate, abortion can be justified on the same grounds that justify other psychiatric therapies. It is not here argued that psychiatric therapy in general is particularly rational; only that the use of abortion for the pregnant depressed woman is completely in keeping with current psychiatric practice, rational or not. To call into question the use of abortion here should logically call into question the use of all other commonly used procedures employed by psychiatrists.

One might argue that since the depression related to unwanted pregnancy generally lifts after delivery, one might "wait it out." This, however, is an ethically questionable argument. The physician's role in society is quite clear. It is to relieve suffering in the patient as quickly as possible. It is not to withhold treatment on the philosophical premise that the pain might remit spontaneously. If that attitude were general, the function of a psychiatrist would be so limited that he would have no practice. Ninety per cent of depressions remit spontaneously. There is no place in the consulting room for the physician who acts largely as a disinterested academic scientist. A second problem with waiting is that there is no guarantee in the individual case that the depression will lift. Guarantees in medicine are not to be found.

A difficulty in the practice of psychiatry is that it depends heavily on the verbalizations of the patient. Bolter (1962:312) has made the point that a pregnant woman seeking an abortion will learn which responses will get an abortion, and emit these responses. This is in keeping with learning theory (more or less) and has validity as far as it goes. However, it is also a tenet of learning theory that such behaviour will be emitted only when the organism stands to gain something of value to itself, which in this case, is relief from stress. Thus the performance of the operant behaviour (symptom-emission) merely demonstrates the perceived need for the procedure (abortion). In other words, if one employs learning theory consistently here, one ends up with the same option one began with.

Society's Response to the Mutable Symptom

A complicating observation is that when a pregnant woman knows she can obtain an abortion, she may not develop much anxiety or depression. This can be explained best in social terms. The unavailability of the abortion is a necessary (but not a sufficient) cause of the depression. This situation has no precise analogy in the rest of medical practice. Here, the symptom is induced as much by specific social events as by internal or random external events. Most psychiatrists have little trouble with this concept, since they have used (perhaps too much) the idea of societal events as pathogenic for decades. Laws, however, are made by all of society, and not by psychiatrists. Canadian society's inability to understand the above concept is represented by the fact that an abortion committee has the right (indeed the duty) to tell certain women that they don't need the procedure badly enough to have it legally. No criteria exist telling one how badly is "badly enough." This horrendous omission stands in marked contrast to the specificity of other laws which must be administered by psychiatrists. For example, in determining whether a psychiatric patient may be hospitalized against his will, the psychiatrist must show that specific behavioural criteria have been satisfied (Mental Health Act). If they have not been, the psychiatrist may not act.

A Cynical View of Canadian Abortion Law

Defenders of Canadian abortion law deny that it is a "cop out" but do not deny that it is a "compromise" (Interdisciplinary Seminar, author's note). The difference between these is difficult to discern. In fact, Canadian legal response to the abortion controversy seems to have been shaped by the obvious impossibility of satisfying two equally implacable philosophies. The solution was to frame a law which dissatisfied each of them about equally, and to leave much of the day-to-day decision-making in the hands of a profession known for its vague and fuzzy conceptualizations. This decision was clever. The individuals and groups with strong feelings about abortion hesitate to raise the issue of changing the law, for fear that it might be changed in a direction further away from their interests. It is difficult to mount an attack on psychiatric indications for abortion without mounting an attack on the general processes of psychiatric decision-making. At the same time, the more influential, wealthy and resourceful women can now legally obtain the abortions they need, so that abortion is no longer an issue which can topple governments.

This has resulted in events which would be humorous if the topic were not so serious. In one Canadian hospital, a set number of abortions are performed per week, and the candidates are chosen by lot. At a governmental level, a western Canadian politician has recently raised questions about the legality of abortions in his province, based not on any specific allegations of wrong-doing, but on the fact that the number of abortions per capita in his province exceeded that of other provinces. These two examples of devotion to the numbers game are cited not to criticize the individuals or institutions involved. In the absence of reliable guidelines as to what is legal and what is not, everyone will be eventually forced to turn to statistics and probability for their opinions and decisions. No other law works in this way.

Implementation Versus Interpretation of a Law

Psychiatrists must be prepared to implement many laws in their practice, but it is quite another thing to expect them to interpret law, which is ordinarily the function of a judge. The difference is best illustrated by examining two other laws which psychiatrists must commonly implement.

Under the Child Welfare Act a physician (indeed any professional) who suspects child abuse in a family is obliged to report his suspicions to the appropriate children's aid society. Failure to do so may result in a substantial fine. Furthermore, the physician is not liable for an error, if he reports his suspicions in good faith. The law is clear and unambiguous. It does not have to be interpreted. The physician does not have to define child abuse prior to reporting his suspicions.

Similar circumstances exist in Ontario's Mental Health Act. A physician may compel a patient to attend hospital for up to five days for assessment, on the suspicion of mental illness. However, the conditions which must exist to make this forcible confinement legal are clearly specified. The physician does not have to define mental illness or give a specific diagnosis. In short, the physician merely executes a law whose interpretation has been settled for him.

In contrast, in Canadian abortion law, the physician (or committee of physicians) must interpret the law. They must decide if mental illness exists, in the absence of a definition of it. They must determine if the illness is severe enough to warrant an abortion, in the absence of a definition of "sufficient seriousness." They must predict the future of the woman's mental health, in the absence of any demonstrated ability to do so. All this adds up to the fact that the physician (or committee) must interpret a law, although most physicians have no training in the interpretation of law.

A Potential Erosion of the Practice of Psychiatry

If Canadian abortion law is largely a compromise, and if psychiatrists are being used to hold it in place, will this have a deleterious effect on the practice of psychiatry? No such effect has been detected after over 10 years of operation of the law. This may be because the law which serves the interests of the government also serves the interests of many of the people affected by it. Nevertheless, the profession's actions with respect to the abortion law have served notice of its potential involvement in other sticky social functions; Canadian psychiatry should be wary of getting involved in too many analogous activities, lest it find itself perceived as mainly an arm of government.

Conclusion

Valid psychiatric indications exist for the termination of a pregnancy; nevertheless, ideally, both government and psychiatry would be better off out of the abortion-granting business. If government wishes to remain involved, it should bring abortion law into line with other laws which physicians must administer, and change the law so that it is merely administered, and not interpreted, by physicians.

However, such changes are unlikely in the near future. In that case, the psychiatrist must continue to further those medical and social processes he thinks are in the best interest of the individual patient; for he has no other mandate. But while doing this, he should remind the country from time to time that his role is at best, needlessly ambiguous, and at worst, partly political.

References

Bolter, S. "The Psychiatrist's Role in Therapeutic Abortion: The Unwilling Accomplice." *Amer. J. Psych.* 1196 (1962):312.

Criminal Code, section 251.3(c).

Hacker, Andrew. "Of Two Minds About Abortion." *Harper's*, September 1979, pp. 16–22.

Interdisciplinary Seminar, Population and Birth Control. University of Toronto, November 20, 1979. Author's note.

Mental Health Act, RSO 1970 Chapter 269. As amended by 1978 Chapter 50 section 8.

Priest, R.G. "The Impact of the Abortion Act." *Br. J. Psychiat.* 121 (1972):293–99.

Report of the Committee on the Operation of the Abortion Law. (Chairman: Robin F. Badgley) Ottawa: Minister of Supply and Services Canada, 1977.

Romm, May E. "Psychoanalytic Considerations." In *Abortion in America*, edited by Harold Rosen. Boston: Beacon Press, 1967.

Watters, Wendell W. *Compulsory Parenthood*. Toronto: McClelland and Stewart, 1976.

Zung, W.W.K. "A Self-Rating Depression Scale." *Arch. Gen. Psychiat.* 121 (1972):293–99.

4

The Canadian Abortion Experience Since the 1969 Abortion Law

Paul MacKenzie

Introduction

In 1969, the law concerning abortion in Canada was changed. During the 1970s, more than 450,000 pregnancies were legally terminated in Canada, and yet many pregnant women experienced difficulty, delay, or rejection in seeking an abortion. Large numbers of people expressed their opinions on abortion, often strongly held, and many advocated further changes in the law, to make it either more or less restrictive. In the course of their jobs, numbers of doctors, nurses, social workers, counsellors, clergy, social scientists, administrators and politicians dealt with consequences of the new law. Thus, for personal or professional reasons, abortion has been a topic of interest and concern to many Canadians in the 1970s and appears likely to remain so in the 1980s.

Abortion may be defined as termination of a pregnancy after implantation in the uterus and before viability of the fetus. Abortions may be spontaneous or induced. Spontaneous abortions or miscarriages occur in 8 per cent to 12 per cent of recognized pregnancies and likely many unrecognized miscarriages occur in early pregnancies in which there is some abnormality of early development. Induced abortions, if done within the law, are often called therapeutic abortions, and if done outside the law, have been called criminal abortions. In recent years, the arbitrary point called *viability* has been moved back from 28 weeks to 20 weeks of pregnancy, measured from the first day of the last normal menstrual period. However, in current practice, survival of a fetus of less than 25 weeks is a very rare event.

In this summary of Canadian experience with the revised abortion law, two main sources have been used: the Annual Reports of Statistics Canada on Therapeutic Abortion from 1970 to 1978, and the Report of the Committee on the Operation of the Abortion Law published in 1977. This Committee was appointed by the Privy Council and given specific terms of reference. The Committee of three, chaired by Robin F. Badgley, presented an extensive report in January 1977 to the Minister of Justice which was published the same year. Included in the report are results of a national population survey on abortion, a national survey of abortion patients, a national survey of physicians on abortions, a national survey of hospitals on abortion and a number of personal accounts of Canadian women who had abortions done before and after the law was changed.

The Committee found that the law was not operating equitably across Canada and that there were sharp disparities in the distribution and accessibility of therapeutic abortion services. It pointed out that these disparities were not due to the federal law which is uniform across the country, but due to the attitudes and interpretations of the law by the Canadian people, the medical profession, and superimposed provincial and hospital regulations. However, the law itself, in requiring a system of therapeutic abortion committees, is responsible for adding considerable delay in abortion processing.

The Canadian Law

The Criminal Law Amendment Act 1968 (Bill C-50) contained a variety of amendments to Canada's Criminal Code which dates from 1892. One of these amendments was section 18 of the Act which added an exception to section 237 of the Criminal Code. The old law made "procuring the miscarriage of a female person" an indictable offense without exception punishable by up to life imprisonment for the abortionist and by up to two years imprisonment for the pregnant woman. The amendment provided an exception when:

(1) A therapeutic abortion committee, appointed by a hospital board, and composed of not less than three members, each of whom is a qualified medical practitioner, has, after considering the case at a meeting, stated in a written certificate that in the opinion of the majority of the committee "continuation of the pregnancy would or would be likely to endanger her life or health."

(2) The abortion is performed by a qualified medical practitioner, other than a member of a therapeutic abortion committee, in a hospital accredited by the Canadian Council on Hospital Accreditation, or approved for this purpose by the Provincial Minister of Health or his equivalent.

The actual wording of the law can be found in the revised Criminal Code of 1970, chapter C-34, section 251.

It will be noted that the essential features of this law are:

(1) it requires a committee of doctors to review abortion applications;

(2) it requires abortions to be performed within hospitals, which excludes free-standing clinics or offices;

(3) it provides only two indications: danger to life of the mother or danger to her health. It does not mention genetic abnormality, rape, incest, social, psychiatric or economic indications. However, it does not define health, leaving this to the doctors on the committee to interpret;

(4) it does not specify a gestational age limit to abortion.

Abortion Statistics

Numbers

The change in Canada's abortion law became effective on August 26, 1969. Prior to that time small numbers of abortions were being done in hospitals for severe medical problems, and increasingly larger numbers for reasons usually described as psychiatric.

In January 1970, 169 legal abortions were reported under the new law. In December 1970, this number had risen to 2,248. The total for 1970 was 11,152. The increasing numbers of abortions over the years 1970 to 1979 are shown in Table 4–1. By 1979 the yearly total was 5,043.

Table 4–1

LEGAL ABORTIONS REPORTED FOR CANADIAN RESIDENTS IN CANADA
1970–1978

Year	Number of Abortions	Rate per 1,000 Women Age 15–44	Ratio per 1,000 Live Births
1970	11,152	2.5	30
1971	30,923	6.6	86
1972	38,853	8.2	112
1973	43,201	8.8	126
1974	48,136	9.5	137
1975	49,311	9.5	137
1976	54,478	10.3	151
1977	57,564	10.6	160
1978	62,290	11.3	174
1979	65,043	11.6	180

Source: Statistics Canada, Therapeutic Abortions, 1970, 1978.

Rates and Ratios

In order to express abortion statistics over a denominator for comparative purposes, the rates of abortion per 1,000 population may be used. However, since the age and sex structures of populations vary, abortions per 1,000 women aged 15 to 44 is more precise where available, since only women in the reproductive age group are susceptible to abortion. The abortion rates shown in Table 4–1 and their increase over the years thus reflect real increases independent of the growth in this segment of the Canadian population. It can be seen that the abortion rate climbed most steeply from 1970 to 1972 and more slowly since that time.

It is possible to compute a rate of abortion per 1,000 pregnancies but data on numbers of pregnancies are not usually as available or as accurate as those on live births, so a ratio of abortions per 1,000 live births is commonly used as an index of the relationship. This ratio can be seen to rise faster than the abortion rates in Table 4–1, since birth rates were falling over the period.

Variations within Canada

A breakdown of abortion rates in 1979 by province and territory (Table 4–2) reveals great differences across the country from a high of 21.1 in British Columbia to a low of 1.7 in Prince Edward Island. These differences have been apparent from the beginning in 1970 and have narrowed only slightly over the years. Differences in demand for abortion and availability of abortion must both be present, and it is difficult to determine how similar the rates would be if availability were uniform across the country.

Table 4–2

ABORTION RATES BY PROVINCE AND TERRITORY, 1970, 1974, 1978

Province or Territory	Abortion Rates per 1,000 Women Age 15–44		
	1970	1974	1979
British Columbia	6.6	19.0	21.1
Yukon	1.6	14.6	19.5
Ontario	3.4	13.7	15.2
Alberta	3.4	11.4	13.9
N.W.T.	NA	9.4	13.7
Manitoba	1.2	6.6	7.0
Nova Scotia	1.7	6.1	7.8
Saskatchewan	1.2	6.5	8.0
Quebec	0.4	3.1	5.6
Newfoundland	0.2	1.6	4.9
P.E.I.	0.8	2.1	1.7
Canada	2.5	9.5	11.6

NA = not available
Source: Statistics Canada, Therapeutic Abortions 1970, 1980

International Comparisons

Since the Supreme Court decision regarding abortion in the United States, abortion laws in that country may be considered more liberal than those in Canada and the abortion rates have been higher. However there are still wide differences between the various states as illustrated in Table 4–3. There are some geographic trends in the continent which can be seen by comparing adjacent states and provinces.

Abortion rates in Canada are relatively low compared to many other countries with legal abortion where data are available (Table 4–4). Canadian rates are much closer to those of England than to those of the United States. International

Table 4–3

ABORTION RATES, SELECTED STATES, 1977

State	Abortion Rate per 1,000 Women Age 15–44
New York	36
California	33
Washington	32
Pennsylvania	23
Michigan	19
Montana	15
Alaska	10
Maine	10
Indiana	8
Mississippi	5
U.S.A.	22

Source: Center for Disease Control. Abortion Surveillance, 1977. Issued September 1979.

comparisons indicate the great influence of the law on legal abortion rates. However the law is not the only factor in determining these rates. Because of the relatively widespread use of contraception and sterilization in Canada, demand for abortion, particularly among married Canadian women, is less than in some other countries. Experience in other countries would suggest that a more liberal law in Canada would result in some further increase in Canadian abortion rates.

Table 4–4

LEGAL ABORTION RATES, SELECTED COUNTRIES, 1978

Country	1976 Abortion Rate per 1,000 Women Age 15–44
Bulgaria	68.3
Cuba	52.1
Hungary	37.0
Singapore	28.9
Denmark	22.3
U.S.A.	28.2
Sweden	19.4
Tunisia	16.5
England & Wales	11.4
Canada	11.3
Scotland	7.0
Czechoslovakia	28.9
Finland	15.8
Norway	5.5

Source: Statistics Canada, 1980.

Other Abortions on Canadian Women

The figures given above are reported legal abortions within Canada. Other abortions to be considered include those done outside of Canada and those done in Canada outside the law.

Available data from the United States and England (Table 4–5) although incomplete, indicate falling numbers of Canadians travelling outside Canada to obtain abortions. This may be attributed to the increasing availability of abortion within Canada and the increasing expense of out-of-country abortions.

Considerable numbers were being done prior to 1969 by doctors in their offices, by lay persons using various methods, and by women on themselves. Their numbers will never be fully known, but in the national population survey, women admitted having tried self-induced abortions at a rate of 8.5 per 1,000 women, and admitted having had someone else perform abortions for them at a rate of 6.6 per 1,000 women, of which 4.3 per 1,000 were in doctor's offices and 2.3 per 1,000 by lay persons. These figures, which apply to women's experience over many years, should not be compared directly with yearly abortion rates. Also, there is likely considerable underestimation in these figures due to reluctance to reveal such activitives and due to recall errors.

There is good reason to believe that illegal abortions have declined greatly since 1970 in Canada, particularly the more dangerous methods done by lay persons and unskilled physicians. The number of deaths from such abortions, which averaged 12.3 yearly from 1958 to 1969 dropped to 1.8 yearly from 1970 to 1974. Infected abortions admitted to hospitals also dropped considerably. The number of criminal charges against abortionists fell from an average of 27 yearly during 1961 to 1970, to 4 yearly from 1971 to 1972. The residual number of illegal abortions presently being done is, of course, unknown.

Table 4–5

LEGAL ABORTIONS REPORTED FOR CANADIAN RESIDENTS OUTSIDE
CANADA, SELECTED YEARS

Year	Abortions in U.S.A.*	Abortions in England
1972	6,573	52
1975	4,394	13
1978	1,802	—

*Thought to be at least 20% under-reported.
Source: Statistics Canada, Therapeutic Abortion, 1978.

Effect on Birth Rate, Births Out of Wedlock and Adoption

The crude birth rate in Canada in 1970 was 17.5 and in 1974 was 15.4 per 1,000 population. The rate of decline in the birth rate did not change spectacularly following the change in the abortion law. This is not surprising since the direct effect of abortion on fertility is relatively small. The indirect effect, of reinforcing preventive attitudes and contributing to increased use of contraception and sterilization may be considerable. Increasing use of contraception and sterilization are the most important direct factors to account for the declining birth rate in Canada.

Given the fact that 61.4 per cent of abortions had been done on single women in 1978, one might suppose that this would have had an impact on the number of births out of wedlock, the number of babies being given up for adoption and possibly the number of teenage marriages. Increasing legal abortion is undoubtedly a major factor in the falling number of babies being put up for adoption in Canada. However, there has been very little effect on the percentage of births out of wedlock. Such births were 7.6 per cent of live births in 1966, 9.6 per cent in 1970, and 9 per cent in 1973. It appears that the use of abortion may have blunted the rise in such births but certainly has not caused a dramatic fall. In 1978, while there were about 45,000 abortions on women who were not married, there were still about 40,870 births out of wedlock.

Characteristics of Women Having Abortions

Age

The incidence of abortions is spread over the female reproductive age group, but with more in the younger age groups compared to the age distribution of live births. About 30 per cent of abortions were on women under age 20 in 1978. The age distribution of abortion cases has not changed significantly over the years for which data are available (Table 4–6).

Compared to many countries, Canada and the United States have a high percentage of abortions in the under-20 age group. Teenage abortion attracts particular interest and attention. The rate of increase in teen abortions in Canada has not been greater than that of abortions in general. The actual numbers of teen abortions by age for 1978 are shown in Table 4–7. A total of 5,144 abortions or 8 per cent of the cases were aged 16 or under. This youngest group had a higher rate of late abortion (25 per cent were after 12 weeks as compared to 15 per cent for all age groups). The higher rate of complications in this group is explained by their later gestational age at abortion.

Table 4-6

PER CENT DISTRIBUTION OF ABORTIONS BY AGE, CANADA 1974–1978

Age Group	1974	1975	1976	1977	1978
Under 20	31.5	31.3	30.7	30.8	30.5
20–24	29.3	29.1	29.6	30.3	30.9
25–29	18.5	19.4	19.8	19.4	19.3
30–34	10.7	10.7	10.9	11.2	11.3
35–39	6.8	6.4	6.1	5.8	5.7
over 39	3.3	3.0	2.9	2.6	2.4
Total	41,227	49,033	54,097	57,131	61,806

Source: Statistics Canada, Therapeutic Abortion, 1978.

Table 4-7

TEENAGE ABORTIONS BY WOMAN'S AGE AND GESTATIONAL AGE
CANADA, 1978

Woman's Age	Number of Abortions Canada, 1978	Per cent with Gestational Age Over 12 Weeks
12 or less	9	55
13	95	24
14	490	27
15	1,510	26
16	3,040	25
17	3,953	25
18	4,877	20
19	4,852	19
Total	18,826	21
All Ages	62,290	15

Source: Statistics Canada, Therapeutic Abortion, 1978.

Table 4–8

PER CENT DISTRIBUTION OF ABORTIONS BY NUMBER OF PREVIOUS
DELIVERIES, CANADA, 1974 AND 1978

Previous Deliveries	1974 all cases	1978 all cases	1978 single	1978 married
0	57	60	85	18
1–3	36	35	13	73
4 or more	6	3	0	7
Unknown	1	2	2	2
Total	100	100	100	100

Source: Statistics Canada, Therapeutic Abortion, 1978.

Parity

In 1978, about 60 per cent of women having abortions had no previous deliveries
as compared to 57 per cent in 1974 (Table 4–8). However, if married women
only are considered, about 80 per cent had previous deliveries. The trend to
slightly lower parity is due to a slight increase in the percentage of abortions
being done on single women.

Marital Status

Single women have had the majority of legal abortions in Canada (61 per cent in
1978, 60.2 per cent in 1977, 58.4 per cent in 1975) while currently married
women have been a minority (27 per cent in 1978). This pattern is similar to that
of the United States but different from the abortion pattern in many other parts of
the world such as Asia and Central Europe where the majority of women having
abortions are married. This again reflects the frequency of pregnancy in the
unmarried in Canada, the difficulty such a pregnancy presents in our culture, and
the relatively high use of contraception and sterilization among the married in
Canada. If only abortions under age 20 are considered, 95 per cent were
performed on single women. Of live births to those under age 20, about 35 per
cent are from single women.

Table 4-9

ABORTION BY MARITAL STATUS AND AGE CANADA, 1978

Age	Per cent Never Married	Per cent Currently Married	Per cent Formerly Married
Under 20	95.4	3.0	1.6
20–29	57.8	28.4	13.8
30–39	18.4	60.7	20.9
40 and over	6.0	77.1	16.9
All Ages	61.3	27.3	11.4

Source: Statistics Canada, Therapeutic Abortion, 1978.

Education

Women obtaining abortions have on average, a higher level of education than those who do not. Above 25 per cent have a college education. Among unwed teenagers who become pregnant, those who have abortions on average have a better academic record than those who carry the pregnancy. One reason for this is that those with career goals or with a potential for higher education are less willing to allow pregnancy to interrupt their education. Those single girls who elect to keep their babies are not always those with the optimum resources to do so. These findings are consistent with attitude surveys on abortion that show women with higher education have a more liberal attitude toward the indications for abortion (Committee on the Operation of the Abortion Law, 1977:456).

Prior Contraceptive Use

In the National Patient Survey in 1976, of 4,754 women who had abortions, 27 per cent had never used contraception, 25 per cent had discontinued using contraception sometime before the present conception, and 47 per cent became pregnant while using a contraceptive method which apparently failed. The methods being used when conception occurred included condom (26 per cent), pill (18 per cent), foam (15 per cent), rhythm (15 per cent), IUD (10 per cent), and diaphragm (4 per cent).

Knowledge and practice of contraception are least among single women aged 16 and under. After age 20, ignorance of contraception is seldom a factor, but contraceptive side effects or anxiety about possible side effects are important reasons for discontinuing methods such as the pill. Unanticipated intercourse, as in resuming a broken relationship, or in establishing a new relationship, may be unprotected by contraception.

Between 5 per cent and 10 per cent of women requesting abortion have discontinued contraception to become pregnant but change their minds after pregnancy begins, often because the relationship with the partner has broken.

Prior Abortion

With the increased number of legal abortions over the past decade, there is an associated increase in reported repeat abortions, which rose from 8 per cent of abortions in 1975 to 13 per cent in 1978. These figures are likely underestimated since there may be reluctance to reveal prior abortions. In the National Abortion Patient Survey of 1976, 18 per cent of patients admitted to prior induced abortion.

It would be wrong to assume that women who have had more than one abortion are necessarily irresponsible in their use of contraception. The use effectiveness of any contraceptive method is less than 100 per cent and the chances of an unplanned pregnancy become high as the proportion of a woman's fertile years during which she is sexually active but not wanting pregnancy becomes high. In fact, 57 per cent of women who had repeat abortions reported using a contraceptive method at the time of conception.

The Abortion Process

Therapeutic Abortion Committees

Hospitals have been reluctant to establish model therapeutic abortion facilities, partly out of fear of attracting numbers for which they are unprepared, and partly out of fear of being known as "abortion mills." By 1973, there were 261 therapeutic abortion committees in Canada. Since then a number have been disbanded and others established resulting in little change in the total number of committees.

Not all hospitals are eligible to have committees. The Committee on the Operation of the Abortion Law took particular interest in this topic. It identified 1,348 non-military hospitals in 1976, of which 789 (58.5 per cent) were ineligible to establish committees for various reasons (small size, specialty functions, lack of accreditation). Of the remaining eligible hospitals, 48 per cent had established committees. The distribution of these committees by province is shown in Table 4-10.

A relatively small number of hospitals handle a large part of the volume of abortions in Canada. In 1978, of 271 hospitals with committees, 41 hospitals reported over 400 abortions each and these hospitals accounted for 71 per cent of all abortions (Table 4-11). There were also 42 hospitals with committees that reported no abortions.

Table 4–10

HOSPITALS WITH AND WITHOUT ABORTION COMMITTEES BY PROVINCE, CANADA, 1976

Province	Total General Hospitals	Exempt by Criteria	Eligible but no Committee	Eligible and have Committee	Per cent Eligible with Committee
Newfoundland	46	35	5	6	55
P.E.I.	8	2	4	2	33
Nova Scotia	45	18	15	12	44
New Brunswick	37	16	13	8	38
Quebec	128	33	64	31	33
Ontario	205	51	45	109	71
Manitoba	78	38	32	8	20
Saskatchewan	133	110	12	10	43
Alberta	119	38	55	26	32
Brit. Columbia	103	16	34	53	61
Yukon & N.W.T.	4	—	2	2	50
Total	906	357	282	267	48%

Source: Report of the Committee on the Operation of the Abortion Law, Ottawa, 1977.

Table 4–11

NUMBER OF HOSPITALS WITH THERAPEUTIC ABORTION COMMITTEES BY NUMBER OF ABORTIONS DONE CANADA, 1978

Categories Based on Number of Abortions per hospital, 1978	Number of Hospitals in Category	Per cent of Abortions in Hospitals in Category
0	42	0.0
1–20	55	0.7
21–100	76	6.1
101–400	57	18.7
401 and over	41	74.4
All Categories	271	100.0

Source: Statistics Canada, Therapeutic Abortion, 1978.

Duration of Pregnancy

The duration of pregnancy is often called the gestational age, and is measured from the first day of the last menstrual period until the day of abortion in weeks. When the date of the last menstrual period is unknown or incompatible with the size of the uterus, then the size of the uterus is usually used to estimate the weeks of pregnancy.

Before 10 weeks of pregnancy, abortion is associated with a very low incidence of complication. As the weeks advance, the risk increases, and the techniques become more complex. Twelve weeks, the end of the first trimester of pregnancy, has been widely regarded as a marker between early and late abortions. Second trimester abortion refers to abortion beyond 12 weeks gestation. The percentage of abortions done in the first trimester has been used as an index in evaluating abortion services.

There is some concern that the extra dilation required between 10 and 12 weeks may occasionally weaken the cervix and lead to preterm delivery in subsequent pregnancies. A reasonable goal would be to maximize the percentage of abortions done up to and including 10 weeks gestation and to use this percentage as an evaluative index. In Canada in 1978, this was only 61 per cent (Table 4–12).

Canadian data on gestational age at abortion are not available from all provinces before 1974. From 1974 to 1978, there has been a gradual increase in earlier abortions and a decrease in later ones (Table 4–13). However, whereas abortions after 13 weeks accounted for 16 per cent of those in Canada in 1977,

Table 4-12

REPORTED LEGAL ABORTIONS BY WEEKS OF GESTATION, CANADA, 1978, U.S.A. 1977

Weeks of Gestation	Per cent Distribution of Abortions, Canada, 1978	Per cent Distribution of Abortions, U.S.A., 1977
10 weeks & under	60.9	75.3
11–12 weeks	23.7	12.6
13–15 weeks	9.3	3.3
16–20 weeks	5.9	4.1
21 weeks & above	0.2	0.9
Unknown	0.0	3.8
	100.0	100.0

they accounted for only 8 per cent of those in the United States. Two provisions in the Canadian law significantly delay the abortion: the requirement that all abortions be done in hospital, and the requirement that applications be reviewed by a therapeutic abortion committee. Local committee rules often add further delays by requiring multiple opinions, psychiatric consultations, and residency requirements.

Table 4-13

REPORTED LEGAL ABORTIONS BY WEEKS OF GESTATION CANADA, 1974–78

Year	<9	9–12	Per cent of Abortions at Stated Weeks of Gestation 13–16	17–20	>20
1974	20.8	58.0	14.6	6.2	0.4
1975	22.4	58.9	13.3	5.2	0.2
1976	24.1	59.0	11.8	5.0	0.1
1977	23.8	60.4	11.0	4.5	0.3
1978	24.7	59.9	11.1	4.1	0.2

Source: Statistics Canada, Therapeutic Abortion, 1978.

In the National Patient Survey conducted in 1976 by the Canadian Committee on the Operation of the Abortion Law, women reported a delay of 2.8 weeks after they suspected they were pregnant until they visited a physician. After this contact, they reported an average of 8 weeks until the operation was done. This time period was taken in seeing other physicians, awaiting committee approval, and awaiting hospital admission for operating time. Since the average gestation at abortion in the group was 10 weeks, there must be some exaggeration in these figures, but they serve to indicate the administrative delays consequent of the requirements of the Canadian law.

Concurrent Sterilization

There has been some decrease in the percentage of the women having abortions who are sterilized during the same operation. This percentage was 12.3 in 1974 and 9 in 1978. Only about 1 per cent of those under age 25 are sterilized but over 45 per cent of those age 45 and over request concurrent sterilization.

Laparoscopic tubal coagulation has become the most popular method of sterilization at the time of abortion.

Deaths, Complications and Sequelae

Deaths

There have been so few deaths from legal abortions reported in Canada that it is not possible to compute a rate. Statistics Canada reported one death in 1974 and

Table 4-14

CONCURRENT STERILIZATION WITH ABORTION, CANADA, SELECTED
YEARS

	1974	1976	1978
Per cent of Abortion Cases sterilized			
all ages	12.3	10.2	9.0
age under 25	1.8	1.4	1.3
age 45 and over	48.6	53.8	45.9
Method of Sterilization			
tubal ligation	59.0	45.5	42.9
tubal coagulation	19.7	36.5	43.8
bilat. salpingectomy	16.7	14.7	10.1
hysterectomy	3.9	2.9	2.3

Source: Statistics Canada, Therapeutic Abortion, 1978.

no deaths in 1975 or 1976. Deaths from spontaneous abortion which have been
running one or two a year in Canada are now more common than deaths from
induced abortion.

A reasonable idea about mortality from therapeutic abortions can be obtained
from the United States data. In 1977, in that country, there were 1.4 deaths per
100,000 abortions. Abortion mortality has been falling as has maternal mortality
in general. Maternal mortality in Canada in 1977 was 5 per 100,000 live births.

The most important factor in abortion mortality is the gestational age. Data on
the effect of gestational age from the United States are shown in Table 4–15 for
the years 1972 to 1977 combined. By method, the death to case ratio was 1.5 per
100,000 curettages, 13.5 per 100,000 installation procedures, and 43.6 per
100,000 hysterotomy / hysterectomy procedures.

Complications

Complications here refer to short-term physical problems developing as a result
of the abortion. Examples are hemorrhage, infection, and perforation of the
uterus. A complication may not be apparent on the day of surgery and the woman
may attend another doctor or hospital for treatment. Therefore, complications as
reported to Statistics Canada are under-reported and give no valid indication of
real rates. The trends are probably valid and show modest reduction in
complications from 3.1 per cent in 1974 to 2.7 per cent in 1978 (see Table 4–16).
More accurate information on rates of complication is available from studies with
good follow-up such as the Joint Program for the Study of Abortion in the
U.S.A. It is interesting to note that hospitals with the largest number of abortions

Table 4-15

DEATH TO CASE RATE FOR LEGAL ABORTIONS BY WEEKS OF GESTATION,
UNITED STATES, 1972–77

Weeks of Gestation	Deaths	Cases	Rate per 100,000 Cases
8 or less	12	2,145,802	0.6
9–10	23	1,393,551	1.7
11–12	20	741,536	2.7
13–15	19	253,890	7.5
16–20	43	295,196	14.6
21 or over	12	58,642	20.5
Total	129	4,887,617	2.6

Source: Center for Disease Control, Abortion Surveillance, 1977.

have the lowest rates of complications in spite of the fact that they are performing more complicated later abortions. This indicates that physician experience is important in reducing the rate of complications.

Most of these complications leave no permanent sequelae although severe infection can impair subsequent fertility, and severe hemorrhage with perforation may lead to hysterectomy.

Table 4–16

NATURE OF ABORTION COMPLICATIONS AND COMPLICATION RATES,
CANADA, 1974–1978

Complication	Rate per 100 Abortions				
	1974	1975	1976	1977	1978
Retained tissue	1.7	1.8	2.3	2.0	1.8
Laceration of cervix	0.3	0.3	0.3	0.3	0.3
Hemorrhage	0.4	0.4	0.3	0.2	0.2
Infection	0.5	0.3	0.3	0.2	0.2
Perforation of uterus	0.1	0.2	0.2	0.1	0.1
Other	0.1	0.1	—	—	—
All complications	3.1	3.2	3.3	2.9	2.7

Source: Statistics Canada, Therapeutic Abortion, 1978.

Concluding Comments

In most animal species there is a high natural reproductive wastage. In humans this wastage is relatively small and most of it is confined to the early weeks of pregnancy. In recent years Canadians have added to nature's indications for abortion certain psychological and social reasons which seem important in the present culture. At the same time the techniques for abortion have become relatively simple and safe. Large numbers of unmarried women are finding themselves with unplanned and unwanted pregnancies, and a significant portion of these women are requesting abortion under these circumstances. Contraceptive education and information appears to have prevented a much larger portion of unmarried women from having such pregnancies. However, preventive measures are not likely to reduce current abortion levels significantly. The problem appears likely to remain with us through the 1980s.

A more liberal law on abortion in the near future seems unlikely in the present political climate. The same could be said for a more restrictive law which would be far less enforceable, now that simple abortion techniques are well known to the public and the medical profession. One might only hope for a more workable law. In the meantime credit must be given to those who have helped to make the present law as workable as possible and who in doing so are bearing a disproportionate burden of the problem of unwanted pregnancy in Canada.

References

Center for Disease Control. *Abortion Surveillance*. Atlanta, September 1979.

Report of the Committee on the Operation of the Abortion Law. (Chairman: Robin F. Badgley) Ottawa: Minister of Supply and Services, 1977.

Statistics Canada. Annual Reports on Therapeutic Abortion, 1970–1978.

Tietze, Christopher. *Induced Abortion*. 3rd ed. New York: Population Council, 1979.

5

Abortion and Contraception

Christopher Tietze

The interfaces of induced abortion with contraception, including surgical sterilization, cannot be adequately explored on the basis of Canadian data, but require consideration on a more comprehensive basis.

Because induced abortion and contraception share the prevention of unwanted or mistimed births as a common objective, a high correlation between abortion experience and contraceptive experience can be expected in populations to which both contraception and abortion are available and where some couples have attempted to regulate the number and spacing of their children. In such populations, women who have practised contraception are more likely to have had abortions than those who have not practised contraception, and women who have have had abortions are more likely to have been contraceptors than women without a history of abortion.

Among women who want to avoid or defer childbirth, but not all of whom practice contraception, the percentage of abortions among all pregnancies tends to be high, because many unwanted pregnancies are aborted. Women who practice contraception consistently and effectively, however, experience fewer unwanted pregnancies and therefore have a lower abortion rate than those who practice contraception ineffectively or not at all (Gaslonde Sainz, 1976).

Because abortion and contraception serve the same purpose, changes over time in the use of these two methods of birth prevention are often in the same direction. A good example is the experience of England and Wales during the seven years from April 1971 through March 1977, shown in Table 5-1. In this table live births during successive calendar years are combined with legal abortions obtained six months earlier, and both births and abortions are allocated to the marital status of the woman at the time of conception, that is, premaritally conceived births are credited to the unmarried women (United Kingdom, 1979:133).

Over the seven-year period the proportion of pregnancies ending in abortion remained virtually constant among the married, but increased from 26 per cent to 40 per cent among the unmarried. The pregnancy rate per 1,000 women aged 15–44 years declined by one-fourth among the married and almost as much among the unmarried, suggesting a substantial improvement of contraceptive practice.

In the United States, a series of four surveys of contraceptive behaviour, covering the decade from 1965 to 1975, presents a similar picture. Shown in Table 5–2 are the percentages of continuously married white women aged 15–44 protected by contraception (including surgical sterilization), the increment from survey to survey, and the average annual increment during each period. The percentages are standardized for duration of marriage (Westoff, 1977).

Table 5–1

LIVE BIRTHS, LEGAL ABORTIONS, AND KNOWN PREGNANCIES, BY
MARITAL STATUS AT CONCEPTION. ENGLAND AND WALES, 1971–77

	Married Women			Unmarried Women[2]		
Year[1]	Live Births	Legal Abortions	Known Pregnancies[3]	Live Births[4]	Legal Abortions	Known Pregnancies[3]
NUMBER OF EVENTS[5]						
1971	646.5	38.5	685.0	136.7	48.0	184.7
1972	598.7	44.5	643.2	126.8	58.1	184.9
1973	560.6	47.6	608.2	115.4	63.5	178.9
1974	532.6	45.9	578.5	107.3	64.9	172.2
1975	503.5	43.7	547.2	99.9	63.1	163.0
1976	490.3	42.2	532.5	94.0	62.7	156.7
1977	476.0	39.6	515.6	93.3	62.1	155.4
PER CENT DISTRIBUTION						
1971	94.4	5.6	100.0	74.0	26.0	100.0
1972	93.1	6.9	100.0	68.6	31.4	100.0
1973	92.2	7.8	100.0	64.5	35.5	100.0
1974	92.1	7.9	100.0	62.3	37.7	100.0
1975	92.0	8.0	100.0	61.3	38.7	100.0
1976	92.1	7.9	100.0	60.0	40.0	100.0
1977	92.3	7.7	100.0	60.0	40.0	100.0
RATE PER 1,000 WOMEN, 15–44						
1971	101.8	6.1	107.9	46.1	16.2	62.3
1972	93.7	7.0	100.7	42.9	19.7	62.6
1973	87.4	7.4	94.8	38.6	21.2	59.8
1974	82.9	7.1	90.0	35.6	21.5	57.1
1975	78.6	6.8	85.4	32.5	20.5	53.0
1976	76.8	6.6	83.4	29.8	19.9	49.7
1977	74.7	6.2	80.9	28.7	19.1	47.8

[1] Twelve months ending March 31 of year shown.
[2] Single, widowed, divorced, and separated women.
[3] Live births plus legal abortions (excludes spontaneous fetal deaths and illegal abortions).
[4] Includes premaritally conceived births (legitimate births occurring within eight months of marriage).
[5] In thousands.

Table 5–2

Year	Per cent Using Contraception	Per cent Increment Total	Annual
1965	66.5	—	—
1970	67.6	1.1	0.2
1973	72.9	5.3	1.8
1975	79.0	6.1	3.0

Between 1965 and 1970, when legal abortion was generally not available in the United States, the annual increment in the number of couples protected by contraception was 0.2 percentage points. From 1970 to 1973, when abortion on request was available to the residents of four states and the District of Columbia, and to all other women who had the means to travel to New York City, Washington, and a few other places and to pay for the service, the annual increment was 1.8 percentage points, rising to 3.0 points after the rulings by the Supreme Court in early 1973 had made abortion increasingly available throughout the country.

The proportion of sexually active unmarried United States women aged 15–19 who reported use of contraceptives at their last encounter rose from 45.4 per cent in 1971 to 63.5 per cent in 1976, while the proportion stating that they "always" used contraceptives rose from 18.4 per cent to 30.0 per cent over the same period (Zelnik and Kantner, 1977).

In Denmark, on the other hand, the authorization of abortion on request in 1973 was followed by a marked increase not only in legal abortions but also in estimated conceptions (based on live and stillbirths nine months later and legal abortions three months later) and an equally marked decline in sales of oral contraceptives (Somers and Gammeltoft, 1976). The transfer of an unknown number of abortions from the illegal to the legal sector cannot be ruled out, however, as a factor in the increase in the number of legal abortions. Sales of IUDs increased, and no information on use of contraceptives other than pills and IUDs is available. After 1975, sales of oral contraceptives increased once more, although not to their earlier levels, sales of IUDs rose further, and the numbers of legal abortions, of births and of pregnancies declined (Denmark, 1979).

An important aspect of the complex relationship between abortion and contraception concerns the number of abortions required to replace one live birth. In reference to a given pregnancy, the answer to this question is, of course, "one," since a pregnancy can be terminated only once, but a different answer is required when one considers an entire population.

The interval between two successive conceptions has three components: (a) the pregnancy itself; (b) a post-gestational anovulatory period during which conception cannot occur; and (c) an ovulatory period during which the monthly probability of conception is more than zero but less than one.

Induced abortion reduces components (a) and (b), because the duration of pregnancy is shortened from about nine months for a live birth to about three months for an abortion and the post-gestational anovulatory period is also shortened following an abortion compared with a live birth, the magnitude of the difference depending on the extent and duration of breastfeeding. The average time required for conception during the ovulatory period (c) is presumably not affected. With breastfeeding of moderate to long duration and without contraception, component (b) is comparatively long and component (c) is short, the net effect being that two to three abortions are required to avert one live birth. If contraception is effectively practiced, (c) is extended relative to (a) and (b), with the result that only slightly more than one abortion is required to avert one birth. Abortion alone is an inefficient method of fertility regulation; however, it becomes progressively more efficient as the expanding use of contraceptives relegates its role to a backstop measure.

Figures 5–1 and 5–2 illustrate two possible transitions, from uncontrolled fertility to near universal family limitation, using highly effective contraception backed up by induced abortion of all pregnancies resulting from contraceptive failure. The horizontal axis represents time, although no part of the scale corresponds to any particular number of years. The vertical axis·shows the numbers of live births, induced abortions, and total pregnancies (excluding spontaneous fetal deaths) during a woman's lifetime. The light grey area represents the births, the darker area the abortions, and both together the pregnancies (Tietze and Bongaarts, 1975).

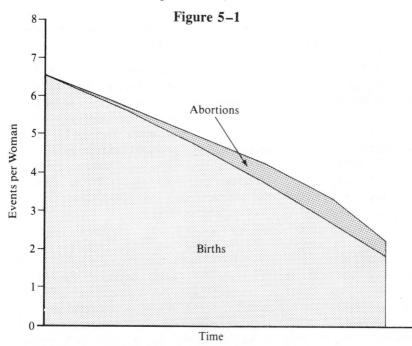

Figure 5–1

Transition from Uncontrolled Fertility to Near-Universal Family Limitation
When Contraception Precedes Abortion

Figure 5–2

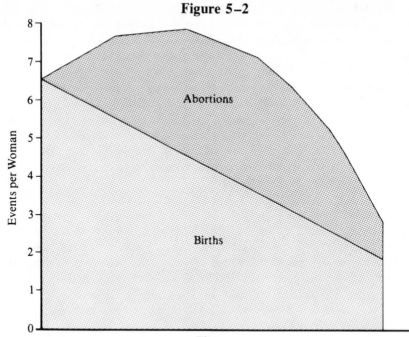

Transition from Uncontrolled Fertility to Near-Universal Family Limitation
When Abortion Precedes Contraception

Figure 5–1 illustrates a transition in which the adoption of contraceptive
practice, gradually increasing in scope and effectiveness, precedes a widespread
resort to induced abortion. Under this assumption, the numbers of births and
pregnancies decline steadily while abortions increase only modestly and late,
never reaching one-fifth of the number of pregnancies. This model probably
approximates the fertility control patterns of nineteenth-century western Europe,
where the decline of the birth rate has been interpreted to be primarily a reflection
of an increased use of contraception, mainly withdrawal (Peller, 1930:184).
According to this view, abortion was rarely used during the nineteenth-century,
partly because of the risks associated with its illegality.

The rates in Figure 5–2 illustrate a situation in which abortion precedes
contraception as a method of family limitation. This might be called the
Latin-American pattern (Requeña, 1966). In this transition the number of births
per woman also declines steadily: in the early stages, more rapidly than in Figure
5–1 and in the later stages, less rapidly. The number of abortions rises steeply to
high values equalling and exceeding births at some point and then recedes
equally steeply with increasing use and effectiveness of contraception. An
increase in the total pregnancy rate during the early stages of the transition is
followed by a sustained downward trend. In the real world, however, the later
stages of the transition lie still in the future.

Table 5–3

FIRST AND REPEAT ABORTIONS NEW YORK CITY, 1972–78

Year	Number of Abortions* First	Repeat	Per cent Distribution First	Repeat
1972	61,200	9,700	86.4	13.6
1973	66,700	14,500	82.2	17.8
1974	67,400	18,500	78.5	21.5
1975	58,300	23,100	71.6	28.4
1976	55,600	28,100	66.4	33.6
1977	53,800	32,900	62.0	38.0
1978	51,800	38,000	57.7	42.3

Year	Women at Risk (1,000s) First	Repeat	Abortions per 1,000 Women First	Repeat
1972	1,584	110	38.6	88.2
1973	1,517	173	44.0	83.8
1974	1,447	238	46.6	77.7
1975	1,382	300	42.2	77.0
1976	1,323	356	42.0	78.9
1977	1,266	409	42.5	80.4
1978	1,212	460	42.7	82.6

*New York City residents only.

Repeat abortions are a matter of concern for those who feel that abortion is unacceptable as a primary method of fertility regulation and should be used only as a backup measure when contraception has failed. As shown in the upper panel of Table 5–3, the number and percentage of repeat abortions has increased rapidly in places such as New York City, where restrictive abortion laws and practices have only recently been replaced by easy access to pregnancy termination (Pakter et al., 1975). This rapid increase does not reflect a progressive change from contraception to abortion as the primary method of fertility regulation but simply the fact that a growing number of women who have had a first legal abortion are at risk of having a repeat abortion. While the number of repeat abortions obtained by resident women rose from less than 10,000 in 1972 to 38,000 in 1978, that is, 3.9 times, the estimated number of women at risk increased from 110,000 to 460,000 or 4.2 times.

Table 5–3 also reveals much higher rates of repeat abortions, per 1,000 women at risk of experiencing them, than of first abortions. This finding should not be interpreted as evidence for a deterioration of contraceptive practice after the first abortion. Rather, the difference reflects the heterogeneity of the populations concerned. With and without contraception, the incidence of unintended pregnancies varies with age, parity, and marital status, and among ethnic and socio-economic groups. In addition, within each group, attitudes and behaviour range as a continuum, from complete rejection of abortion under all circumstances, to acceptance of abortion in some situations (e.g., for termination of out-of-wedlock pregnancy or for family limitation, but not for child spacing within marriage), to acceptance of abortion of all unintended pregnancies. Other factors being equal, the difference between first-abortion rates and repeat-abortion rates increases with the degree of heterogeneity of the population with regard to abortion practices (Tietze and Jain, 1978).

References

Denmark: National Health Service. *Statistik om Prevention og Aborten 1978.* Copenhagen, 1979.

Gaslonde Sainz, S. "Abortion Research in Latin America." *Studies in Family Planning* 7(8):211–217.

Pakter, J. et al. "Legal Abortion: A Half-Decade of Experience." *Family Planning Perspectives* 7(6):248–255. November/December 1975. Supplemented by unpublished data supplied by the New York City Department of Health.

Peller, J. *Fehlgeburt und Bevölkerungsfrage.* Stuttgart: Hippokrates-Verlag, 1930.

Requeña, M. "Condiciones determinantes Del Aborto Inducido." *Revista Medica de Chile* 94(1966):714–722.

Somers, R.L. and M. Gammeltoft. "The Impact of Liberalized Abortion Legislation on Contraceptive Practice in Denmark." *Studies in Family Planning* 7(1976):218–223.

Tietze, C. and J. Bongaarts. "Fertility rates and abortion rates: Simulations of family limitation." *Studies in Family Planning* 6(1975):114–120.

Tietze, C. and A. Jain. "The mathematics of repeat abortion: Explaining the increase." *Studies in Family Planning* 9(1978):293–299.

United Kingdom: Office of Population Censuses and Surveys. *Birth Statistics 1977.* London: HMSD, 1979.

Westoff, C.F. and E.F. Jones. "Contraception and Sterilization in the United States, 1965–75." *Family Planning Perspectives* 9(1977):153–157.

Zelnik, M. and J.F. Kantner. "Sexual and Contraceptive Experience of Young Unmarried Women in the United States, 1976 and 1971." *Family Planning Perspectives* 9(1977):55–71.

Part 2

Emotional and Psychological Aspects of Abortion

Introduction

Not only do professionals and the general public differ on the moral aspects of abortion, they also lack a consensus on how women are affected psychologically, emotionally and sexually by the interruption of their pregnancies. Although massive data on the psychological outcome of abortion exist, the earlier studies are largely polemic and statistical and offer few secure guidelines. Furthermore, since earlier studies were done on women who sought abortions under a more restrictive system, which permitted termination of pregnancy only if it posed a threat to their life or mental stability, one cannot generalize from these findings to women who now seek abortions mainly for socio-economic reasons. The evaluation of psychological sequelae of induced abortion is further complicated by the complex set of variables that is believed to influence their outcome. These include the woman's age, marital status, religion, attitude towards abortion and motherhood, circumstances of and reaction to her pregnancy, relationship with her sexual partner, parity, pre-existing psychiatric conditions or morbid personality, gestational age, concurrent sterlization etc. Finally, an objective assessment of post-abortal reactions is not possible as long as abortion is treated differently from other surgical procedures.

Some attempts have been made to evaluate the unforeseen consequences for the women who are refused a legal abortion and for the resulting children. But the research studies on this are exceedingly rare. The central focus of this section is the psychological effects on women who are granted abortion and on those who are denied abortion.

Zimmerman provides an extensive review of the research studies on the psychological reactions of legal abortion, and she notes that a consensus seems to emerge, at least among the more recent investigators, that most women do experience some degree of psychological distress, but these reactions "are not nearly as serious and painful as previously thought." The severity of these reactions is determined by the woman's psychosocial state, support level, degree of ambivalence over pregnancy and abortion, and her coping mechanisms. A Canadian study by Greenglass that examined the psychological consequences for women who underwent therapeutic abortions reached similar conclusions. Employing objective tests, the author compared these women with three control groups and found no severe adverse reactions in her sample women nine months following their abortions. Perceived social support and pre-existing psychiatric history were strongly associated with the abortion outcome. The author concludes that the abortion experience, *per se*, does not result in psychologically adverse reactions in a woman, and for better understanding of post-abortal reactions, future research investigations should focus on the social and legal aspects of abortion in Canada.

Simon did an extensive review of research studies dealing with the psychological aftermath for women who refused or were refused an abortion, and the implications for their resulting children. This is truly an encyclopedic work. The author found strong evidence suggesting that certain women can be adversely affected by the consequences of refused abortion, and the resulting children, particularly the male offspring, are susceptible to acute illness and untoward personality development. The author notes physicians' biases against some women because of their age or marital status and cautions against this practice.

Pregnancy termination can be traumatic in itself for some women, but when it is performed in conjunction with a sterilization operation, the chances of psychological and medical risks increase considerably. Also, there is a danger of implied pressure on the women to seek sterilization as a pre-condition. Despite the pessimistic evaluation of the combined procedures, Osborn notes that a sizable proportion of Canadian women obtain sterilization operations concurrently with abortion. The author describes the socio-demographic characteristics of these women, their contraceptive behaviour and the reasons for seeking abortion and/or sterilization.

6

Psychosocial and Emotional Consequences of Elective Abortion: A Literature Review

Mary K. Zimmerman

Studies of the psychological and emotional consequences of elective abortion began to accumulate in the mid-1950s. Since that time, there have been several major shifts in the focus of this research, as well as a dramatic reversal in the overall conclusions reached by investigators. These changes, in part, reflect the application of more systematic and sophisticated research methods. In part, they also appear to reflect changes in the societal reaction to abortion — changes in attitudes and moral values as well as the more obvious legal and institutional changes.

A review of psychological and emotional sequelae studies also reveals a growing recognition by investigators that, while the psychological consequences of abortion are not nearly as serious and painful as previously thought, they emerge from a broader and more complex psychosocial process. Thus, in addition to studying the woman and her emotional-psychological status, recent studies have also examined the nature of her interpersonal relationships and social situation.

My purpose in reviewing the psychosocial literature on abortion is to provide an overall perspective on these developments. I have two specific objectives. The first is to summarize the research efforts of the past three decades, placing special emphasis on the orientation and findings of studies published since 1975. The second is to direct attention to the methodological problems involved in abortion sequelae research, and to the difficulties involved in evaluating and drawing conclusions from these studies. While it is true that by now many of these problems are recognized, they remain an important issue in abortion research.

Research Through the Mid-1960s

Beginning in the 1940s and continuing into the 1960s, investigations of the psychological sequelae of abortion consisted almost exclusively of physicians' clinical reports. These reports concluded almost without exception that abortion inevitably causes trauma, posing a severe threat to psychological health (Taussig, 1942; Deutsch, 1945; Dunbar, 1954; Wilson, 1954; Galdston, 1958; Bolter, 1962).

Typically, these investigations were impressionistic accounts based on small groups of patients. Basic to most was the underlying assumption that abortion constituted a mental health problem, "a sick woman and a sick situation" as one investigator phrased it (Galdston, 1958). This view of the abortion patient as abnormal or deviant was consistent with the broader societal definition of abortion as a crime, and with the fact that legal abortion, if allowed at all, was restricted to patients with serious medical or psychiatric indications. From a clinical standpoint, this view of women seeking and undergoing abortion was consistent with the commonly accepted Freudian interpretation of what constituted normal (and abnormal) female personality development. Specifically, according to the Freudian framework, the desire for motherhood represents a woman's successful resolution of the Oedipal crisis and normal compensation for the lack of a penis. Any rejection of the wish for motherhood (e.g., abortion), therefore, signified abnormal psychological adjustment and generally was expected to lead to further personality disturbance.

Undoubtedly, abortion was a particularly difficult experience to deal with given the social milieu of those years; however, it is also clear, from a scientific point of view, that early reports of an abortion's negative psychological effects were subject to considerable bias. The basic problem was weak research methodology, allowing the investigators' own culturally learned views on the morality of abortion and on the proper role of women in society to significantly influence their interpretations and conclusions.

Two specific methodological problems can be identified. The first is measurement. In the early abortion sequelae reports, assessment of psychological well-being was determined through clinical judgments, with virtually no use of other more systematic or standarized procedures. Post-abortion psychopathology was typically assumed to be the result of the abortion experience itself, and was not examined relative to the patient's psychological status prior to the abortion. Comparison or control groups, which would have helped address the issue of causality, were not used.

The second problem is one of representative sampling. Patients studied in these early reports cannot be considered to represent all women who underwent abortion during those years. As mentioned previously, study groups were small and limited to women from one hospital or medical practice. Adequate socio-demographic descriptions of these women were seldom given; however, the likelihood is high that certain age, income, religious and cultural groups were disproportionately present. Despite this, research findings were not qualified in this respect, and the results often were assumed to indicate the impact of abortion for all women.

An equally serious factor confounding the representativeness of study groups in the United States was that, since abortion was severely restricted by law at this time, only about 1 per cent of all abortions were performed legally in hospitals (Zimmerman, 1977). Thus, not only did study groups constitute a tiny proportion of all abortion recipients, they also constituted groups specially selected for psychopathology and other health problems.

One frequently cited study which stands in exception to this trend is Ekblad's (1955) study of 470 Swedish women who underwent legal abortions in 1949–1950. These women were interviewed shortly after their abortion and again two to three years later. The majority (65 per cent) reported that they were satisfied with their experience and had no psychological problems at follow-up. Ten per cent had no regrets but felt the abortion itself had been unpleasant; 14 per cent had a mild degree of self-reproach and 11 per cent regretted the operation and felt very guilty about it. Of this last group, however, Ekblad found that from a psychiatric point of view the reactions were mild. In fact, only 1 per cent of those studied had their work ability affected.

Another finding of the Ekblad study was that guilt was correlated with the degree of pre-abortion psychiatric disturbances. Such a finding illustrates the importance of systematic measurement strategies in abortion research, in this case the need to be careful that pre-existing psychological problems which persist after the abortion are not mistaken for problems caused by the abortion.

Studies of the Late 1960s and Early 1970s

Psychiatric studies of abortion sequelae received strong criticism in the late 1960s and early 1970s (Simon and Senturia, 1966; Fleck, 1970; Walter, 1970; Beck, 1971; Pohlman, 1971; David, 1972; Osofsky and Osofsky, 1972 and 1973; Sarvis and Rodman, 1973; Friedman, Greenspan and Mittleman, 1974; Blumberg and Golbus, 1975). Of particular concern were the related problems of weak methodology and the intrusion of ideological bias against abortion. As one reviewer put it, "It is . . . sad to have to report that psychiatrists oblivious to their contamination by irrational traditions, albeit deeply ingrained social attitudes . . . justify blanket refusal of abortions because of alleged subtle, buried psychological aftermaths based often on a single case report — aftermaths rarely of a clinical magnitude" (Fleck, 1970:45). Another reviewer pointed out the pervasiveness of this trend: "A whole generation of professional health workers refuses to let the myth die out that abortion will irreparably harm a women . . ." (Walter 1970:482). It should be noted that many of these critical reviews came from physicians themselves, often psychiatrists.

Along with questioning the validity of existing research, the late 1960s and early 1970s brought new, more rigorous studies of abortion sequelae. Measurement was more precise; causality was more cautiously considered. Questions of the psychological status of women seeking abortion and the psychological impact of abortion were better separated. Study populations were larger and, if not more representative, at least their characteristics were better described. Sampling efforts in the U.S. were helped by the liberalization of some states' abortion laws, beginning in 1967, which created a more open abortion climate and a more accessible patient population. This situation was enhanced further in 1973 with the U.S. Supreme Court's decision that the states could no longer restrict first and, for the most part, second trimester abortions.

Studies conducted in the late 1960s and early 1970s reversed the conclusions reached in previous reports. Echoing the Ekblad study, the new studies consistently found that abortion's harmful psychological consequences, if they existed at all, were almost always mild and short-term (Peck and Marcus, 1966; Niswander and Patterson, 1967; Simon et al., 1967; Patt, Rappaport and Barglow, 1969; Margolis, 1971; Barnes et al., 1971; Niswander, Singer and Singer, 1972; Ford, Castelnuovo-Tedesco and Long, 1972; Smith, 1973). In fact, abortion could be constructively therapeutic (Notman, 1973; Payne et al., 1973). Compared to childbirth, abortion was found to be no more psychologically damaging, perhaps less so (Athanasiou et al., 1973).

An important finding which emerged from these studies was that psychological or emotional problems following abortion appeared to be due largely to factors existent prior to the abortion rather than to the abortion experience *per se*. This observation was possible only because adequate ''before'' measures were incorporated in research designs. Relevant to this point, it should be noted that abortion-seeking women have not been found to exhibit greater pre-abortion psychological disturbance when compared to other groups of women (Kane et al., 1973).

Research Since 1975

Studies since the mid-1970s have continued to support those discussed above. Similar findings also have been reported from research conducted in Canada (Greenglass, 1976) and England (Gillis, 1975; Lask, 1975).

As a response to the dramatic shift in researcher's conclusions regarding the psychosocial impact of abortion, the latter half of the 1970s brought expressions of concern that perhaps the extent of abortion-related psychological distress was being underestimated. One line of reasoning held that sample populations, though improved over earlier ones, might still be yielding biased results. Adler (1976) reviewed 17 articles on abortion's psychosocial sequelae published between 1966 and 1973, and found that many had, by follow-up, lost between one-third and one-half of the original study participants. She then analysed these studies along with data of her own, with the hypothesis that attrition might function to bias studies in the direction of under-reporting negative sequelae — that women who refuse to participate or who drop out before follow-up experience more abortion-related psychosocial problems. The evidence Adler presented provided only weak support for her contention. Her research, however, underscores (a) the need to account for study drop-outs, (b) the caution required in interpreting results obtained with significant sample attrition, and (c) the importance of continued efforts to improve research methods in abortion research.

Clinicians, too, have expressed concern, cautioning their colleagues against "over-reacting" to the earlier, biased studies by underestimating the complexity of abortion situations, and by failing to recognize patients' problems (Mester, 1978; Cherazi, 1979).

Balancing the fear that more negative sequelae exist than are recognized is the fact that abortion is often reported to have been a positive maturational experience, a "turning point" resulting in increased responsibility and awareness (Notman, 1973; Payne et al., 1976; Zimmerman, 1977; Abrams, DiBiase and Sturgis, 1979).

Overall, the dominant orientation of psychosocial research on abortion since around 1975 has been to explore in some detail the factors which lead either to better or to poorer post-abortion adjustment. Frequently, research findings are presented along with recommendations for abortion counselling. Several types of studies have been conducted: (a) studies analysing the social and psychological situations and adjustment process of women undergoing abortion (Adler, 1975; Schregardus, 1976; Payne et al., 1976; Freeman, 1977; Zimmerman, 1977; Belsey et al., 1977; Shusterman, 1979); (b) studies of second trimester abortions (Blumberg, Golbus and Hanson, 1975; Rooks and Cates, 1977; Kaltreider, Goldsmith and Margolis, 1979); and (c) studies of the impact of abortion and subsequent contraception practices and on psychological reactions to subsequent pregnancy (Margolis et al., 1974; Kumar and Robson, 1978; Abrams, DiBiase and Sturgis, 1979).

The remaining portion of this review is devoted to a discussion of the research in each of these three areas.

Studies continue to find very few serious negative consequences as a result of abortion. Investigators who have conducted in-depth studies of abortion experience have been careful to point out that abortion is, nonetheless, stressful and emotionally difficult for most women (Freeman, 1978; Zimmerman, 1977). Reflecting this orientation, studies published since the mid-1970s have explored in greater detail various correlates and sources of abortion-related psychological distress. Findings to date can be organized into three influential factors: (a) ambivalence over pregnancy and/or abortion; (b) the nature of relationships with others, particularly the specific reactions of others to the abortion; and (c) techniques of coping with the stress of an abortion experience. Generally, the findings indicate that relatively greater psychosocial distress following abortion occurs in those with more decision ambivalence, those with unstable personal relationships, those who receive hostile or non-supportive reactions from others close to them, and those who accept stress, turning their feelings inward as opposed to those who cope through denial, repression, or by attributing problems to external sources.

Ambivalence (confusion, vacillation, etc.) in response to the pregnancy and/or the abortion decision is clearly a key factor in short-term post-abortion adjustment. Payne et al. (1976) found that ambivalence at the time of decision-making related to subsequent psychological conflicts. For the most part these conflicts occurred in the first two months, and had subsided by six months following the abortion. Freeman (1977) found that 39 per cent of women in her study having abortions said they had wanted to become pregnant. These women were the most likely to experience depression soon after their abortion; however, at four months post-abortion, while more of these women had not resolved their feelings, the difference was no longer statistically significant. Zimmerman (1977) found that confusion and vacillation in decision-making was part of an overall "disruptive" pattern of experiencing abortion which led to more troubled thoughts and unresolved issues in the period 6 to 10 weeks after abortion. Those in her study with less ambivalence had better adjustment. Zimmerman concluded, through retrospective analysis, that the entire disruptive pattern (including ambivalence) related to a woman's lack of social integration or "affiliation" prior to becoming pregnant. Indicators used to determine low social integration (e.g., few close friends or family ties, poor work or school pattern) also have been found by other investigators to be predictive of poor psychological adjustment to abortion (Payne et al., 1976; Belsey et al., 1977). These findings suggest that pre-abortion social and social-psychological factors, as well as pre-existing psychological problems, can influence abortion adjustment.

The quality of a woman's relationships with others, specifically the extent to which she receives support and does not receive hostile reactions, is another factor predictive of psychological adjustment to abortion. Adler (1975) and Shusterman (1979) both found that women with higher levels of social support experienced less post-abortion distress. Approaching the issue in a slightly different way, Zimmerman (1977) found that negative or hostile reactions from significant others were strongly related to confusion in decision-making and, in turn, to more post-abortion distress. She also found that a majority of those with such distress were those whose relationships with the male disintegrated after the abortion. It has been observed by other investigators that psychosocial problems after abortion are often due to the disruption of the woman's relationship with the man rather than to the abortion itself (Ekblad, 1955; Payne et al., 1976).

A third factor which appears to relate to psychological distress following abortion is personality. On a global level, studies continue to support previous researchers' observations that women with "healthier" pre-abortion personality characteristics do somewhat better — for example, those with positive self-images, including emotionally expressive and mastery-achievement attributes (Freeman, 1977). More specifically, Schregardus (1976) examined psychological response to abortion according to two major styles of coping, "repression" and "sensitization." Both before and after abortion, "repressors" exhibited less anxiety, higher self-esteem, and fewer mood shifts. It is noteworthy that both Brewer (1978) and Kaltreider, Goldsmith and Margolis (1979) have pointed to denial as an important coping mechanism in adjusting to abortion. In the latter study, the authors compared two types of second trimester abortion procedures. They suggested that abortion by instillation, which involves labor and expulsion, produces more negative psychological sequelae than abortion by dilation and extraction, because it disrupts the "normal" coping process of denial.

A second area of current abortion research is the psychosocial sequelae of second trimester abortions. For the most part, it has been assumed that later abortions are psychologically more difficult to experience and, therefore, lead to more problems afterward. Brewer (1977), however, concluded that despite the difficulties surrounding these abortions, the psychological after-effects were not as severe as expected (five of 25 patients in his British pilot study reported post-abortion depression; however, only one of these had to take time off from work for this reason and none sought psychiatric care).

Kaltreider, Goldsmith and Margolis (1979) examined the psychological consequences depending on the type of second trimester abortion procedure. Comparison was made between the dilation and extraction method (D and E) and intra-amniotic or instillation method. Patients exhibited no significant psychological differences prior to abortion; however, the instillation patients reacted with more anger and depression afterward. Physicians and nurses have reported D and E procedures to be more emotionally difficult for themselves than instillation, and it is thought that this fact may encourage the use of instillation despite more emotional risks for the patient (Rooks and Cates, 1977; Kaltreider, Goldsmith and Margolis, 1979).

Another aspect of second trimester abortion research involves the psychological sequelae of abortions conducted due to the results of genetic screening. In a study of such cases, Blumberg, Golbus and Hanson (1975) found that both husband and wife experienced negative reactions to a much greater extent than reported for other types of abortions. Depression was experienced by 92 per cent of the women and 82 per cent of the men in the study. These findings provide additional support for the view discussed earlier that wanting a child, and the ambivalence produced by having to abort the pregnancy, result in more severe psychological distress afterwards.

The third area of investigation for psychosocial research on abortion is the impact on attitudes and behaviour related to subsequent childbearing. One aspect of this area about which little is known is how a previous abortion affects psychological adjustment to pregnancy. Since a large portion of abortions are conducted on women with no children, who are likely to bear a child later on, this is an important question. Kumar and Robson (1978) in a preliminary report cite results indicating that abortion may lead to higher rates of ante-natal depression in primiparae, as well as intensified fears of fetal abnormality. They did not find, however, that the higher incidence of depression carried over into the post-abortion period. This issue is one which merits further investigation.

Perhaps the most commonly asked question about the impact of abortion relative to subsequent child-bearing has to do with subsequent contraceptive behaviour. Margolis et al. (1974) found 91 per cent of their study group using contraception six months after an abortion. More recently, in a one-year follow up study, Abrams, Dibiase and Sturgis (1979) reported 76 per cent.

Conclusion

Abortion sequelae research is no longer preoccupied with the question of abortion being a psychologically damaging procedure. Clearly, it is not harmful for most women. It is, however, commonly associated with some degree of distress — mild depression, doubts, or generally troubled thoughts — for several weeks or months. For this reason, studies have begun to look more deeply at which women experience greater distress and why. Psychosocial differences in ambivalence over pregnancy and abortion, social support levels, and defensive coping styles have all been found to influence psychological consequences. Further exploration into such factors, psychological as well as socio-environmental, is needed. Future studies should consider a range of possible contributing factors simultaneously in order to assess which are most important.

In general, there has been a vast improvement in the scientific quality of abortion sequelae research since the 1950s. The two problems of measurement and sample representativeness remain of concern; however, the latter problem appears to require more attention, particularly in terms of addressing the potential effects of attrition rates. The quick reversal in findings and in informed opinion about the extent of negative sequelae gives testimony to the importance of methodologically sound investigations in so controversial an area.

References

Abrams, Marilyn, Vilma DiBiase and Somers Sturgis. "Post-abortion Attitudes and Patterns of Birth Control." *The Journal of Family Practice* 9(1979):593–99.

Adler, Nancy. "Sample Attrition in Studies of Psychosocial Sequelae of Abortion: How Great a Problem?" *Journal of Applied Social Psychology* 6(1976):240–59.

Athanasiou, R. et al. "Psychiatric Sequelae to Term Birth and Induced Early and Late Abortion: A Longitudinal Study." *Family Planning Perspectives* 5(1973):227–31.

Barnes, Ann et al. "Therapeutic Abortion: Medical and Social Sequels." *Annals of Internal Medicine* 75(1971):881–86.

Beck, M.B. "Abortion: The Mental Health Consequences of Unwantedness." In *Abortion: Changing Views and Practices*, edited by R.B. Sloane. New York: Grune and Stratton, 1971.

Belsey, Elizabeth et al. "Predictive Factors in Emotional Responses to Abortion: King's Termination Study-IV." *Social Sciences and Medicine* 11(1977):71–82.

Blumberg, Bruce, Mitchell Golbus and Karl Hanson. "The Psychological Sequelae of Abortion Performed for a Genetic Indication." *American Journal of Obstetrics and Gynecology* 122(1975):799–808.

Blumberg, Bruce and M. Golbus. "Psychological Sequelae of Elective Abortion." *Western Journal of Medicine* 123(1975):188–93.

Bolter, S. "The Psychiatrist's Role in Therapeutic Abortion: The Unwitting Accomplice." *American Journal of Psychiatry* 119(1962):312–16.

Brewer, Colin. "Induced Abortion After Feeling Fetal Movements: Its Causes and Emotional Consequences." *Journal of Biosocial Science* 10(1978):203–8.

Cherazi, Shahla. "Psychological Reaction to Abortion." *Journal of the American Medical Women's Association* 34(1979):287–88.

David, H.P. "Abortion in Psychological Perspective." *American Journal of Orthopsychiatry* 42(1972):61–68.

Deutsch, H. *Psychology of Women*. Vol. 2. New York: Grune and Stratton, 1945.

Dunbar, F. "A Psychosomatic Approach to Abortion and the Abortion Habit." In *Therapeutic Abortion*, edited by H. Rosen. New York: Julian Press, 1954 (re-released in 1967 as *Abortion in America*).

Ekblad, Martin. "Induced Abortion on Psychiatric Grounds: A Follow-up Study of 479 Women." *Acta Psychiatrica et Neurologica Scandinavica*, Supplement 99(1955).

Fleck, S. "Some Psychiatric Aspects of Abortion." *Journal of Nervous and Mental Disease* 151(1970):42–50.

Ford, C., P. Castelnuovo-Tedesco, and K.D. Long. "Women Who Seek Therapeutic Abortion: A Comparison with Women Who Complete Their Pregnancies." *American Journal of Psychiatry* 129(1972):546–52.

Freeman, Ellen W. "Influence of Personality Attributes on Abortion Experiences." *American Journal of Orthopsychiatry* 47(1977):503–13.

Freeman, Ellen W. "Abortion: Subjective Attitudes and Feelings." *Family Planning Perspectives* 10(1978):150–55.

Friedman, C.M., R. Greenspan, and F. Mittleman. "The Decision-Making Process and the Outcome of Therapeutic Abortion." *American Journal of Psychiatry* 131(1974):1332–37.

Galdston, I. "Other Aspects of the Abortion Problem: Psychiatric Aspects." In *Abortion in the United States*, edited by I. Galdston. New York: Hoeber-Harper, 1958.

Gillis, Aron. "A Follow-up of 72 Cases Referred for Abortion." *Mental Health and Society* 2(1975):212–18.

Greenglass, Esther R. "Therapeutic Abortion and Psychiatric Disturbance in Canadian Women." *Canadian Psychiatric Association Journal* 21(1976):453–60.

Kaltreider, Nancy, Sadja Goldsmith and Alan Margolis. "The Impact of Midtrimester Abortion Techniques on Patients and Staff." *American Journal of Obstetrics and Gynecology* 135(1979):235–38.

Kane, F.J. et al. "Motivational Factors in Abortion Patients." *American Journal of Psychiatry* 130(1973):209–93.

Kumar, R. and Kay Robson. "Previous Induced Abortion and Ante-Natal Depression in Primiparae: Preliminary Report of a Survey of Mental Health in Pregnancy." *Psychological Medicine* 8(1978):711–715.

Lask, Bryan. "Short-term Psychiatric Sequelae to Therapeutic Termination of Pregnancy." *British Journal of Psychiatry* 126(1975):173–77.

Margolis, Alan et al. "Therapeutic Abortion Follow-Up Study." *American Journal of Obstetrics and Gynecology* 110(1971):243–49.

Margolis, Alan et al. "Contraception After Abortion." *Family Planning Perspectives* 6(1974):56–60.

Mester, Roberto. "Induced Abortion and Psychotherapy." *Psychotherapy and Psychosomatics* 30(1978):98–104.

Niswander, K.R. and R. Patterson. "Psychologic Reaction to Therapeutic Abortion I: Subjective Patient Response." *Obstetrics and Gynecology* 29(1967):702–06.

Niswander, K.R., J. Singer, and M. Singer, "Psychological Reaction to Therapeutic Abortion II: Objective Response." *American Journal of Obstetrics and Gynecology* 114(1972):29–33.

Notman, M.T. "Pregnancy and Abortion: Implications for Career Development of Professional Women." *Annals of the New York Academy of Science* 208(1973):205–09.

Osofsky, H. and J. Osofsky, eds. *The Abortion Experience: Psychological and Medical Impact.* New York: Harper and Row, 1973.

Osofsky, J. and H. Osofsky. "The Psychological Reaction of Patients to Legalized Abortion." *American Journal of Orthopsychiatry* 42(1972):48–60.

Patt, S., R. Rappaport, and P. Barglow. "Follow-up of Therapeutic Abortion." *Archives of General Psychiatry* 20(1969):408–14.

Payne, E. et al. "Methodological Issues in Therapeutic Abortion Research." In *The Abortion Experience: Psychological and Medical Impact,* edited by H. Osofsky and J. Osofsky. New York: Harper and Row, 1975.

Payne, Edmund C. et al. "Outcome Following Therapeutic Abortion." *Archives of General Psychiatry* 33(1976):725–33.

Peck, A. and H. Marcus. "Psychiatric Sequelae of Therapeutic Interruption of Pregnancy." *Journal of Nervous and Mental Disease* 143(1966):417–25.

Pohlman, E. "Abortion Dogmas Needing Research Scrutiny." In *Abortion: Changing Views and Practices,* edited by R.B. Sloane. New York: Grune and Stratton, 1971, (originally in *Seminars in Psychiatry,* August, 1970).

Rooks, Judith Bourne and Willard Cates, Jr. "Emotional Impact of D&E vs. Instillation." *Family Planning Perspectives* 9(1977):276–77.

Sarvis, B. and H. Rodman. *The Abortion Controversy.* New York: Columbia University Press, 1973.

Schregardus, Darell J. "A Study of Defensive Style and Its Interaction with Perception and Experience of Stress." *Dissertation Abstracts International* 38(1977):400–401.

Shusterman, Liza Roseman. "Predicting the Psychological Consequences of Abortion." *Social Sciences and Medicine* 13(1979):683–89.

Simon, N. and A.G. Senturia. "Psychiatric Sequelae of Abortion: Review of the Literature." *Archives of General Psychiatry* 15(1966):378–89.

Simon, N. et al. "Psychiatric Illness Following Therapeutic Abortion." *American Journal of Psychiatry* 124(1967):59–65.

Smith, Elizabeth. "A Follow-up of Women Who Request Abortion." *American Journal of Orthopsychiatry* 43(1973).

Taussig, F.J. "Effects of Abortion on the General Health and Reproductive Functions of the Individual." In *The Abortion Problem*, edited by H. Taylor. Baltimore: Williams-Wilkins, 1942.

Walter, G.S. "Psychologic and Emotional Consequences of Elective Abortion." *Obstetrics and Gynecology* 36(1970)482:91.

Wilson, D.C. "The Abortion Problem in the General Hospital." In *Therapeutic Abortion*, edited by H. Rosen. New York: Julian Press, 1954 (re-released in 1967 as *Abortion in America*).

Zimmerman, Mary. *Passage Through Abortion: The Personal and Social Reality of Women's Experiences*. New York: Praeger Publishers, 1977.

7

A Canadian Study of Psychological Adjustment After Abortion*

Esther R. Greenglass

The study of the psychology of abortion in women is significant for a number of reasons. With women's social role undergoing such rapid social change, particularly with regard to their fertility, systematic knowledge of the psychodynamics of abortion should shed light on how contemporary women cope with a major fertility decision. Psychological adjustment after abortion should be explored, not only for its own sake, but also so that informed social and legal decisions about abortion can be made on the basis of knowledge rather than personal bias. And finally, because abortion, unlike other operative procedures, involves political, religious, moral, and social overtones, frequently one finds a polarization as well as ambivalence associated with attitudes that people hold towards the woman having an abortion. Frequently, the woman who undergoes abortion cannot but reflect this ambivalence herself. Abortion counselling, which occurs far too infrequently in Canada, is an integral part of the abortion procedure in many of the teaching hospitals in parts of the United States. Effective counselling programs have to build on a systematic body of information relating to the psychological adjustment of abortion.

Despite extensive worldwide research on the psychological sequelae of abortion which has been going on for 45 years, systematic knowledge of the psychological effects of abortion is not forthcoming because of the relative lack of sound research which tends to be permeated with researchers' subjective opinion. An additional problem relates to the difficulty in generalizing results of studies done in countries which vary considerably in the grounds on which therapeutic abortions are granted. So, for example, because therapeutic abortion in Canada is legally granted on health grounds, women having abortions in Canada may differ from those granted abortion on request, as is the case in the

*This study is part of a larger project sponsored by Canada Council Grants S71-0471, S73-0846 and S74-1322.

United States. This is of particular importance when studying psychological sequelae of abortion since hospital therapeutic abortion committees likely favour women with a history of poor adjustment when considering abortion applicants.

Several early investigations of women obtaining legal, therapeutic abortions conclude that the psychological effects are unfavourable (e.g., Taussig, 1936; Romm, 1954; Lidz, 1954). However, since these conclusions tend to be based on the investigators' own clinical experiences, they are questionable because of reliability and validity difficulties associated with this kind of subjective data. In other studies done in Sweden where untoward effects of abortion have been reported (Arén, 1958; Arén and Amark, 1961), the methodology used was not described adequately, and once again, clinical impressions and subjective interviews were the bases of data collection. Further, these studies tend not to use control groups when assessing psychological effects of abortion. Moreover, a review of the studies concluding that abortion causes mental illness suggests that there is little in the way of objective and scientifically valid data to support this conclusion.

Several other studies, however, indicate no severe psychological effects of therapeutic abortion. For example, the results of a survey of 32 psychiatrists in California suggest that women who have abortions do not generally experience severe or even moderate psychiatric symptoms afterwards (Kummer, 1963). When asked whether or not they had ever encountered serious psychiatric difficulties in women who had legal or illegal abortions, 75 per cent of the doctors said they had not. Twenty-five per cent said they had encountered difficulties only rarely. In this study however, the results of illegal and legal abortions were not reported separately. Secondly, because of inadequate information on the methodology employed, that is, how the woman's emotional condition was assessed, it is difficult to evaluate the validity of these findings. Two other studies conclude that abortion may actually result in improvement of the woman's mental health and in a reduction in psychopathology (Brody et al., 1971; McCance et al., 1973). In both of these prospective studies, psychopathological symptoms were evaluated objectively among women who applied for therapeutic abortion. Comparisons were then made between women who had abortions and those whose applications for abortion had been refused. In the Brody et al. study, initially, abortion applicants showed more psychological disturbance than a group of "controls" (women in the same stage of pregnancy). After the abortion, women who had abortions had MMPI profiles approaching normalcy; refused applicants remained as disturbed as they were initially. And in the study by McCance et al. in Aberdeen, women who obtained abortions showed more lifting of depression and lessening of hostility than those compelled to carry an unwanted pregnancy to term. Thus, the mental health of a woman faced with an unwanted pregnancy stands a greater chance of improving when she has an abortion than when she is forced against her will to carry a pregnancy to term. On the basis of her rather extensive review of the literature, Roseman Shusterman (1976) concludes that there is stronger evidence that therapeutic abortion is basically untraumatic (if not favourable) than that it leads to psychopathology.

Yet, there are other data to suggest that a woman's adjustment after abortion is dependent on circumstances surrounding the abortion. Some of these include the woman's reason(s) for abortion, and the extent of emotional support the woman has in the abortion decision (Freeman, 1978). Along the same line, when the doctor and attending nurse are seen as non-supportive or critical of the woman, negative effects are more likely to result (Walter, 1970). It is further suggested that a woman's adjustment after abortion may be dependent on her future fertility plans. For example, when "older" married women who have two or more children undergo concomitant abortion and sterilization because they feel they have had "enough" children, they show a relative absence of neurotic symptoms afterwards (Malmfors, 1958; Pare and Raven, 1970). This outcome is quite understandable in light of the probable absence of ambivalence about abortion among women who have concomitant sterilization and thus plan *not* to have children after abortion. But the situation is very different for many women who may want to have a child at some future date, but because of overwhelming immediate circumstances, have opted to abort the present pregnancy. For these women, it is expected that abortion would generate ambivalence which may result in some unfavourable psychological sequelae.

In examining psychiatric impairment after abortion, one of the major factors that should be considered is the woman's overall mental health before the abortion. For example, in Malmfors (1958) study of Swedish women who had undergone abortion, 12 per cent of the women were reported to have suffered mental health impairment afterwards, but all of them had various neurotic complaints before the abortion. A woman in poor psychological health may be vulnerable to any operation or upset in her routine. Thus, in assessing psychiatric disturbance after abortion, it is necessary to take account of the woman's pre-abortion psychiatric state.

A Study of Psychological Adjustment After Abortion

The present study was undertaken in order to identify those variables that relate to a woman's adjustment after therapeutic abortion (see *After Abortion*, by E.R. Greenglass for complete study). The respondents were 188 women living in Canada who were interviewed from 1972 to 1973 an average of 36 weeks after their abortions. Eighty-five per cent of the women had their abortions within the first 12 weeks of their pregnancy and the rest had them at 13 weeks of pregnancy or later. While most of the interviews were conducted in Toronto, the sample included women both from Toronto and surrounding areas. Table 7–1 presents the demographic characteristics of women who participated in the study. On the whole the sample varies considerably on demographic variables. And, in the main, the proportion of women in each marital status closely resembles that of women obtaining therapeutic abortions in Canada. In 1977, for example, 60 per cent of women obtaining therapeutic abortions in Canada were single, 29 per cent were married, and 10 per cent were divorced, separated or common-law at the time of abortion (Statistics Canada, 1977). Women who had abortions were also closely matched with three groups of women who did not have abortions (controls) as to age, religion, education and socio-economic status. One group consisted of 20 single women who had never been pregnant. Another comprised 23 married women who had given birth 5 to 17 months before the interview (approximately the same time interval as between the abortion and the interview). A third control group consisted of 40 married women who did not have any babies less than 18 months old, or who had not been pregnant within the last 18 months. These control groups were included in order to compare psychological adjustment after abortion among single women, and among married women after they had carried a fetus to term and given birth.

Measures of Psychological Adjustment

The main psychological test of adjustment was the Differential Personality Inventory (DPI) (Jackson and Messick, 1970), a true-false questionnaire designed to assess a relatively normal person's degree of neurotic or emotional disturbance in personality functioning on 27 scales. The scales are described here under five general headings: first, there are those that measure physical and somatic complaints such as insomnia, headache-proneness, health concern, and hypochondriasis, among others. A second set of scales measures the person's broodiness, depression, and self-depreciation. A third group of scales assesses the degree of disturbance in social interaction by, for example, degree of cynicism, desocialization, familial discord, hostility, ideas of persecution, irritability, rebelliousness, and socially deviant attitudes. Seven scales are used to assess perceptive, intellectual and affective disturbance by measuring, for example, disorganization of thinking, impulsivity, panic reaction, feelings of unreality, etc. Five other scales measure shallow affect, sadism, and repression.

On another measure the woman was asked to indicate how she perceived herself on a variety of characteristics. These took the form of a series of pairs of opposite adjectives such as warm-cold, which were listed with space between them so that the woman could indicate with a check mark just where on the continuum she saw herself on a given characteristic. The assumption was that if a woman saw herself as a warm person, for example, she would place her check mark closer to the "warm" end of the scale than the "cold" end. Some of the bipolar adjectives were: warm/cold, satisfied/dissatisfied, bad/good, healthy/unhealthy, sure/shifting, guilty/not guilty, peaceful/troubled, unworried/worried, sad/happy, full/empty. On another test, the woman's attitudes toward abortion in general were assessed. It consisted of 11 attitudinal statements, including seven that described possible after-effects of abortion. The woman was asked to indicate her degree of agreement or disagreement with these after-effects on a 7-point scale that went from 1, "agree strongly," to 7, "disagree strongly," point 4 being "neither agree nor disagree." Examples of these statements are:

"Women feel shame after having an abortion"; "Women do not feel depressed after having an abortion."

Table 7–1

DEMOGRAPHIC VARIABLES OF WOMEN WHO HAD ABORTIONS

Variable	Categories	Frequency	Per cent
Marital Status	Single	100	53.2
	Married	63	33.5
	Divorced or Separated	25	13.3
		188	100.0
Age	24 years old or less	91	48.4
	25 years old or more	97	51.6
		188	100.0
Education	Non-university	130	69.1
	University	58	30.9
		188	100.0
Religion	Protestant	82	43.6
	Catholic	34	18.1
	Jewish	13	6.9
	Agnostic and Atheist	49	26.0
	Other*	10	5.3
		188	99.9†
Woman's full-time occupational status‡	High	27	28.1
	Low	69	71.9
		96	100.0
Husband's full-time occupational status	High	28	49.1
	Low	29	50.9
		57§	100.0

*Includes Buddhist, Humanist, Hindu, Christian, Spiritualist, Greek Orthodox, Unitarian, Pantheist, etc.
†Does not add up to 100 per cent due to rounding.
‡High status occupations include those labeled as professional, proprietal, managerial, financial, semi-professional and technical. Low status occupations include those labeled clerical, sales, artisan, foreman, skilled factory, repair and service.
§57 of 63 married women reported their husbands working full-time.

Psychological Adjustment after Abortion

Comparisons between abortees and controls suggest that abortion is not associated with profound or widespread psychological disturbance afterwards, either for married or for single women. For example, of the 27 scales assessing psychological functioning, married abortees obtained significantly higher scores than the two married control groups on only two of the scales — rebelliousness and depression.*Single women who had abortions showed more rebelliousness and more shallow affect (a pronounced tendency to be unemotional) than those who did not have abortions. It should be pointed out however, that since the average DPI scores of all respondents were well within the normal range of scores obtained by the majority of those on whom the DPI had originally been standardized (Jackson, 1971), the relatively greater psychological disturbance found for abortees was not great enough to be called "abnormal."

Nevertheless, there was greater depression among married women who had abortions. Other research suggests that the depression observed here might well have been transient, and that had the women been interviewed a longer time after the abortion than they had been here (an average of nine months), married abortees would not have been found to be more depressed. For example, while symptoms such as depression, guilt and anxiety may occur in some women immediately following abortion, these symptoms have been found to either disappear or diminish considerably within a few weeks or months (Senay, 1970; Ford et al., 1971). And, in an American study where the amount of time until follow-up was considerably longer — 13 to 26 months — women who had abortions were not more depressed than those who had delivered a child (Athanasiou et al., 1973). In the Aberdeen study cited earlier, where length of time until follow-up was also longer than in the present study (18 months), women who had abortions showed more lifting of depression afterwards than women compelled to carry a pregnancy to term because they were refused a legal abortion (McCance et al., 1973). In light of these findings, it seems likely then that married abortees in the present study experienced a relatively transient depression. One possible explanation for the married woman's depression may involve one of the basic norms of marriage — namely that prescribing reproduction. By having an abortion, married women (in contrast to their single counterparts) may have perceived themselves as having violated this basic norm, at least as far as this pregnancy was concerned. Thus, married women may feel they have failed to live up to societal, and possibly their own expectations regarding appropriate feminine behaviour in marriage, and as a result, they feel depressed. One married woman, for example, admitted that she was depressed afterwards and said, "I would not like to have children for myself, but I would like one (child) for my husband and daughter."

Both married and single women who had abortions scored higher on rebelliousness than controls. A person scoring high on rebelliousness is one who "frequently is uncooperative, disobedient, and resistant when faced with rules and regulations; reacts against discipline and criticism" (Jackson, 1971). Is it possible that women in Canada who have abortions are made to feel "deviant,"

---

*Detailed statistical elaboration of the results may be obtained from the book, *After Abortion*; t-tests and analyses of variance were used and only results significant at the .05 level or better are reported here.

since frequently the grounds on which they must convince a therapeutic abortion committee to grant them an abortion are psychiatric in nature? The woman may then feel she *is* abnormal or deviant regardless of her original reasons for wanting an abortion. Feelings of shame for having had an abortion can be seen in remarks in the hospital of one separated woman after her abortion. She said, "one mother after another came into my room. Their reactions were bad. They were uncomfortable and so was I. They knew I had an abortion." Alternatively, given that there is still considerable ambivalence associated with abortion in Canada, it may be that women must be somewhat rebellious and nonconformist in the first place in order to obtain an abortion. It will be recalled that single women after abortion were found to have greater shallow affect. Single women were also more rebellious, and they, as well as their married counterparts, felt they were deviant after their abortions. But for single women there is probably another factor contributing to this feeling — namely, the admission of having engaged in sexual intercourse. While there may be pressures on women to have pre-marital intercourse, single women are not supposed to admit publicly that they do so. In this social context, abortion may be perceived as a shameful act. Thus, one possible interpretation of the results is that single women develop an unemotional attitude both towards themselves and life in general as a kind of defense against painful feelings of shame.

Antecedent Conditions and Psychological Adjustment After Abortion

While relief has been found to be one of the main psychological reactions to abortion (Illsley and Hall, 1976; Institute of Medicine, 1975), nevertheless the decision to abort may involve considerable difficulty for some women who may vary considerably in the degree to which they resolve their emotions after. In order to construct a more comprehensive view of the psychology of abortion, it is necessary to investigate the relationship between certain antecedent conditions and consequent psychological reactions. Some of the antecedent factors include the woman's reason(s) for abortion, how the abortion decision was reached, and the reactions of "significant" others to the woman undergoing abortion.

Reason(s) for Abortion

In this study, when women were asked why they had an abortion 64 per cent gave "social" reasons. These included financial factors, age, poor relationship with the man, and problems related to having and raising an illegitimate child. As expected, social reasons tended to be given by single, separated and divorced women. Approximately 29 per cent of the women gave "motivational" reasons which included "not wanting a (another) child," and the psychological health of the women. The remaining women gave a physical reason for their abortions such as, possible fetal abnormalities and the women's health. Married women tended to give physical and motivational reasons. Analyses of DPI scores as a function of "reason for abortion" showed that there were differences on only one scale — broodiness. Women who were aborted for physical reasons had the highest scores when compared with those giving motivational or social reasons. Women who aborted for physical reasons, in contrast to the others, probably wanted the child and thus likely regretted not being able to carry their pregnancy to term. But, despite their strong wish for a child, they had decided (most likely after consulting their doctor) to terminate their pregnancy because of rubella, or some other threat to the fetus, or to themselves.

The Abortion Decision

In the present study, women made the decision to have an abortion in one of three ways: 48 per cent said they had made the decision themselves, 45 per cent said the decision was made along with one or two people close to them (their male partner, a family member or a friend), and about 6 per cent said they were pressured into the abortion but that they themselves were against it. Women who were pressured into the abortion experienced the most psychological disturbance after, and they held the most negative attitudes toward abortion. These women, who were mainly young and unmarried, had the highest scores on hypochondriasis, ideas of persecution, and self-depreciation. They also saw themselves as more dissatisfied, unhealthy, more shifting, guilty, worried, and unhappy than the others. Their attitudes toward abortion were also markedly negative, as evidenced in their stated belief that women who have abortions will have negative psychological and physical after-effects. Thus, the abortion experience for a woman pressured into it is an ambivalent one — on the one hand, she sees abortion as a negative thing, but on the other, she has had an abortion herself. Such ambivalence may be the factor responsible for the woman's greater psychological disturbance afterwards.

In contrast, support from others in the abortion decision is clearly a factor related to more favourable psychological adjustment after. When the woman reported she made the decision with people close to her who also supported her, she showed the least hypochondriasis, ideas of persecution and self-depreciation, and she also perceived herself the most satisfied, healthy, sure, happy and the least guilty when compared to the others. The relationship between support from others (parents or the male partner) for the abortion decision and a positive adjustment afterwards has also been reported by Bracken et al. (1974). Similarly, Freeman (1978) found, in a sample of largely young unmarried women, that those who had resolved their abortion experience at follow-up four months later, perceived support from their partners for the decision.

Attitudes of Physician and Staff Toward the Woman

All of the women were asked to describe the attitudes towards them of the doctor who performed the abortion, as well as the attending nurse. These were categorized by independent observers as positive, negative or neutral. Sixty-two per cent of the women perceived their physician's attitude as positive and 65 per cent described the nurse in the same way. Examples of some of these attitudes were, "he (the doctor) treated me as a person . . . nothing to be ashamed of." And, another woman described the nurse's attitude as "fantastic." A sizable number of respondents described the attitudes of the doctor and nurse as negative — 23 per cent perceived the physician's attitude as negative, and 18 per cent described the staff as negative. One young single woman said of her doctor: "he (the doctor) felt it was a shame. Throughout the abortion he kept making comments about my situation and commented on the sex of the baby. It was upsetting." Another single woman said, "the nurses didn't like us" (women who had abortions). Psychological adjustment varied with the woman's perception of the attitudes of those attending her. Women who perceived their physician's attitude as negative had higher scores than the others on feelings of unreality, health concern, hypochondriasis, rebelliousness and somatic complaints. But women who perceived positive attitudes on the part of the physician obtained the lowest scores on insomnia, impulsivity, rebelliousness and somatic complaints. They also had the best self-image. Women who described their reported by 30 per cent of the women (or of the 56, 27 had received psychiatric the others. Similar results were obtained for the relationship between adjustment and the woman's description of the nurse's attitudes. It is possible that medical personnel were reacting negatively to a woman who might have been somewhat neurotic before her abortion? While it is difficult to disentangle the "real" attitudes of those attending the woman from her perceptions of them, the nature of some of these attitudes as described by the women suggests that this is not likely. Many of the comments, as quoted by the woman, were not directed specifically toward the woman but rather appeared to reflect attitudes which condemned abortion in general.

Clearly, these results have important implications for the way in which physicians and attending staff treat women who experience abortion. The mental health of a woman having an abortion would be seriously endangered if she were to encounter a physician or a nurse with a critical, disapproving or punitive attitude. In hospitals efforts should be made to prevent contact between women having abortions and staff who disapprove of or reject women undergoing abortion. Only individuals who can support the woman in her decision to have an abortion should be allowed to attend her.

Fertility Plans and Psychological Adjustment

To what extent does psychological adjustment vary with a woman's fertility plans? When asked whether or not they planned to bear children in the future, about one-half of the women said they did, 38 per cent said they did not, and 11 per cent were unsure. These groups differed in other ways as well; the vast majority of those planning to have children at a future date had no children at the time of abortion and most were single. And of women planning to have no children in the future, most had at least one child and were married. Women with fertility plans showed a more unfavourable psychological adjustment after abortion than the others. Specifically, they appeared to suffer more from physical complaints (health concern and somatic problems), and they tended to show more perceptual distortion and emotional instability (such as broodiness, ideas of persecution, and mood fluctuation). They also held more unfavourable attitudes towards abortion and its after-effects than the others. For example, they attributed depression, guilt and psychological problems to hypothetical women who have abortions. And they tended to disagree with the statement that "women in general feel no regrets after having an abortion." Women who planned to have children also agreed less than the others that "a woman can feel completely psychologically fulfilled if she does not have children." It would appear that abortion for the woman planning on having children is an ambivalent event. While practically all these women freely chose abortion, most were single and had the abortion not because they did not want children, but because having a child *at that time* would likely have entailed a good deal of social and financial hardship. These same women expressed a wish to bear children at some time in the future. The data suggest that this wish was a central part of their perceptions of themselves as women, as seen by their affirmation of the statement that having children was important for a woman's complete psychological fulfillment.

There is then, a dissonance of conflict in the woman having an abortion who at the same time plans to bear children later. On a conscious level, abortion is for her the only practicable solution to what could become an intolerable social situation should she deliver the child. When asked, most of these women stated that they believed themselves still able to conceive after the abortion. Yet even with this belief, the woman who plans to bear children may feel on an unconscious level that having an abortion will hinder her in fulfilling herself completely. Their negative attitudes toward abortion, and their belief that it is associated with psychological problems in other women, may be the result of projection. Being unable to reconcile their ambivalence, these women may then attribute or project uncomfortable feelings onto others who have abortions, thus attempting to relieve their anxiety.

As was discussed earlier, the unfavourable psychological sequelae observed after abortion among women in this study may well be transient. Nevertheless, the finding that women planning to have children in the future may have some psychological disturbance after their abortion, even if only short-lived, should be of practical interest to those involved in abortion counselling. Counselling could be directed towards encouraging the woman to verbalize her ambivalence and helping her reconcile her dissonant wishes in an atmosphere of emotional support and understanding. Group discussion with others who experience similar dissonance may also prove effective in helping the woman work through her ambivalence. Here the woman could learn that her feelings may not be unique to her, and provided the group leader (counsellor) focuses on the women's strengths rather than their weaknesses she may also learn coping strategies from others in a similar situation.

Abortion and Psychiatric Disturbance

In order to objectively assess the extent and severity of psychiatric disturbance after abortion, three criteria were employed. These were: whether or not the woman had sought psychiatric or psychological help, had been hospitalized for emotional disturbance, and / or had attempted suicide. These measures were used to assess psychiatric disturbance both before and after the abortion since previous research has shown that women with serious psychiatric problems prior to their abortions are more likely than those with no psychiatric history to have difficulties afterwards (Simon et al., 1967; Ekblad, 1955; Jansson, 1965).

The results showed that the majority of the women (166 or 88 per cent) had no psychiatric disturbance after abortion. Most (15) of the remaining 22 women who reported disturbance afterwards had only sought psychiatric help on an outpatient basis. Two had been hospitalized for emotional disturbance, and five had attempted suicide after the abortion. Psychiatric disturbance before abortion was reported by 30 per cent of the women (or of the 56 — 27 had received psychiatric help, 8 had been hospitalized, and 21 had attempted suicide an average of 66 months before the abortion). To what extent did women with disturbance prior to abortion also have psychiatric disturbance afterwards? Of the 56 women who reported disturbance before, 21 per cent showed some signs of disturbance afterwards. And, of the 132 women with no psychiatric history before the abortion, 7 per cent experienced some disturbance afterwards (see Table 7–2).

Table 7–2

WOMEN WITH (NO) PRE-ABORTION PSYCHIATRIC DISTURBANCE WHO
REPORTED (NO) POST-ABORTION PSYCHIATRIC DISTURBANCE

	Pre-abortion psychiatric disturbance		
	Absent N = 132	Present N = 56	Total N = 188
Post-abortion Psychiatric Disturbance Absent N = 166	122 *73.5% †92.4%	44 26.5% 78.6%	166
Present N = 22	10 45.5% 7.6%	12 54.5% 21.4%	22
Total	132	56	188

*Row percentage
†Column percentage

These results suggest again that abortion is not a traumatic event for most women. The vast majority of women reported that they did not have emotional problems afterwards requiring psychiatric intervention. And, of those who did report some disturbance afterwards, the majority had only consulted a psychiatrist or a psychologist on an outpatient basis for an average of three months after the abortion. While one might be tempted to draw a causal relationship between the abortion and the appearance of some subsequent disturbance, it is noteworthy that for four out of the five women who attempted suicide, circumstances other than the abortion *per se* were likely the precipitating factors. Three of the women said they had attempted suicide because of difficulties with the man, or because of "family circumstances." One woman, for example, said that her boy-friend was against her obtaining an abortion and had become so violent in his attempt to stop her that she had to call the police. In the fourth case the woman had attempted suicide before the abortion and the pregnancy (suggesting that she might have been unstable prior to the abortion), and she also believed her mother had forced her into having the abortion against her will. Thus, researchers and counsellors in the area of abortion should be aware that often, circumstances other than the abortion may be the reasons for attempted suicide afterwards.

Not all women are equally susceptible to psychiatric disturbance after their abortions. Moreover, women with a psychiatric history were three times as likely to have some disturbance afterwards as those who did not report past psychiatric difficulties. It is quite possible that coping in general, and with an abortion in particular, may be more difficult for the woman who has had psychiatric problems previously. Moreover, given the ambivalence that characterizes the norms and attitudes relating to abortion in Canada, abortion may be particularly anxiety-provoking for these women. Or, psychiatric disturbance may simply represent a continuation of problems that were present before the abortion.

Finally, it is necessary to comment on what appears to be a relatively high proportion of women (11 per cent) who had attempted to commit suicide before their abortions. It is suggested that hospital therapeutic abortion committees may more likely grant abortions to women whom they consider are suicidal (because of their psychiatric history). Further, the finding that approximately 30 per cent of the women had experienced some psychiatric difficulty prior to their abortion suggests that legal abortions are either not sought or granted to women in general. It may be that therapeutic abortion committees cull women who appear the most troubled from those applying for legal abortion. One of the implications of this practice is that legal abortion is probably being granted in strict accordance with the law, and that frequently, applications of women may be rejected because they do not appear "sick enough" to be granted an abortion. But if a woman seeks an abortion because of intolerable social conditions, does this mean her "need" for abortion is any less? Should she be forced to bear a child against her will, her undesirable social situation may eventually precipitate a psychiatric state. While such practices on the part of therapeutic abortion committees may facilitate their decision-making, they do not take into account the woman's needs, and as such, may actually present a danger to the woman's mental health.

Conclusions and Implications

The results of this study generally support the conclusion that abortion does not lead to severe psychological disturbance afterwards. However, women do vary in the extent to which they resolve their feelings afterwards, and when symptomatology does appear, it can be traced to various antecedent factors associated with the abortion. For example, lack of support for the abortion decision, and critical or disapproving attitudes on the part of medical personnel attending the women were found associated with some transient symptomatology. Conversely, when the abortion decision was made along with others close to the woman who also supported her, or when medical personnel were positive towards the woman undergoing abortion, psychological adjustment was greatly enhanced.

Moreover, feelings of "deviance" expressed by both married and single abortees alike probably derive largely from the nature of the law regulating granting of therapeutic abortions in Canada which rely primarily on "psychiatric" reasons. So even if a woman seeks an abortion because of intolerable social circumstances, she may come to see herself as deviant or abnormal because her reasons will likely be redefined as psychiatric by the committee in order to neatly fit the legal grounds required for abortion in this country. Thus, some of the untoward psychological effects of abortion observed in this study could be considerably lessened if hospital therapeutic abortion committees were abolished and the woman were allowed to decide with her doctor whether or not she will have an abortion.

Ambivalence about the abortion may occur among women forced into it against their will, as well as among those who plan to bear children in the future. These results have important implications for abortion counselling which should be available to women both before and after their abortions. Group counselling may be particularly effective in helping the woman work through any ambivalent feelings she may have, in an atmosphere of emotional support from others which should also counteract somewhat feelings of having been put down or criticized as a result of having had an abortion. Finally, counsellors in this area should be aware that frequently, circumstances other than the abortion *per se* may be the precipitating factors in the appearance of any psychiatric disturbance.

References

Arén, P. "Legal Abortion in Sweden." *Acta Obstet. Gynecol. Scandinav.* 36(1958): Supp. 1.

Arén, P., and C. Amark. "The Prognosis in Cases in Which Legal Abortion Has Been Granted But Not Carried Out." *Acta. Obstet. Gynecol. Scandinav.* 36(1958):203–78.

Athanasiou, R., L. Michelson, W. Oppel, T. Unger, and M.A. Yager. "Psychiatric Sequelae to Term Birth and Induced Early and Late Abortion: A Longitudinal Study." *Fam. Plan. Perspect.* 5(1973):227–31.

Bracken, M., M. Hachamovitch, and G. Grossman. The Decision to Abort and Psychological Sequelae. *J. Nerv. Ment. Dis.* 158(1974):154–62.

Brody, H., S. Meikle, and R. Gerritse, "Therapeutic Abortion: A Prospective Study." *Amer. J. Obstet. Gynecol.* 109(1971):347–52.

Ekblad, M. "Induced Abortions on Psychiatric Grounds: A Follow-up Study of 479 Women." *Acta Psychiat. Neurol. Scandinav.* Supp. 99(1955):1–238.

Ford, C., P. Castelnuovo-Tedesco, and K. Long. "Abortion: Is it a Therapeutic Procedure in Psychiatry?" *J. Amer. Med. Assocn.* 218(1971):1173–78.

Freeman, E.W. "Abortion: Subjective Attitudes and Feelings." *Fam. Plan. Perspect.* 10(1978):150–55.

Greenglass, E.R. *After Abortion.* Don Mills: Longman Canada Ltd., 1976.

Illsley, R., and M. Hall. "Psychosocial Aspects of Abortion: A Review of Issues and Needed Research." *Bull. World Hlth. Org.* 53(1976):83–106.

Institute of Medicine. *Legalized Abortion and the Public Health.* Washington, D.C.: National Academy of Sciences, 1975.

Jackson, D., and S. Messick, *The Differential Personality Inventory.* New York: Research Psychological Press, 1970.

Jackson, D. "Differential Personality Inventory Trait Descriptions for Manual." Unpublished manuscript, 1971.

Jansson, B. "Mental Disorders After Abortion." *Acta Psychiat. Scandinav.* 41(1965):87–110.

Kummer, J. "Post-abortion Psychiatric Illness — A Myth?" *Amer. J. Psychiat.* 119(1963):980–83.

Lidz, T. "Reflections of a psychiatrist." In *Therapeutic Abortion*, edited by H. Rosen, pp. 276–83. New York: The Julian Press, Inc., 1954.

Malmfors, K. "Other Aspects of the Abortion Problem." In *Abortion in the United States*, edited by M. Calderone, pp. 133–35. New York: Hoeber and Harper, 1958.

McCance, C., D.C. Olley, and V. Edward. "Long-term psychiatric follow-up." In *Experience with Abortion*, edited by G. Horobin, pp. 245–300. London: Cambridge University Press, 1973.

Pare, C.M.B., and H. Raven. "Follow-up of Patients Referred for Termination of Pregnancy." *The Lancet* 1(1970):635–38.

Romm, M. "Psychoanalytic considerations." In *Therapeutic Abortion*, edited by H. Rosen, pp. 209–12. New York: The Julian Press, Inc., 1954.

Roseman Shusterman, L. "The Psychosocial Factors of the Abortion Experience." *Psych. Women Quart.* 1(1976):79–106.

Senay, E.C. "Therapeutic Abortion: Clinical aspects." *Arch. Gen. Psychiat.* 23(1970):408–15.

Simon, N., A. Senturia, and D. Rothman. "Psychiatric Illness Following Therapeutic Abortion." *Amer. J. Psychiat.* 124(1967):97–103.

Statistics Canada. *Therapeutic Abortions*, p. 21. Ottawa: Information Canada, 1977.

Taussing, F.J. *Abortion, Spontaneous and Induced*. St. Louis: C.V. Mosby Co., 1936.

Walter, G.S. "Psychologic and Emotional Consequences of Elective Abortion: A Review." *Obstet. Gynecol.* 36(1970):482–90.

8

Women Who Are Refused and Who Refuse Abortion

Nathan M. Simon

Not all women requesting abortion have their pregnancies terminated. Some women are refused abortion, some women refuse to go through with the procedure when offered, and others are barred by cultural and economic factors from access to abortion. There are relatively few studies of women and their offspring who have been refused or refuse to go through with an abortion. These women make up a population group that is difficult to study carefully. Most of the studies reported are either uncontrolled or have control groups which differ markedly from the study group. Few studies use objective criteria and most rely on subjective evaluations.

Women who request abortion all share the quality of having a pregnancy that, at least initially, is unwanted to a degree as to make interruption a desirable course of action. Women who request interruption of pregnancy, however, are not homogeneous in the degree to which their pregnancies are unwanted. They represent a continuum that extends from a group who are irrevocably committed to a course of action that would result in the termination of the pregnancy, to a group who consider interruption as one of several possible courses of action or whose interest in interruption is, because of the special circumstances of the pregnancy, only transitory. The discussion that follows will examine a number of studies which have attempted to examine consequences to women who are refused abortion, women who refuse abortion, women who have almost no access to abortion, and the children born to these women.

The Women Who Are Refused and Who Refuse Abortion

Ambivalence about pregnancy is a very common phenomenon. Even women who have stable marriages and want additional children experience periods during a pregnancy when negative thoughts about the pregnancy are conscious and where the wish not to be pregnant appears. For some women a specific pregnancy may be a complete catastrophe. For others all pregnancies may be. Studies of women who felt negatively enough about their pregnancy to apply for abortion and then were refused an abortion or did not go through with the abortion, can give some information on the outcome of these unwanted pregnancies.

Hook (1963) studied 249 Swedish women 7½ to 11 years after they had been turned down for therapeutic abortion. Eleven per cent of these women had illegal abortions after their applications were refused, and another 3 per cent had spontaneous abortions. At the time of follow-up, Hook found that 53 per cent of the women had serious problems for several years after the pregnancy and finally "adjusted." There were another 24 per cent who still had pathological symptoms that were related to the pregnancy. Hook concluded that one-third of the women should have had abortions in order to avoid serious problems related to the pregnancy. What Hook does not explain is why the other 43 per cent who had serious and persistent problems should not have been aborted. Eighteen months after their applications were refused, 7 per cent of the women were unfit to work because of mental problems. In the period between eighteen months and the time of final follow-up an additional 13 per cent were unfit to work for the same reason. There was a difference between women with "deviating personalities" — psychiatric difficulties — prior to their application, and women who were described as normal. There was 42 per cent poor adjustment in the group of women who had deviating personalities and 12 per cent poor adjustment in the women described as normal.

These data indicate the high price paid in persisting psychological problems by women who are judged to have deviating personalities prior to their pregnancy. However, a significant portion of normal women (12 per cent) also paid a high price in terms of poor psychological adjustment. Another fact of importance is the high percentage of women who sought and successfully obtained abortion in a subsequent pregnancy. In subsequent pregnancies 50 per cent of these women, even though they had been refused before, actively sought and obtained abortion.

Arén and Amark (1961) followed 142 women who had permission to have legal abortions but chose not to have the procedure. Follow-ups were conducted three to five years later. Seventeen of the women refrained because sterilization was a necessary condition for the abortion. The authors felt that in 89 per cent of the cases the decision to have the child was justified, but in 11 per cent an abortion seemed indicated in retrospect.

A most important factor in this study and one that has been over-looked generally, is the fact that most of the women in this study voluntarily chose not to be aborted. Fifty per cent changed their minds regarding therapeutic abortion and another 25 per cent were "persuaded" by their gynecologists not to have the abortion. This group differs from the women studied by Hook. These women, while ambivalent about their pregnancies, still felt positively enough about them to turn down the abortion and go to term. This study when compared to Hook's emphasizes the importance of the woman's motivation. It should be added that in 57 women who became pregnant again in this series, only 42 per cent carried to term. The remaining 58 per cent had either legal, illegal or spontaneous abortions. This is far from a ringing endorsement for their prior decision to not go through with a legal abortion.

Sim (1968), an outspoken opponent of therapeutic abortion, published some data which seem to support my interpretation of the Hook and Arén-Amark data. As far as can be interpreted from his writings, Sim has never recommended therapeutic abortion. He reported a series of 54 women of mixed diagnoses whom he had followed during pregnancy. This was a highly selected sample. These women, all married, were referred to him by general practitioners who knew of his interest in treating women with serious psychiatric illness during pregnancy. Only four of these women wanted to have their pregnancies terminated by a therapeutic abortion. That is, 93 per cent were apparently interested in continuing their pregnancy, while only 7 per cent wanted their pregnancies interrupted. One woman had recurring admissions to psychiatric hospitals following the pregnancy; another woman developed a puerperal psychosis. Sim does not indicate whether either of these women wanted to continue their pregnancy or wanted an abortion. Sim's data indicate that in the group of women he studied, 93 per cent of whom did not want an abortion, the pregnancy could be "managed" by a psychiatrist who never recommended interruption.

Clark et al. (1968) studied a group of 426 women referred for therapeutic abortion during the period 1961 to 1967 in London. A group of 229 women referred during the period 1961 to 1964 were studied. In 120 of this group, termination of pregnancy was recommended by the examining psychiatrist and in 109 termination was not recommended. Abortion was recommended more frequently for women over age 41 (17 out of 19) and less often in women under 21 (35 out of 70). Single and younger women were more frequently refused abortion. The women were followed-up at periods of time from six months to six years after they were seen for the consultation that decided whether or not they were to have an abortion. No specific data are given about average length of follow-up. The follow-ups were done by the general practitioners who originally referred the patients to hospitals for consideration of the therapeutic abortion. Thirty-two of the 109 women whose abortion requests were rejected obtained abortions elsewhere (12 legally and 20 illegally), six women reported spontaneous abortions (a rate at least two times higher than the usual rate); and 55 women delivered live babies. Thirty-nine (71 per cent) of these babies were kept by their mothers, 11 (20 per cent) were placed for adoption and six (10 per cent) were in the care of some governmental agency. However, in 16 women (15 per cent) the outcome was unknown. Of the 55 women who gave birth, 29 were judged to have improved as far as the psychological stress they had experienced was concerned and only 3 were judged to be worse at the time of follow-up; 22 of the women judged improved had accepted their babies. Seven women were judged to demonstrate greater psychological impairment at the time of the follow-up. The authors report that two other women not included in this series, referred too late in pregnancy to be terminated, committed suicide after their abortion request was refused.

Clark's study is a retrospective one. The authors did not explain what criteria were used to evaluate either improvement or disability. The outcome for 15 per cent of the women who gave birth is not known and the psychological assessment following termination of pregnancy is not known for an additional 15 per cent of the sample. The study demonstrates (a) the success with which women are able to terminate pregnancies even if they are initially refused an abortion, (b) the high rate of "spontaneous" abortion, (c) the high rate of adoption or placement of babies born to women who have been refused abortion, and (d) the sizable portion (30 per cent) where outcome is unknown because no follow-up data are available.

Pare and Raven (1970) did a follow-up study of 271 women who had been referred for termination of pregnancy for psychiatric indications and 82 women who were seen only by gynecologists for what apparently were non-psychiatric indications for interruption. The follow-ups were done one to three years after the initial contact with the hospital, and 250 of the 270 women referred for psychiatric reasons were contacted. Of these, 130 had an abortion recommended and 128 actually had the abortion performed, and 120 had the abortion request refused. Of these women, 36 per cent arranged to have abortions elsewhere, 3 per cent had spontaneous abortions and 61 per cent gave birth to live babies. Twenty per cent of the babies were given for adoption. Two of the women who had illegal abortions died, although in neither case was a death directly attributable to the abortion (the authors do not indicate the cause of death).

Of the 82 women who were seen only by gynecologists (where presumably there was not a psychiatric indication), information was obtained on 71 at follow-up. Twenty-two of these women had abortions and 49 had been initially refused abortion; 39 per cent (19 women) who had been refused abortions initially were able to obtain abortions elsewhere (illegally in most cases). Of the 30 women who continued their pregnancy to term there were 28 live births and 2 stillbirths (7 per cent, a high rate of stillborn). Three women who gave birth had severe depressions shortly after their delivery.

In both the psychiatric and gynecological series, stress of continued pregnancy was greatest in single women and those estranged from their husbands. One-third of the women who gave birth resented having to do so and reported feelings of resentment towards their babies.

This study is again a retrospective one and again there is lack of objective criteria in determining outcome. However, the results are remarkably like the Clark study. There is a relatively high rate of unknown outcomes, a large percentage of the women refused abortion initially managed to obtain abortion elsewhere, a high rate of spontaneous abortion, and a large percentage of babies were placed for adoption. The authors comment that of the women who continued their pregnancy, 34 per cent at follow-up felt the burden for having a child and still regretted the pregnancy had not been terminated. The author stated that six of these women should have undoubtedly had their pregnancies terminated because their ability to cope with an extra child was over-estimated, and depressive and/or phobic reactions resulted and were still present at follow-up. Four of the women from the psychiatric series were admitted to psychiatric hospitals because of severity of symptoms, two during pregnancy and two after delivery (one of these had several hospitalizations over the three-year follow-up period).

Smith (1973) reported on 154 women who called a referral agency requesting help in obtaining an abortion in St. Louis, Missouri. These women were interviewed at the time of initial contact by medical students using a standardized interviewing technique, and 125 of these women had abortions, while 29 did not. When contacted one to two years later four of the 29 women who had decided against abortion were discovered to have had spontaneous abortions, a rate of 14 per cent (somewhat higher than the 10 per cent estimated rate for spontaneous abortion in the United States). Twelve women delivered live babies; eight of these women kept their babies and four women placed their babies for adoption. However, the outcome of nine women (31 per cent of the group who did not choose abortion) was unknown at follow-up. Smith states that age, race, and religion did not appear to be significant factors in the decision to continue the pregnancy. Length of pregnancy at the time of the initial contact with the referring agency was of importance. All of the women who continued their pregnancies were over 12 weeks pregnant at the time of initial contact with the agency. Smith speculates that women who seek abortion later in pregnancy have more ambivalence about terminating pregnancy than do women who request abortion earlier.

Smith later studied a group of 175 women who had applied to a problem pregnancy counselling and abortion service in St. Louis and decided to continue their pregnancies after the initial contact. These women were invited by letter to participate in a study of women's health problems. There were 49 letters returned because of incorrect addresses or lack of forwarding address; 30 letters were not returned but the women could not be contacted by phone; 96 women were contacted by phone to arrange an interview. Ten refused — two of whom denied ever contacting the agency. There were 86 (49 per cent of the sample) women interviewed by a social worker using a semi-structured interview schedule. These women were similar in socio-demographic characteristics to the group that did not participate. All 86 women delivered live babies, but one died shortly after birth due to multiple congenital anomalies and another at a few weeks of age of Sudden Infant Death Syndrome; 12 (14 per cent) were placed for adoption. Most women felt the decision to continue the pregnancy was a shared one with the sexual partner's influence regarded as strongest. Seventy-two per cent of the women were satisfied with their decision, 10 per cent had regretted it but no longer did, and 18 per cent regretted the decision to continue and wished they had terminated the pregnancy. About half of the women (mostly married) reported their relationship with their sexual partners improved, but 25 per cent had ended the relationship, 15 per cent reported deterioration of the relationship, and 25 per cent sought professional help during or after the pregnancy (mostly for depression, anxiety, and marital problems). One subject, who had a history of depression, made a suicide attempt shortly after delivery. Twenty-one per cent of the women felt the pregnancy had a negative effect on their lives. Of 29 women married at the time of original contact, two were divorced at follow-up. Twelve of 48 single women were married at follow-up, all to the fathers of the child.

Smith's study demonstrates the problems in follow-up (only 49 per cent of the original sample): a high rate of adoptive placement (14 per cent), a high rate of treatment for psychological problems, and approximately 20 per cent unhappy about their decision and describing the effect of the pregnancy on their lives as negative.

Meyerowitz et al. (1971) studied 168 women in Rochester, New York who were referred for psychiatric consultation as possible candidates for therapeutic abortion. The psychiatrists recommended that 108 of these women in which the psychiatric recommendation was in favour of the abortion actually have the procedure performed. There were six spontaneous abortions, one woman changed her mind, five women were rejected by the obstetricians as not meeting their criteria, and outcome was unknown for three women. Of the 60 women where the psychiatrist did not recommend abortion, 23 carried to term, 4 had spontaneous abortions, 21 had abortions elsewhere, and there was no information obtained on 12 (20 per cent, a sizable portion of this subsample).

The follow-up data were obtained indirectly from obstetricians, family doctors, psychiatrists, and hospital admission records. Women in the upper social classes were much more successful in obtaining abortions elsewhere than women in the lower classes (by a ratio of 3 to 1) and white women were more successful than black women (by a ratio of 20 to 1). Of the 23 women who delivered live babies, seven had little or no distress during pregnancy, one had a severe depression, was hospitalized and had her baby placed for adoption, and for five (over 20 per cent) there was no information available. Table 8-1 shows subsequent psychosocial adaptation of the women in this sample. There appears to be little difference between outcomes in the abortion and pregnancy-to-term group, but the data are difficult to interpret because there is a large number of unknowns in the abortion group. The second-hand and third-hand, unsystematic manner in which the data were collected also makes interpretation extremely uncertain.

The authors believe that it is valuable to reassess persistent or worsening distress that appears in women after an initial abortion request has been rejected. They reconsidered three women who became more anxious and depressed after initial psychiatric consultation in which the abortion request had been denied. They recommended in all three of these cases that abortion be performed. This study also illuminates the bias present in most places where legal abortion decisions are adjudicated in some way. Older women and women with greater than five pregnancies are more likely to be approved for abortion, and single women over the age of 15 and under the age of 30 are more likely to be refused.

Drower and Nash (1978) were one of the first to do a prospective study. All the women who presented themselves at the Grote Schuur Hospital, Cape Town for consideration of psychiatric assessment for therapeutic abortion from February,

Table 8–1

SUBSEQUENT PSYCHOSOCIAL ADAPTATION

Adaptation	Induced Abortion		Pregnancy to Term	
	N =	%	N =	%
Better	47	41.2	7	30.4
Same	23	20.2	13	56.5
Worse	7	6.1	1	4.3
No Information	37	32.5	2	8.7
Total	114	100	23	100

Source: Meyerowitz, 1971.

1974 to May, 1975 were studied. They were all interviewed by the same social worker and psychiatrist. Follow-up was conducted by the same psychiatric social worker 12 to 18 months after initial contact. Standardized data were collected; there was a standardized psychiatric interview initially, and follow-up interviews were conducted by the same social worker. When this was not possible, data were collected by telephone or letter or from collateral sources; sexual partners or relatives were also interviewed. One complicating factor of this study, not commented on by the authors, was the fact that women who refused termination of pregnancy were offered counselling services to assist them in dealing with the problems growing out of refusal.

Drower and Nash's study done in South Africa nearly ten years after the Meyerowitz study reveals a similar pattern. Very young women (under 16), older women (over 30), and women with more than four children all were more likely to have abortions. Women with previous sexual partners were significantly more likely to be refused abortion. This again raised the question of a bias operating among decision makers in places where abortion requests are dealt with by a committee or must meet legal criteria.

Drower and Nash studied 90 women who had applied for abortion on psychiatric grounds and had been refused. They were able to contact 69 (78 per cent) of them 12 to 18 months after the initial request was refused. Fifty-five per cent (38 women) of these 69 women had their pregnancies go to term; six women placed their babies for adoption and 32 women kept their babies; 20 per cent (14 women) were able to have legal abortions elsewhere, 16 per cent (11 women) had miscarriages (again note the high rate), 13 per cent (nine women) attempted to have an illegal abortion that was not successful, and 9 per cent (six women) had illegal abortions that did terminate the pregnancy.

Three women attempted suicide, five had increased use of alcohol, tobacco, and other drugs, eight had increased use of tranquillizers, seven had adverse personality changes, and one had greater social isolation.

Drower and Nash believe that psychiatric sequelae are more likely to occur in women who have been unstable before the pregnancy at issue and that in those women continuation of pregnancy is likely to have a more adverse effect than therapeutic abortion (this is in agreement with Meyerowitz). Drower and Nash perceptively point out that some women present themselves for therapeutic abortion in order to resolve their ambivalence about the pregnancy and are actually relieved when abortion is refused.

Drower and Nash's study again demonstrates the large percentage of women who will seek termination of pregnancy even after refused initially. For this sample there is a somewhat lower rate of adoptive placement which may very well reflect different socio-cultural conditions in Cape Town. The 22 per cent sample attrition rate also reflects a problem seen repeatedly in studies related to abortion and unwanted pregnancy. Being pregnant, adolescent, black, and poor in the United States, especially before 1973, but even now in most cases, is the equivalent of having an abortion request refused or refusing an abortion.

The problems relating to pregnancy in adolescents are complex. To point out that child-bearing begins at 13 or 14 in some primitive cultures, as one author has done recently, is not exactly relevant to the emotional stresses an adolescent will face in the United States when she becomes pregnant. I do not wish to oversimplify or attribute causality where only relationships are present, but the following seems relevant. Most early adolescents are singularly unprepared psychologically to assume the functions of caring for and raising a child and almost invariably none of them does. Out-of-wedlock children of white adolescent girls are almost invariably placed for adoption. Out-of-wedlock children of black adolescent girls are almost invariably cared for by the girl's mother or mother surrogate. In Waters' (1969) series only 10 per cent of the girls (who were nearly all black) returned to school. He saw the pregnancies in these girls as a critical point in the development of the "symptom of failure" which characterizes their later lives. Well over one-half of all teenage marriages are precipitated by pregnancy. Failure rates in teenage marriages are higher than marriages contracted by older partners.

Kane (1973) reported data on 132 white, adolescent, pregnant women he studied in Durham, North Carolina. Ninety-nine of these adolescent girls had abortions, while 33 of them were at the time of the study resident in maternity homes where they were planning to carry their pregnancies to term. The age, education, and religion of these two groups of young women were well matched. However, the abortion group came from families in which the head of household had significantly more education and more often was a white-collar worker. Both the group planning to carry to term and the abortion group showed more parental absence before the age of 18 than would have been expected for a group of similarly-aged women for the entire state of North Carolina. In this group of adolescents guilt over the use of contraceptives was common — guilt that was related often to conscious planning for sexual activity in advance. The authors diagnosed more of the continued pregnancy group as severe acting-out character disorders or girls for whom pregnancy was a manifestation of rebellious, angry attitudes. The continued pregnancy group also demonstrated a marked polarization of scores on a test which measured feminine and masculine traits. That is, the continuing pregnancy group clumped at either extreme of the possible scores of this paper-and-pencil test. The authors speculate that pregnancy in these young women was either an expression of very strong feminine trends or a reassurance that their tom-boy behaviour did not mean they were homosexual. The study illustrates the importance of cultural and socio-economic factors in the decision to continue an unwanted pregnancy rather than to choose an abortion.

Furstenberg (1976) studied (by structured interview) 404 women who had never been pregnant before under the age of 18 who registered at a prenatal clinic in Baltimore during 1966 to 1968. These young women were also interviewed three times subsequently: one year after the birth of the baby, in 1970, and in 1972 when the child was about five-years-old. Data were obtained on 331 women (81 per cent) at the final interview. These women were compared with a group of their former classmates, 221 women (61 per cent of those contacted) who were interviewed in 1970 and 1972. About 90 per cent of both groups were black women. The author found the "adolescent mothers" consistently experienced great difficulty in realizing their life plans, when compared with their classmates who did not become pregnant pre-maritally in their early teens. Marital instability, school disruption, economic problems and difficulties in family size regulation and childrearing were some of the complications brought on by their premature, unscheduled childbearing.

Furstenberg's data on the children born to these teenage mothers is uninterpretable because (a) the outcomes (live birth, spontaneous abortion, still birth, induced abortion) of the index pregnancies are not stated; (b) information on only 323 children is available at the five-year follow-up; and (c) there are inconsistancies in the numbers within the paper itself. Furstenberg found 304 children alive at five-years, 15 were known to be dead and four placed for adoption (their vital status could not be determined). Furstenberg reports 85 per cent of the mothers "rather" content with motherhood after the child was born, but this is derived from a sample in which there has been nearly 20 per cent attrition of the subjects being studied. There is also an unknown attrition rate (on vital status outcome) for the children. The death rate of 5 per cent by age five is at best, a most conservative estimate.

The Risk of Suicide

Suicide and attempted suicide are risks associated with unwanted pregnancy. Whitlock and Edwards (1968) have reviewed the literature on this subject thoroughly. They state, "suicide in pregnancy is not so uncommon as widely believed." The studies they mentioned in their excellent review of the literature have rates from 1 per cent to 20 per cent for the incidence of pregnant women among all women who committed suicide. The incidence of pregnancy among women attempting suicide ran from about 6 per cent to 12 per cent. Whitlock and Edwards' own study of attempted suicide of 483 women (Brisbane, Australia) showed a rate of 7.2 per cent of pregnant women for all women under the age of 45. Whitlock and Edwards thought that about half of the 30 women's pregnancies were related to the suicide attempt. They also estimated that since 7 per cent of the women in the population are pregnant at a given time in Australia, the incidence of pregnant women in their sample then could be accounted for primarily as a matter of chance distribution.

In Hook's study, (1963) 31 of the original 294 reported applicants reapplied for termination of pregnancy, for the same pregnancy, after they were initially refused; 24 were approved. Of these, 14 had voiced serious suicidal threats to friends or members of their family. This would indicate that the Swedish Abortion Boards are sensitive to the threat of suicide and tend to be more responsive to those women whom they consider serious suicidal threats and, therefore, grant more of them permission for legal abortion. It means that the group of women who are not aborted have been culled for the most serious suicidal threats. Lindberg (1963) came to a similar conclusion in his study. Therefore, it is not surprising that there are relatively few suicide attempts following refusal of an abortion application in Sweden. There were three suicide attempts in Hook's sample.

One thing frequently overlooked in evaluating women for termination, is that pregnancies themselves very often are suicidal or self-destructive gestures on the woman's part. In our own study (Simon et al., 1967), of 12 women who were aborted for medical indications, 11 knew about their illnesses before they became pregnant. They had been warned not to get pregnant and had been instructed about contraception. Many of these women were chronically depressed. Their pregnancies in the circumstances of their physical illnesses contained serious self-destructive elements. Even in those women who were not physically ill, pregnancies were often extraordinary exercises in masochism. Typical of this group was a 28-year-old, white, divorced woman, diagnosed borderline schizophrenic, with two latency-aged sons. She permitted her ex-husband to return to live with her episodically, even though he drank constantly and beat her frequently. She made no efforts at contraception, even though she knew a pregnancy would interfere with her efforts to support herself.

Granacher (1963) thought that in four of the nine women (in a series of 496) who died following refusal of therapeutic abortion, the strain of pregnancy had a probable connection with death. It should also be clear that some women are behaving in a suicidal way when they expose themselves, often repeatedly, to the incompetents and frauds who perform many of the illegal abortions. Lindberg found that in women who were likely to be deserted by their male partners, women with hysterical traits and those who made explicit threats about illegal abortion, the risk of "desperate" (i.e., illegal or dangerous self-induced) abortion was considerable.

Suicides and suicide attempts do occur in pregnant women, and, from Whitlock and Edwards' work it appears that at least in half of the cases, the suicide or suicide attempt is related to the pregnancy. An impulsive suicide attempt in a pregnant woman is something difficult to guard against or prevent. The presence of serious suicidal thoughts and/or history of previous suicide attempts in a woman who has an unwanted pregnancy should put the psychiatrist on guard. Even Anderson (1966) who is not a strong advocate of interruption emphasizes this and reports on a suicide who was turned down for therapeutic abortion.

The Children of Women Denied Abortion

The other major area of interest in evaluating the effects of unwanted pregnancies that are carried to term is the personal and social development of children born to women who consciously made efforts to have the pregnancy terminated. The literature presents somewhat of a paradox. There is, on the one hand, only one carefully controlled, well-designed study that has provided quantitative data on this issue. Although this study is an outstanding one, it is retrospective. On the other hand, there is voluminous psychiatric literature that recounts individual case studies of unwanted children. The suffering, pain, and sorrow on the part of mother, child, father, the family and often the community are documented with monotonous regularity. These effects are most difficult to demonstrate statistically but are visible to all who look.

Granacher's follow-up of 496 Swiss women who were refused abortions revealed that only 60 per cent of the married women and 43 per cent of the unmarried women had positive attitudes towards their children. He also observed that the physical and mental development of the child was satisfactory in 78 per cent of the married mothers and in 56 per cent of the unmarried mothers. The differences between the groups increased with age.

Forssman and Thuwe (1966) compared 120 Swedish children born after application for therapeutic abortion was refused with another 120 children who were the next same-sexed children born in the hospital when the women denied abortion gave birth. The follow-up period was 21 years. The 120 children in the study group when compared with the control group, had more insecurity in their family life, higher psychiatric utilization, demonstrated more anti-social and criminal behaviour, needed more public assistance, were more frequently exempted from military service, more frequently were under-achievers as far as educational levels and married earlier. The authors concluded that children born under those circumstances run the risk of having greater social and mental handicaps than their peers.

There are other data of importance in the Forssman-Thuwe study not commented on by the authors. The original sample of women refused legal abortions was 196. Sixty-eight women, or 35 per cent, had some type of abortion, either spontaneous or illegal. There were 128 women who went to term and produced a total of 134 children; four of these children, (3 per cent) were stillborn; eight died in the first year and another two before the third year of life. The infant mortality in the first year of life for this sample is 6.1 per cent. For all of Sweden in 1948 the first-year infant mortality rate was 2.3 per cent. Since these were all unwanted pregnancies, one can wonder if the hostility engendered by lack of acceptance of the unwanted pregnancy is reflected not only in a high spontaneous abortion and illegal abortion rate, but also in the high rate of infant mortality.

David (1972) and Cameron and Tichenor (1976) have criticized the Forssman-Thuwe study because the control group of mothers was not well-matched with the study group (Cameron and Tichenor contend that the difference between the study and control children can be accounted for entirely because the study mothers were of lower social class and sought more psychiatric care). Both critics have made valid points, but Cameron and Tichenor unfortunately mar their criticism by (a) basing some of their reasoning on inference — e.g., "if the data were examined more closely, then one would find" — and (b) by quoting from two retrospective studies on parental attitudes to children that are more flawed by design problems than the Forssman-Thuwe study. Cameron and Tichenor's statement that "social outcome for children is most probably independent of the mother's attitude toward the pregnancy" appears to be more a wish on their part and not a fact, especially since Dytrych et al.'s (1975) study of Czech children born to women denied abortion had been published nearly one year before their paper appeared and they did not find it necessary to refer to it, even though they cite David's 1973 paper which describes the Czech study in some detail. Cameron and Tichenor seem typical of those who appear to ignore data that does not fit their own preconceived position.

The Dytrych work is a landmark study of unwanted pregnancy in the care with which it was designed and carried out and the richness of the data it has provided to date. Czechoslovakia liberalized its abortion laws in 1957 permitting district abortion commissions to terminate unwanted pregnancies on medical and social grounds during the first three months of pregnancy. During the first ten years after the enactment of this legislation, 92 per cent of the women applying were granted abortions upon initial application, 6 per cent on appeal, and 2 per cent were refused. Dytrych studied the cohort of 638 women who had been refused abortion initially and again on appeal in 1961 and 1962 in Prague. The study itself was done in 1971. Eighty-three women who were not residents of Prague, and four who were citizens of another country were excluded. Another 239 women were excluded from the study for the following reasons: 43 obtained legal abortions from another district, 80 had spontaneous abortions (this makes up one-third of the subsample and is two times the expected rate in Czechoslovakia), six turned out to be not pregnant, 31 moved out of Prague before delivering, 62 had no record of giving birth (25 per cent of this subsample and 11 per cent of the entire sample), nine gave false addresses, and eight were untraceable. The high proportion of women who did not carry the pregnancy to term stands out — 51 per cent using the most conservative figure and 75 per cent if one includes those without any record of giving birth. There were 316 women who gave birth to a total of 317 live children. Six children died before the study began, five in the first year of life for a mortality rate of 16 per 1,000 live births. Nineteen of the children were given up for adoption, 39 moved out of Prague, and two were permanently placed in a child-care institution. It is of some interest that four of the women denied that a child had been born to them.

Two hundred and forty-seven mothers and children were located. Seven mothers refused to participate in the study and six were unable to participate (three of those were dead). Eventually, 220 children were matched to controls who were similar in respect to age, grade in school, sex, birth order, number of siblings, mother's marital status, and father's occupation. The research data were collected by staff who did not know whether the child and family were in the study or in the control group.

The authors point out that the study group was made up of women who were not at the extreme end of the scale in their desire to bring their pregnancy to an end. The extreme cases of unwantedness were represented by women who obtained abortions, denied having given birth, or placed their child for adoption or in the permanent care of others. The children in this study were living with their parents or at least with their mothers. Detailed and carefully structured collection of data distinguishes this study. The data included hospital, clinic, and school records, structured interviews with mothers, children, fathers, other family members, teachers, and classmates, physical examination by pediatricians, and psychological examination with the use of several standard tests. More than 400 different measures were obtained for each matched pair of children. The children averaged nine nine years of age when studied. The mothers and children involved in the study did not know that the study was designed to examine the outcome of pregnancy for which abortion had been requested and denied. They were given an explanation for the study which disguised the real motive of the researchers but which allowed a high level of participation.

The study children demonstrated significantly more acute illness than the controls and more chronic illness as well, though the difference there did not reach statistical significance although it did indicate a trend. The study children were described by their mothers more often as being bad-tempered (this was statistically significant) and as naughty and stubborn (a trend). When personality characteristics were rated by mothers and teachers there was an agreement between them that the study group showed less desirable characteristics. Specifically this rating showed statistically significant differences for both conscientiousness and excitability, with the study children rated less favourably on both of these variables. When school grades were examined, the differences were consistently in favour of higher grades for the control children (Table 8–2). The differences in grades reached statistical significance, however, only for the grades for study of the Czech language. The authors write,

Not only is performance in language generally assumed to be an indicator of intelligence, but it is also usually related to social development, particularly within the family. As the social standing of the two family groups was roughly equal, the children's poor performance in language is attributable to their social environment. On the other hand, marks in arithmetic which under normal conditions have the highest correlation with intelligence and are less vulnerable to environmental factors demonstrate very small differences.

The differences in grades appeared even though the IQs of the two groups were not significantly different.

Table 8–2

AVERAGE SCHOOL GRADES OF STUDY AND CONTROL CHILDREN
(5 POINT SCALE, 5-HIGHEST)

Subject	Study	Control
Czech*	2.83	3.01
Arithmetic	3.20	3.29
Physical Training	3.81	3.85
Drawing	3.33	3.43
Music	3.73	3.74
Arts and Crafts	3.58	3.62

*P < .05 + Test.
Source: Dytrych et al., 1975.

Table 8–3

AVERAGE NUMBER OF VOTES RECEIVED FROM CLASSMATES BY STUDY
AND CONTROL CHILDREN BY SPECIAL CHARACTERISTICS

Characteristic	Study	Control
Best Friend	2.74	2.90
Refused as Friend*	3.15	2.69
Fights a Lot	3.15	2.95
Has Sense of Humour†	2.65	2.15
Audacious	2.65	2.53
Cowardly	2.84	2.39
Intelligent	2.21	2.58
Reclusive	2.10	2.08
Brags a Lot	2.56	2.43

*P < .05 MN paired Chi-Square.
†Synomymous with Clowning, Showing Off.
Source: Dytrych et al., 1975.

Another variable identified in the school study that reached statistical significance was one of a group that related to personal characteristics and was noted as ''refused as a friend.'' Study children were as a group more often refused as friends than the control group. This rating was derived from other students in the class (Table 8–3). Overwhelmingly, mothers, teachers, and classmates rated study children less favourably on personal characteristics.

A consistent difference between study boys and study girls was demonstrated, with the boys showing either poorer performance or more of an undesirable characteristic. For example, when chronic disease patterns were analysed by sex, the study boys showed more chronic disease than control boys and this difference was statistically significant. When mothers rated pre-school behaviour, statistically significant differences appeared between the study and control boys, with the study boys rated more naughty. Teacher ratings of initiative, self-control, diligence, concentration, tidiness, intelligence and grades revealed in each catorgory that study boys received poorer evaluations than control boys, with the differences reaching a level of statistical significance for the first two of these variables. Sociograms done by classmates which dealt with a number of personal characteristics also showed study boys faired more poorly than control boys.

Teachers and social workers (who gathered much of the study data) were asked to assess the children's families on four variables — cultural level, internal family life, care of the child, and co-operation with the school. The teachers and social workers both rated study families inferior to controls on all four variables, with the differences reaching statistical significance in the last two variables. In addition, social workers rated study mothers as significantly less informed about the child and significantly more detached from the child.

Other variables that distinguish study and control families were, (a) study mothers who had three to four abortions made up 8 per cent of that group, while control mothers with three to four abortions only made up 2 per cent of the group, and (b) abortions after the birth of the child in this study were significantly higher among study mothers than control mothers.

Strikingly, 38 per cent of the mothers of the study group children denied having asked for an abortion when they were pregnant with the study child. They were more likely to deny this with a female psychiatrist than with a male psychiatrist.

Dytrych concluded that to sum up the differences between study and control children concerning performance, attitude, and behaviour, a common denominator is an increased defensive position against stress and frustration among the study children. The boys are especially vulnerable. The patterns develop and consolidate into permanent personality traits. At the time of the study these traits were still mostly within the bonds of social viability. Nevertheless, there may be a question concerning the future development of these children. The authors emphasized again in their conclusions that they have examined the children and women who do not represent the most negative prospective mothers.

Baldwin and Cain (1980) reviewed 11 carefully designed longitudinal studies of teenage parents (mostly poor and black) and their children, and concluded that children born to teenagers suffer intellectual deficits, largely because of the economic and social impact of early childbearing on the young parents. Such children are likely to spend part of their childhood in one-parent households and have children themselves while still adolescent. Several of the studies reviewed demonstrated the greater vulnerability of male children — for example, lower IQ scores and more intense psychiatric symptoms.

The risks of unwanted pregnancy extend farther beyond the social and mental handicaps that Forssman and Dytrych allude to. In 1966 there were 10,920 murders in the United States and one out of 22 of these were filicides. Resnick (1969), in reviewing literature on child murders from 1751 to 1960, reported on 131 filicides in which the victim was one day or older. The number of filicide-mothers was twice as great as filicide-fathers. Fourteen per cent were classified by Resnick as being motivated because the child was an "unwanted child," in 21 per cent the parent was acutely psychotic, in 38 per cent the filicide was associated with suicide, and 12 per cent were "accidental" and were usually the result of a fatal battered child syndrome. Twenty-seven per cent of the victims were under six months of age and 48 per cent under two years. In another paper, Resnick reported on 37 neonaticides (the victim murdered in the first 24 hours of life by a parent). The murders were committed by the mother in 34 cases. Of the maternal neonaticides, 83 per cent were classified as being motivated because the child was unwanted and 11 per cent because the mother had an acute psychosis. Illegitimacy is the most common reason given for neonaticides. Other reasons are extramarital paternity, rape, and seeing the child as an obstacle to parental ambition. One group of these women, described as extremely passive, exhibited pathological denial about the pregnancy. A second group described as having strong drives with little ethical restraint, sought and were denied abortion during the pregnancy.

Anthony's (1959) report of group therapy of 12 mothers with murderous impulses toward their children, suggests that even where the impulses are not acted on directly, the damage can be considerable. The children were in concomitant group therapy. Half the children were overtly disturbed; two severely so. Several of the children acted out the mother's wish by making suicidal gestures.

Both Holman (1975) and Irwin (1975) who have studied battered children believe that there is some relationship between an unwanted pregnancy and the likelihood that a child will be subject to severe abuse. Holman studied 28 cases, of which 10 were girls and 18 boys. In his series 10 parents admitted they resented the pregnancy and the child was unwanted. Two of them had requested termination of the pregnancy and had been refused. Irwin studied 67 cases over a four-year-period and reported that 70 per cent of these were unwanted pregnancies. Fifty-eight per cent of his series of abused children were boys. Several authors have commented on the high incidence of male children among abused, battered children. This higher incidence of male children combined with the high rate of unwanted pregnancies makes one think of the findings of Dytrych and Baldwin and Cain where greater vulnerability of male children is demonstrated.

Neilson et al. (1973) made a perspective study of 165 randomly selected women who appeared at an ante-natal clinic. They were studied at mid-pregnancy, two days after giving birth to their babies, and six months post partum, and then four years later. They discovered that in 71 of the cases followed that there was a correlation between unwanted pregnancy and bed wetting in the children.

Summary

The literature on women who have been refused abortions, who themselves refuse abortion or do not avail themselves of abortion, and the children born of women who have been refused abortion has been reviewed. There is still a great need for researchers to focus their efforts precisely on the problem of unwanted pregnancy by designing and carrying out prospective studies. The studies reviewed are often difficult to compare with one another because populations differ or there is little agreement in objective criteria used or dependent variables measured. However, the evidence strongly suggests that there is a group of women in whom an unwanted pregnancy can be a serious, devastating event that can have far reaching consequences for herself and for her child. There has been in the past a rather systematic bias against offering abortions to women in their twenties and a greater readiness to abort women with unwanted pregnancies who are younger than 15 and over 40 and who have several children. The best study of the effects on the development of children who were born to parents who wished abortion indicates that these children appear to be more vulnerable to chronic and acute illness and compare unfavourably with children who are born to mothers in which the pregnancy was desired. Male children seem to be consistently at higher risk if they are born to a mother who had wished an abortion or where pregnancy was unwanted.

References

Anderson, E.W. "Psychiatric Indications for Termination of Pregnancy." *J. Psychosom. Res.* 10(1966):123–34.

Anthony, E.J. "A Group of Murderous Mothers." *Acta Psychother.* 7(1959):1–6.

Arén and C. Amark. "The Prognosis in Which Legal Abortion Has Been Granted but Not Carried Out." *Acta. Psychiat. et Neurol.* 36(1961):203–78.

Baldwin, W. and V.S. Cain. "The Children of Teenage Parents." *Fam. Plan. Perspect.* 12(1980):34–43.

Cameron, P. and J.C. Tichenor. "The Swedish Children Born to Women Denied Abortion study: A Radical Criticism." *Psych. Reports*. 39(1976):391–94.

Clark, M., I. Forsoner, D.A. Pond and R.F. Tredgold. "Sequels of Unwanted Pregnancy." *Lancet* 2(1968):501–03.

David, H. "Abortion in Psychological Perspective." *Am. J. Orthopsych.* 42(1972):61–67.

Drower, S.J. and E.S. Nach. "Therapeutic Abortion on Psychiatric Grounds: Part I." *S. A. Med. J.* 54(1978):604–08.

Drower, S.J. and E.S. Nash. "Therapeutic Abortion on Psychiatric Grounds: Part II." *S. A. Med. J.* 54(1978):643–47.

Dytrych, Z., Z. Matejcek, V. Schuller, H.P. David, H.P., and H.L. Friedman. "Children Born to Women Denied Abortion." *Fam. Plan. Persp.* 7(1975):165–71.

Forssman, H., and I. Thuwe. "One Hundred and Twenty Children Born After Application for Therapeutic Abortion Refused." *Acta. Psychiat. Scand.* 42(1966):71–88.

Furstenberg, F.F., Jr. The Social Consequences of Teenage Pregnancy." *Fam. Plan. Persp.* 8(1976):140–64.

Furstenberg, F.F., Jr. Personal communication.

Granacher, M., as reported in Hook, K. "Refused Abortion." *Acta. Psychiat. Scand.* 39(1963):16–17.

Hook, K.: "Refused Abortion." *Acta. Psychiat. Scand.* 39(1963):1–156.

Hoover, J.E. "Uniform Crime Reports, 1966." Washington, D.C.: U.S. Government Printing Office, 1966.

Holman, P.R. "Early Life of the Battered Child." *Arch. Dis. Child.* 50(1975):78–80.

Irwin, C. "The Establishment of a Child Abuse Unit in a Children's Hospital." *S. A. Med. J.* 51(1975):1142–46.

Kane, F. and P.A. Lachenbruch. "Adolescent Pregnancy: A Study of Aborters and Non Aborters." *Am. J. Orthopsych.* 43(1973):796–03.

Lindberg, B.J., as reported in Hook, K. "Refused Abortion." *Acta. Psychiat. Scand.* 39(1963):14–16.

Meyerowitz, A., Satloff, and J. Romano. "Induced Abortion for Psychiatric Indications." *Am. J. Psych.* 127(1971):1153–59.

Nilson, A., P.E. Almgren, E.M. Kohler, L. Kohler. "The Importance of Maternal Attitudes and Personality." *Acta. Psych. Scand.* 49(1973):114–30.

Pare, C.M.B. and H. Raven. "Follow-up of Patients Referred for Termination of Pregnancy." *Lancet*. 1(1970):635–38.

Resnick, P.: "Child Murder by Parents: A Psychiatric Review of Filicide." *Amer. J. Psychiat.* 126(1969):325–34.

Resnick, P. "Murder of the New Born: A Psychiatric Review of Neonaticide." Read at Annual APA Meeting, 1969.

Sim, M. "Psychiatric Disorders of Pregnancy." *J. Psychosom. Res.* 12(1968):95–100.

Simon, N.M., D. Rothman and A.G. Senturia. "Psychiatric Illness Following Therapeutic Abortion." *Amer. J. Psychiat.* 124(1967):59–65.

Smith, E.M. "Women Who Request Abortion." *Am. J. Orthopsych.* 43(1973):574–85.

Smith, E.M. Personal communication.

Waters, J.L. "Pregnancy in Young Adolescents: A Syndrome of Failures." *So. Med. J.* 62(1969):655–58.

Whitlock, F.A. and J.E. Edwards. "Pregnancy and Attempted Suicide." *Compr. Psychiat.* 9(1968):1–12.

9

Sterilization of Abortees

Richard W. Osborn

Introduction

The delivery of a child, experience of a therapeutic abortion or other obstetrical and gynecological events are emotionally as well as physically stressful. While these stresses are too well known to require comment it is none the less true that some of these events are more stressful than others. This is clearly true of surgical sterilization which has its own medical risks and marks the end of a woman's reproductive career. Although considered a relatively safe elective procedure, current laparoscopic or other tubal ligation procedures carry a risk to the health or life of the patient. A complication rate of 2.4 per cent for sterilization cases has been noted (Cheng and Rochat, 1977). Sterilization is likely to be even more stressful if it is performed in conjunction with another critical event such as an abortion or delivery.

Therapeutic abortion is held to be associated with a low level risk to the health or life of the woman. A complication rate of 3.6 per cent reported by Cheng and Rochat (1977) is typical of most evaluations of the procedure. The low level of complications observed in Canada is in agreement with these findings from other settings (COAL, 1977).

To minimize the problems which arise from the unique stresses of sterilization it is a frequent practice of hospitals and physicians to discourage the simultaneous undertaking of delivery or abortion and sterilization. In part this pattern reflects established medical practice. Higher mortality risks have been associated with concurrent sterilization in Britain (Kestelman, 1978) due to infection, pulmonary embolism and complications of general anesthesia. A review of sterilizations done in Aberdeen from 1969 to 1976 showed accidental pregnancies with a two-fold increase for those whose sterilization was post-abortion (Hughes, 1977). However, many of these operations were performed by inexperienced staff and were accompanied by more frequent surgical difficulties. These and other studies provide the basis for the conclusion reached by a review panel that complication and mortality rate increases are associated with concurrent sterilization (Scientific Group, World Health Organization, 1978).

Not all studies support the World Health Organization conclusion. A review of 284 cases by Chang showed no significant increase in operation time or complications of concurrent sterilization compared with laparoscopic sterilization of non-pregnant women (Cheng, 1977). A larger study by Cheng and Rochat concludes that the combined abortion-sterilization approach offers special advantages including a reduction of inconvenience to the patient, possible diminution of psychological stress, lowered risk from a second anesthetic procedure, reduction in the possibility of pregnancy occurring and a lowering of severe work load on the medical facility (Cheng and Rochat, 1977). These advantages, plus the low level of the additional risk associated with the combined procedure, increase the likelihood of concurrent sterilization being performed in suitably equipped medical centres. There continues to be some speculation, however, that an agreement to be sterilized is occasionally used as a precondition to performing an abortion. Further, the vulnerability of a woman at either delivery or an abortion make it somewhat easier for her to agree to the sterilization procedure at that time although she may regret it at a later date.

For the above reasons the occurrence of sterilization with the sample of abortion patients is an event of particular importance. Of direct concern is the variability of this practice among population sub-groups as it provides insight to alternative patterns of the delivery of health services. Additionally this problem affords an insight into the questions of contraceptive usage and therapeutic abortion.

Sample Characteristics

In 1976 the Government of Canada chose to undertake a study of abortion under the Committee on the Operation of the Abortion Law (COAL). The Report from COAL was published in 1977. The present author was the consultant responsible for the collection and analysis of the data from abortion patients that was part of the report. A random survey could not be attempted due to confidentiality of abortion patients' names and limitations on funds and time. Patients in a total of 24 hospitals in eight provinces were surveyed. The approach was to ensure regional representation, a balance among hospitals as to size, and to provide a mixture of hospitals which were affiliated with medical faculties and hospitals without training functions. Within each selected hospital, attempts to control bias in selection of patients were employed including assuring a mixture of private and non-private patients. Interviewers were trained in January, 1976 and data collection began the next month and lasted until May, 1976. A total of 4,754 questionnaires were returned to COAL. No centre reported difficulties in refusal from patients or in gaining access to cases.

In the total sample of abortion patients 9 per cent of the women obtained a sterilization operation at the time of the therapeutic abortion. The women obtaining this permanent method of conception control are different in many respects from those who are obtaining an abortion alone. A majority of the abortees report having had no live births, are under 24 years of age and are

Table 9–1

DEMOGRAPHIC CHARACTERISTICS OF STERILIZATION AND TOTAL SAMPLE
ABORTION WOMEN, CANADA, 1976

Characteristic	Sterilized	Total Sterilized & Non-sterilized
	N = 395	N = 4459
Number Live Births	%	%
0	10.6	64.4
1	9.4	15.1
2	32.9	11.7
3	24.8	5.5
4 +	22.3	3.2
Age		
24 and under	12.0	62.9
25–29	22.3	20.9
30–34	27.6	9.1
35 and over	38.1	7.2
Education		
Primary	15.7	7.8
Secondary	66.6	67.0
Post secondary	17.6	25.2
Marital Status		
Single	12.4	64.4
Married	69.8	25.0
Widowed, Separated, Divorced	17.8	10.5
Religion		
Catholic	32.9	34.5
Protestant	46.9	46.0
Jewish	2.8	2.2
Other	6.0	9.3
None	114.0	8.0
Region of Occurrence		
Atlantic Provinces	6.3	5.5
Quebec	10.1	14.5
Ontario	48.9	44.9
Prairie Provinces	19.0	15.9
British Columbia	22.0	19.2

single. In contrast, nearly two-thirds of the sterilized women are aged 30 and
over, one-half have had three or more children, and 70 per cent of these women
were married. As is shown in Table 9–1 the educational levels of the sterilized
women were similar to those of the total sample except for a somewhat higher
level of women who had only achieved primary education, and a corresponding
deficit in the highest level of education among the sterilized group. Few

differences are seen between the total sample and the sterilized group with regard to religion or to region of residence and occurrence of the abortion operation. The dominant characteristics, therefore, of the sterilized sample are (a) higher number of live births, (b) older age, (c) somewhat deficient with regard to education, and (d) most are married.

The differences just reviewed between the sterilized population and those of the entire abortion sample are more clearly seen in a comparison of sterilized versus the non-sterilized groups within the sample. The proportions sterilized rise directly with number of live births with a large increase noted between one and two births. By the third or fourth or more previous live births level the proportions sterilized increase to 40 per cent and 60 per cent respectively. Not surprisingly, as is clear from Table 9–2, a parallel increase occurs with increasing age with 27 per cent and 47 per cent of the women in the 30 to 34 year and 35 and over years categories reporting concurrent sterilization. As has been noted above, a large portion of those who are sterilized were married, and as shown in the present table, approximately 25 per cent of the married group were sterilized.

Table 9–2

STERILIZED AND NON-STERILIZED ABORTION PATIENTS BY SELECTED
DEMOGRAPHIC CHARACTERISTICS, CANADA, 1976

Characteristics	Sterilized	Non-sterilized
	%	%
Number Live Births		
0	1.5	98.5
1	5.5	94.5
2	24.9	75.1
3	40.0	60.0
4+	60.3	39.7
Age		
24 and under	1.7	98.3
25–29	9.4	90.6
30–34	26.8	73.2
35 and over	47.0	53.0
Education		
Primary	17.7	82.3
Secondary	8.7	91.3
Post Secondary	6.2	93.8
Marital Status		
Single	1.7	98.3
Married	24.9	75.1
Widowed, separated, divorced	15.0	85.0

Table 9–3

CONCURRENT STERILIZATION LEVELS FOR COMPLETED LEVEL OF
EDUCATION BY NUMBER OF LIVE BIRTHS, ABORTION PATIENTS,
CANADA, 1976

| Number Live Births | Proportion at each education level | | | Statistical Significance "p" of x^2 |
	Primary	Secondary	Post-Secondary	
0	3	1	2	.31
1	8	5	5	.88
2	15	27	23	.21
3 or more	45	47	49	.10

Of some interest is the finding that the proportion sterilized decreases directly with increasing level of education. Nearly 18 per cent of those with primary schooling were sterilized as compared to 9 per cent of those at the secondary level and 6 per cent of those who had achieved a post-secondary level of schooling. Reasons for the clear association with education are not immediately obvious. In order to examine this question more completely additional analyses of the data were undertaken. The previously noted, clear relationships between sterilization and woman's age and prior number of live births suggested one line of investigation. It is possible that the association noted between education and sterilization may be an artifact of the other demographic influences. In order to examine this possibility the influence of previous live births was removed and the relationship between education and sterilization observed within each of the levels of reported births. As can be seen from Table 9–3 the proportions sterilized increase with number of live births but are nearly constant across each educational level within the live birth category. The differences in the level of sterilization for each educational group do not obtain statistical significance at any of the four levels of live births. It is reasonable to conclude that the relationship observed above with education and sterilization is a result of a higher level of previous live births to women of lower education, and that it is the previous births rather than some aspect of educational attainment which accounts primarily for the observed relationship.

Reproductive Data

The second major set of influences on the decision to terminate a woman's reproductive career are those prior fertility and contraceptive experiences which have influenced her decision to accept sterilization. An examination of the behaviours of those women who do choose concurrent sterilization is important not only for our understanding of this particular problem but also of sterilization behaviour in general and the study of therapeutic abortion. Data from the present survey permit a close examination of the previous reproductive experiences of sterilized and the non-sterilized elements in the study population. A review of the data shown in Table 9–4 clearly identifies the areas of uniqueness as well as those areas of common elements shared between sterilized and non-sterilized abortion patients. Prior experience with a therapeutic abortion is unrelated to sterilization as there is little difference in the proportion who have had such a prior event. There is no indication that women are seeking sterilization as a result of their inability to control reproduction which would have led to an earlier abortion episode. What is quite pronounced in the data is that the woman does not wish the present pregnancy nor does she wish to be pregnant in the future. Admittedly, these are retrospective data about the desirability of the present conception but it seems quite clear that while the majority of the sample would wish a pregnancy at a later date, and hence are using abortion for spacing of their reproductive

Table 9–4

REPRODUCTION STATUS FOR STERILIZED AND TOTAL SAMPLE
RESPONDENTS, CANADA, 1976

Previous Therapeutic Abortion Experience	Sterilization Respondents	Total Sample
	N = 395	N = 4459
Yes	11.5	13.6
No	88.5	86.4
Attitude towards Pregnancy		
wanted pregnancy now	5.4	6.1
wanted pregnancy later	11.5	72.3
does not want to ever be pregnant	83.1	21.6
Previously Pregnant		
Yes	98.6	44.9
No	1.4	55.1
Method Use at time of Conception		
Yes	55.0	46.8
No	45.0	53.2
Method Effectiveness for Current Users at time of Conception (2112 cases)		
High (pill, IUD, sterilization)	29.7	29.8
Medium (Barrier methods)	45.2	48.0
Low (rhythm, withdrawal)	25.1	22.2
Method Effectiveness for Discontinued Use Women (1160 cases)		
High	85.7	82.9
Medium	14.3	13.2
Low	—	3.8

behaviours, the sterilized patient in 83 per cent of the cases does not want to ever be pregnant. As would be expected from the previous data showing the high age and higher level of live births among sterilized women, the proportion who have been previously pregnant is much higher among the sterilized as compared to the total sample of abortion patients.

Women obtaining concurrent sterilization differ from the general group of those having an abortion in an additional way, that is, they were far more likely to have been using contraception at the time of the present conception that has led to seeking an abortion. Given the greater reproductive experience of the sterilized women it is not surprising that this group should report a higher level of contraceptive experience. However, when consideration is given to the effectiveness of the method employed, few differences are seen between the two population groups. Those who are sterilized were equally likely to have used effectiveness of the method employed, few differences are seen between the two those individuals who had discontinued using contraceptives prior to the present conception there is little difference in the proportion who were making use of highly effective methods. Moreover, nearly all of the discontinued users had been employing the most effective methods which, for the most part, was the use of the oral contraceptive pill. These data, in Table 9–4, reveal a population who are contraceptively experienced but who clearly did not wish to permit the pregnancy to continue and sought to end their reproductive careers.

Women who discontinued contraception and placed themselves at higher risk of becoming pregnant had for the most part been using the most effective available methods for controlling reproduction. Of concern at the present time, given high and continuing levels of demand for therapeutic abortion, are those factors that lead women to discontinue what would be a very efficient method of regulating fertility. A series of questions was presented to each woman who indicated she had stopped use of contraception to determine the reasons for her discontinuation.

Several aspects of the problem of non-use of contraception are illustrated by the data in Table 9–5. The most commonly mentioned reasons for discontinuation of method use were: side effects from the method, physician suggesting cessation of use, and fear of continued use of the method. This is consistent with the earlier findings that the oral contraceptive pill was the most frequently discontinued method. Side effects from the method of contraception is the most frequently mentioned reason but there is no statistical difference between the sterilized and non-sterilized woman in reporting this reason. Statistically significant differences in responses are seen for three items: not planning to have sex, where a higher proportion of non-sterilized women gave the reply, and, the two pill-related items of the physician suggesting stopping and fear after long periods of method use. These latter two items, in combination with the frequently mentioned reporting of side effects identify some potentially significant problems for the population.

Among these problems is the role of the physician in maintaining conception

Table 9–5

REASONS FOR CONTRACEPTIVE DISCONTINUATION, STERILIZED AND
NON-STERILIZED ABORTION PATIENTS, CANADA, 1976

Reason Given	Proportion mentioning items		Statistical Significance (p=)
	Sterilized	Non-sterilized	
Side effects of method	58.7	48.6	0.16
Not planning to have sex	10.0	25.4	0.006*
Partner objection	4.3	4.7	1.00
Thought I could not get pregnant	15.9	15.4	1.00
Method unavailable	15.7	13.7	0.77
Broke up with partner	5.8	10.1	0.34
Doctor suggested stopping method	33.8	20.8	0.02*
Afraid to continue after long use	36.8	23.3	0.02*

*Significant at .05 level or greater.

control. It is clear that some women believe that a physician suggested discontinuation of the highly reliable oral pill method. Sound medical reasons for stopping pill use are seldom present. Additional investigations are needed as to why this action is recommended and what methods of contraception are prescribed for replacement.

Major Influences In Sterilization Behaviour

It is evident from the above that both demographic and reproductive variables play a significant role in the decision to seek sterilization at the time of abortion. What is not clear is the relative influence of these variables or the part played by aspects of behaviour which could be modified through counselling or patient education. To examine the relative influences of each of the variables these data were examined with a stepwise multiple regression statistical program. This method of analysis provides a statistical test and an order for the variables into most important to least important in explaining variation of the dependent variable. In the present instance we are interested in the relative importance of each of the predictive variables in explaining variation in the status of sterilized and non-sterilized abortion patients.

It would be expected that age, number of live births and other reproductive status variables would influence sterilization. What is clear from Table 9–6 is that the prime determinant of sterilization is the woman's desire to not ever have another pregnancy. The correlation between not wanting an additional pregnancy, which was measured by assigning a score to each women of yes or no as to whether or not she ever wanted to be pregnant, was $r = 0.467$. This is a relatively strong association between these two items. Equally it is clear from the table that the second strongest influence was the number of live births, followed

Table 9–6

DEMOGRAPHIC AND REPRODUCTIVE STATUS DETERMINED OF
CONCURRENT STERILIZATION OF ABORTION PATIENTS, CANADA 1976

Variable	Multiple Correlation Coefficient	Change in r-squared	F-ratio
Pregnancy wanted	.467	.218	391.18
Number live births	.535	0.68	166.95
Age	.539	.004	32.73
Use of highly effective method	.540	.001	5.76
Education	.541	.001	6.27
	Total Variance Explained = .292		

by age, use of a highly effective contraceptive method and education of the respondent. Use of a moderately effective method and other variables are not shown here as they did not reach statistical significance, indicating that their influence on variation in sterilization behaviour was not important.

Some Concluding Remarks

Evidence from the present study makes it abundantly clear that women who receive a sterilization operation concurrently with a pregnancy termination do so because they have reached the end of their reproductive careers. The typical sterilization recipient is married, over 30 years of age and has two or more children. This is a somewhat lower set of age and parity levels than was commonly thought to be characteristic of women a decade or more ago and may reflect an increasing liberalization of sterilization norms.

Concurrently sterilized abortion recipients are more likely than other abortion patients to have been using contraception and have a higher concern over long term use of contraception, and they were more often influenced by a physician to discontinue contraception. The impression is of a population with a relatively high level of motivation to control fertility but who have received inadequate advice or have concerns over their method of conception control. Popular and scientific reports have emphasized the risks in contraceptive use and it is understandable that women follow the advice of their physician in discontinuation of taking the pill. The costs of the resultant unwanted pregnancies are considerable, and additional efforts need to be directed towards the provision of continuous conception control during changes from use of one method to another.

There is clear evidence that the women who were sterilized wished to end their reproductive careers. What is problematic is the behaviours of the even larger group of non-sterilized women who reported they did not want ever to be pregnant. This group was over one-fifth of the entire sample and represents a significant number of women who do not wish to reproduce in the future and who must rely upon current methods of conception control to achieve this goal. It is likely that additional efforts should be directed towards meeting the long-term needs of these women.

Acknowledgments

This research was supported, in part, by the Ontario Ministry of Health, Demonstration Model Grant DM 444 "Therapeutic Abortion in Ontario." The analysis was made possible with the assistance of Ms. Jacqueline Latter and Dr. Rhonda Love, of the Division of Community Health, University of Toronto.

References

Chang, Y.S. "Laparoscopic Sterilization as an Outpatient Procedure: A Review of 1,500 Cases." *Korean Journal of Obstetrics and Gynecology* 20(1977):69–80.

Cheng, M.C.E. and R.W. Rochat. "The Safety of Combined Abortion-Sterilization Procedure." *American Journal of Obstetrics and Gynecology* 129(1977):548–52.

Hughes, G.J. "Sterilization Failure." *British Medical Journal*(November 1977): 1337–39.

Kestelman, P. "Legal Abortion Mortality." *IPPF Europe, Regional Information Bulletin* 7(1978):8–9.

Report of the Committee on the Operation of the Abortion Law. (Chairman: Robin F. Badgley) Ottawa: Minister of Supplies and Services, 1977.

World Health Organization, Scientific Group, *Induced Abortion*. WHO Technical Report Series, No. 623, 1978.

Part 3
Women Seeking Abortion

Introduction

Who are the women who seek abortion? Statistics from Canada and the U.S. show that young unmarried women account for the highest proportion among the abortion seekers, with teenage women under 20 constituting the largest group. Widespread use of abortion has generated a number of concerns. Has availability of abortion weakened women's contraceptive resolve? Do they view abortion as another method of birth control? What kind of women seek multiple abortions? The papers included in this section address these questions.

Cates compared the socio-demographic profiles of women seeking abortion in Canada and the U.S. He observed parallel trends in the demand for legal abortion, which showed a dramatic increase immediately following the liberalization of abortion laws in both countries, followed by moderate increases in the incidence and rates of abortions. Generally, the largest proportion of these abortions is performed on pregnancies among young and unmarried women who seek first-trimester termination. Significantly, the percentages of teenagers obtaining abortion are almost identical in both countries. However, there are some differences. The abortion laws in Canada are more restrictive than those in the U.S. and permit lawful abortions only in approved hospitals. These factors partly account for the overall abortion rates being lower for Canada in comparison to the U.S. Also, the women having abortions in Canada tend to be slightly older (especially after age 24), of lower parity, are more likely to be married, and obtain their abortions later in gestation than their American counterparts.

The issue of erratic use or non-use of contraceptives by a great proportion of unmarried young aborting women has recently become a matter of great concern. Two Canadian studies included in this section examine the etiological variables which contribute to ineffective contraception among abortion patients. They are unanimous in their observation that effective contraceptive activity is largely a function of psychological and attitudinal factors. Chapman-Sheehan and Devlin, for instance, in their study at the McMaster University Medical Centre noted that ineffective or non-use of contraception does not result from the lack of factual information on birth control but from psychological inaccessibility to the contraceptive means. Adolescent women were found to be more vulnerable to psychological inaccessibility than older women. The authors based their conclusions on the contraceptive behaviour of three abortion groups — users of highly effective contraceptives, users of ineffective methods and non-users.

Pearce used standardized personality tests in addition to questionnaires to elicit information from his abortion patients at the Foothills Hospital in Calgary, and he identified three crucial variables associated with effective contraception. These are (a) availability of sexual and contraceptive information, (b) availability of contraceptive services, and (c) emotional maturity or formal operational thinking. The author stresses the role of formal operational thinking in effective contraception, since this trait enables a young unmarried woman to conceptualize the consequences of unprotected sex more realistically, and thus allows her to take rational and deliberate action contraceptively.

The growing incidence of repeat abortions in North America has generated concern that the availability of abortion has weakened contraceptive vigilance of sexually active women so that they view abortion as an alternative rather than as a supplement to contraception. The study by Berger and her associates does not support this contention. The authors compared a sample of women having first abortions and those undergoing repeat abortions, in terms of their demographic and personality characteristics, history of contraceptive usage, relationship with their partners, frequency of coital activity and reaction to abortion. The only variables that distinguished initial or repeat abortion women were age, education, marital status, and number of living children. The authors concluded that "overall, the results indicated that repeaters are more similar than dissimilar to the initials." The authors used the Tietze model as a framework for their analysis. This model views an unwanted pregnancy and consequent abortion as resulting from structural and technological failure of contraceptives rather than from deep-seated psychological motives.

10

Women Obtaining Abortion: A Comparison Between the United States and Canada

Willard Cates, Jr.

Introduction

Legally induced abortion is among the most common surgical procedures performed in the United States (Forrest et al., 1979). Largely because abortion is such a controversial issue, we know more about its epidemiology than that of any other surgical procedure. We know the number of women who obtain abortions, their age, race, parity and marital status, where they obtain the procedure, the stage of gestation when their abortion is performed, and finally the methods of abortion used to terminate their pregnancies. In this chapter, I describe the number and characteristics of women obtaining abortions in the United States in 1977, and compare them with similar characteristics of women obtaining abortions in Canada during the same year.

Number of Women Obtaining Abortions

Since 1969, the United States has passed through three stages regarding the availability of legal abortion: until the middle of 1970, legally induced abortion was generally not available; from mid-1970 through early 1973, legal abortion had limited regional availability, largely on the East and West Coasts; after 1973, there has been general national availability because restrictive abortion laws were declared unconstitutional.

Prior to 1969, the best estimates of the number of induced abortions in the United States ranged from 200,000 to 1.2 million (Calderone, 1965); nearly all of these were illegally induced. Since 1969, the number of legal abortions has increased 50-fold — from approximately 22,000 in 1969 to over 1.3 million in 1977 (Figure 10–1). This increase was initially accompanied by a progressive decline in the estimated number of illegal abortions.

In 1977, the number of legal abortions reported to the Center for Disease

Control (CDC) was 1,079,430, a 9 per cent increase over 1976. The abortion ratio increased 4 per cent in 1977, to 325 per 1,000 live births. These figures reveal a slowing of the percentage increase in the number and ratio of abortions, which may reflect: (a) the continued gradual replacement of non-physician (illegal) procedures by physician (legal) procedures, (b) the more effective use of contraception by reproductive-age women, (c) increasing use of sterilization, thus placing fewer women at risk of unwanted pregnancy, (d) improvements in sex education and changes in the attitudes of reproductive-age women and men, (e) changes in public funding policy for abortion, or (f) reporting artifact.

The number of abortions reported to the CDC was probably less than the number actually performed in 1977. In public health surveillance the number of reported cases is generally lower than the number obtained through surveys. The magnitude of under-reporting can be estimated by comparing the total number of abortions reported to the CDC with the total number obtained through the Alan Guttmacher Institute (AGI) nationwide survey of abortion facilities (Forrest et al., 1979). For 1977, as in previous years, the CDC's total was approximately 17 per cent lower than the AGI total. Thus, under-reporting could probably produce some biases in the CDC data. Abortions performed in physicians' offices are probably under-reported more often than those performed in hospitals or facilities. Because physicians probably perform abortions in their offices at earlier gestational ages of pregnancy than other facilities do, the under-reporting of these data may bias the gestational age distributions toward the later stages of pregnancy.

Canada reported 57,600 women obtaining legally induced abortions in 1977, approximately 1/20 the number performed in the United States. However,

Figure 10–1

Relationship Between Legal and Illegal Abortion, United States, 1969-1977

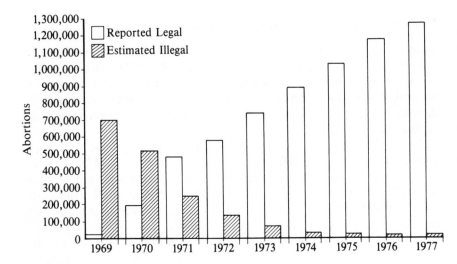

because the number of reproductive age women in Canada is less, their abortion rate (10.6 abortions/1,000 women aged 15–44) was one-half that of the United States (22.2). Possible reasons for the lower rate of women obtaining abortions in Canada, compared to the United States, are: (a) the administrative burdens of obtaining abortion in Canadian hospitals, (b) decreased percentages of unintended pregnancies, and (c) under-reporting of procedures performed in non-hospital facilities.

Characteristics of Women Obtaining Abortions

Women who obtained abortions during 1977 in the United States were most commonly young, white, unmarried, and of low parity, sought their abortions close to home in non-hospital facilities, and had their abortions performed by suction curettage at 12 menstrual weeks gestation or earlier. These characteristics are similar to those of women obtaining abortions in Canada during the same year. In the United States, the age, parity, and marital status distributions for women having abortions have remained relatively constant since 1973. However, over the past four years, changing trends have been observed for state of residence, race, and gestational age.

The general availability of abortion services since 1973 has progressively allowed more women to obtain abortions within their state of residence; between 1973 and 1975, many states performing abortions before 1973 reported decreases in the number of abortions performed for non-residents, while those states that began performing abortions after the Supreme Court decision of January 22, 1973, have progressively reported more abortions for state residents. For example, in 1972, 44 per cent of women had abortions outside their state of residence, usually in New York or California, where abortion laws were liberalized in 1970. In 1976 and 1977, 90 per cent of women obtaining induced abortions were able to have their procedure performed in their state of residence, presumably because the service was more readily available and less expensive. By obtaining abortions close to home, women had the advantages of both having their procedures performed at earlier gestational ages and of being in proximity to follow-up services provided by abortion facilities.

In 1977, 70 per cent of all reported abortions were performed in non-hospital facilities, continuing an increase evident since 1974 (Forrest et al. 1979). Over the past four years, the number of legally induced abortions performed in hospitals declined, so therefore all of the increase in the number of procedures was obtained by the growth of non-hospital facilities. The percentage of abortions performed in physicians' offices has remained steady at about 4 per cent while the percentage performed in outpatient clinics increased from 61 per cent in 1976 to 66 per cent in 1977. Hospital facilities accounted for a larger proportion of providers in non-metropolitan areas than in metropolitan areas, but even in non-metropolitan areas non-hospital facilities accounted for 6 out of every 10 reported abortions (Forrest et al. 1979).

The age distribution of women having abortions in the United States has

Figure 10–2

Per Cent Distribution[1] of Reported Legal Abortion By Age, Selected States,[2]
1975-1977

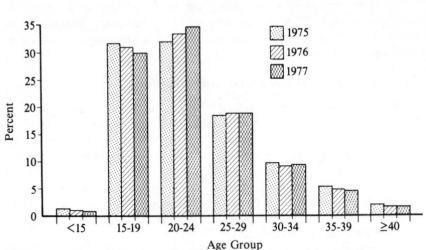

[1] Based on total number with age known.
[2] All states with data available for 1975 (34 states), 1976 (36 states), and 1977 (37 states).
Source: Table 6 of 1975, 1976, and 1977 Abortion Surveillance Reports.

Figure 10–3

Per Cent Distribution[1] of Reported Legal Abortions, By Race, Selected States,[2]
1975-1977

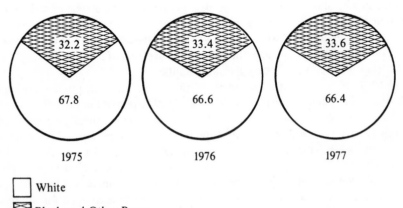

[1] Based on total number with race known.
[2] All states with data available for 1975 (31 states), 1976 (33 states), and 1977 (33 states).
Source: Table 8 of 1975, 1976, and 1977 Abortion Surveillance Reports.

remained constant since 1971; approximately one-third are 19-years-old or younger, one-third are 20 to 24-years-old, and one-third are 25-years-old or older at the time of the procedure (Figure 10–2). In 1977, approximately 410,000 abortions were obtained by women up to 19-years-old, for a rate of approximately 37/1,000 teenage women (Forrest et al. 1979), representing one of the highest abortion rates for teenagers in the world (Tietze, 1979). Very young teenagers under the age of 15 had more abortions than live births. Women in the 25 to 29-year-old age group continued to have the lowest abortion ratio, indicating that pregnancies of this group were more likely to be planned and therefore carried to term.

Compared to women in the United States, Canadian women obtaining abortions had a slightly older age distribution, especially after age 20. In Canada, the percentage of teenagers obtaining abortion in 1977 was nearly identical to that in the United States (31 per cent). However, a smaller percentage of women aged 20 to 24 obtained abortions in Canada, 30 per cent versus 35 per cent in the United States. Similarly, a higher percentage of Canadian women 25 years of age or older obtained abortions in 1977 than in the United States.

Although the majority (66 per cent) of abortions in 1977 in the United States involved white women, the percentage of abortions for women of black and other races continued to increase compared with previous years (Figure 10–3). Moreover, women of black and other races continued to have higher abortion ratios than whites. In 1977, a larger percentage increase occurred in their abortion ratio than in the ratio reported for white women. This may have been due to several factors: (a) women of minority racial groups may have unwanted pregnancies proportionately more often than white women, thus reflecting the need for family planning services for minority racial groups, and (b) women of minority racial groups may be more likely to obtain abortions in facilities where abortions are reported by race; for example, under-reporting of abortions performed in physicians' offices may disproportionately reduce the number reported for white women.

Since 1973, almost three times as many abortions in the United States have been performed for unmarried as for married women (Figure 10–4); moreover, in 1977 the legal abortion ratio for unmarried women (1,480/1,000 live births) was nearly 16 times higher than for married women (93). This large difference in abortion ratios between married and unmarried women does not take into account those women who conceived premaritally and subsequently gave birth while married. This situation would tend to shift live births from the unmarried to the married category, thereby increasing the abortion ratio for unmarried women to a greater degree than for married women because of the large number of live births to the latter. In Canada in 1977, women obtaining induced abortion were slightly more likely to be married (30 per cent) than in the United States (24 per cent).

Many women having abortions in the United States in 1977 had no living children at the time of the procedure (Figure 10–5). An inverse relationship existed between the number of living children and the percentage of abortions

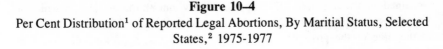

Figure 10–4

Per Cent Distribution[1] of Reported Legal Abortions, By Maritial Status, Selected
States,[2] 1975-1977

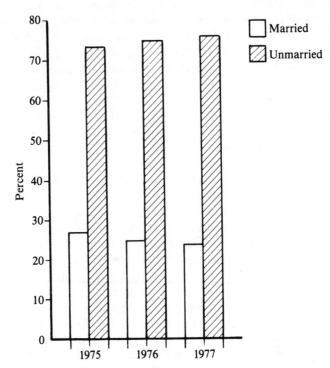

[1] Based on total number with maritial status known.
[2] All states with data available for 1975 (31 states), 1976 (34 states), and 1977 (34 states).
Source: Table 10 of 1975, 1976, and 1977 Abortion Surveillance Reports.

obtained by women; 53 per cent of abortions were for women with no living
children, and 3 per cent were for women with five or more children. In 1977,
women with one living child had the lowest abortion ratio (190/1,000 live births)
and those with no living children had the highest (415). In Canada, a higher
percentage of women obtaining abortions (60 per cent) had no living children at
the time of their procedure.

In 1977, 22 per cent of abortions in the United States were obtained by women
who reported having had at least one previous induced abortion. This continued
the increasing trend toward repeated induced abortions reported for 1975 (16 per
cent) and 1976 (18 per cent). Of women who had abortions in 1977, 17 per cent
had one previous abortion; 3 per cent two abortions; and 1 per cent three or more.
Because the population at risk of having multiple abortions has increased, it
would be expected that an increased percentage of abortions performed would be
obtained by women who had undergone one or more previous procedures. Thus,
the increasing percentage of repeat abortions probably reflects the cumulative

Figure 10–5

Per Cent Distribution[1] of Reported Legal Abortions, By Number of Living Children, Selected States,[2] 1975-1977

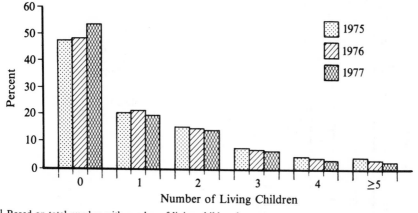

Number of Living Children

[1] Based on total number with number of living children known.
[2] All states with data available for 1975 (24 states), 1976 (28 states), and 1977 (29 states).
Source: Table 13 of 1975, 1976, and 1977 Abortion Surveillance Reports.

increase in the number of women at risk of repeat procedures since legal abortion became more widely available in the United States.

An increasing proportion of abortions have been performed at eight or fewer menstrual weeks' gestation since 1974 (Figure 10–6), with a concurrent decrease in the percentage of procedures at other gestational ages. In 1977, over 50 per cent of abortions were performed at eight or fewer menstrual weeks' gestation, while only 0.9 per cent of abortions were for pregnancies of 21 weeks or more. Because abortion morbidity and mortality are directly related to gestational age (Grimes and Cates, 1979), the trend toward abortions at earlier gestational ages means that abortion is becoming an even safer procedure within the United States. In Canada, women are obtaining abortions somewhat later in gestation. In 1977, 24 per cent of Canadian women obtained abortions at eight weeks or less, and 16 per cent at 13 weeks or more. This compares to 51 per cent and 9 per cent, respectively, in the United States.

In 1977, women obtaining abortions had their procedures performed by curettage (suction, sharp, and dilation and evacuation) 93 per cent of the time (Figure 10–7). Saline and prostaglandin instillations made up 4 per cent and 1 per cent respectively, while hysterotomy/hysterectomy procedures accounted for only 0.2 per cent of all abortions in 1977. Within the first 12 weeks, curettage procedures are the most common method used (99 per cent) for pregnancy termination. In the 13 to 15 week interval, 73 per cent of all procedures were by curettage (dilation and evacuation), followed by saline instillation (17 per cent) and prostaglandin instillation (6 per cent). Saline instillation was the most commonly used procedure at 16 or more weeks' gestation, with curettage

Figure 10-6

Per Cent Distribution[1] of Legal Abortions, By Type of Procedure, Selected States,[2] 1975-1977

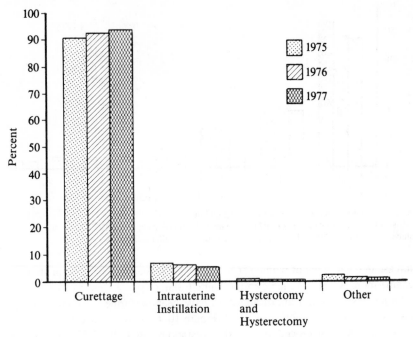

Type of Procedure

[1] Based on total number with type of procedure known.
[2] All states with data available for 1975 (32 states), 1976 (34 states), and 1977 (35 states).
Source: Table 15 of 1975, 1976, and 1977 Abortion Surveillance Reports.

procedures and instillation of prostaglandin or other agents (e.g., urea) accounting for about 16 per cent and 30 per cent, respectively, in 1977.

In Canada, similar distributions of curettage and instillation procedures were performed in 1977 as in the United States. However, the percentage of hysterotomy/hysterectomy procedures was over five times more frequent (1.1 per cent versus 0.2 per cent). After 13 weeks, in Canada, similar percentages of dilation and evacuation procedures were performed as in the United States. However, instillation procedures in Canada were more likely to have prostaglandin or urea used as the abortifacient, rather than saline, when compared to the United States.

Summary

In summary, in 1977 in the United States nearly 1.1 million women had reported legal abortions; based on surveys, the actual number who obtained abortions was

Figure 10-7

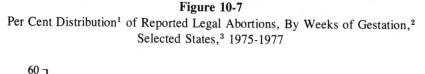

Per Cent Distribution[1] of Reported Legal Abortions, By Weeks of Gestation,[2] Selected States,[3] 1975-1977

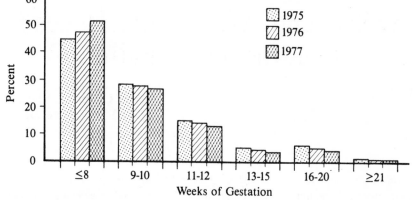

[1] Based on total number with weeks of gestation known.
[2] Weeks from last menstrual period.
[3] All states with data available for 1975 (35 states), 1976 (37 states), and 1977 (38 states).
Source: Table 16 of 1975, 1976, and 1977 Abortion Surveillance Reports.

over 1.3 million. These women were mostly young, white, and of low parity, and had abortions in the first trimester by suction curettage. The increasing availability of abortion services in the United States since 1973 has enabled about 90 per cent of women who obtain abortions to do so in their state of residence. Compared to Canadian women, women in the United States who obtain abortions are more likely to be in the 20 to 24 year age group, of higher parity, and obtaining their abortions earlier in gestation.

References

Calderone, M.S. *Abortion in the United States*. New York: Paul B. Hoeber, 1958, pp. 178–80.

Center for Disease Control. Abortion Surveillance 1977. Issued September 1979.

Forrest, J.D., E. Sullivan, and C. Tietze. "Abortion in the United States, 1977–1978." *Fam. Plann. Perspect.* 11(1979):329–41.

Grimes, D.A., W. Cates, Jr. "Complications from Legally Induced Abortion: A Review." *Obstet. Gynecol. Surv.* 13(1979):177–91.

Tietze, C. *Induced Abortion*. New York: The Population Council, 1979.

11

Access and Availability Issues in Contraceptive Failure

Sharon Chapman-Sheehan
M. Corinne Devlin

Historically, man has always wished to control family formation, and within that unit, the number and spacing of children. By the 1970s, advances in social policy[1] and pharmacotechnology brought to this practical problem a theoretical solution.

Regrettably, the steady increase in the rate of unwanted pregnancies, as estimated by combining induced abortions and illegitimate births, suggested that the sought-after individual, family and social goals of willing childbearing and childrearing were far from realized.

As workers in the Reproductive Regulation Clinic of the McMaster University Medical Centre, we became convinced through literature review and clinical experience that the explanation for the phenomenon of unwanted pregnancy is not simple but complex, not unifactoral but multifactoral, and lies in a broader understanding of the issues involved in the access to and the availability of birth-control methods and services.

Objectives

Using Canadian clinical material, the study examined the correlation between three variables: knowledge of birth-control methods, availability of birth-control services, and the woman's psychological accessibility to the use of birth-control methods and services.

For the purpose of this study, knowledge referred to the possession of information related to various methods of contraception and their relative effectiveness. Availability of services referred to the perceived existence of birth control services and knowledge of how to employ these facilities. Effective contraception was categorized as the consistent use during sexual intercourse of

---

[1] In 1969, the Federal Government of Canada enacted two pieces of legislation. The first legalized distribution of birth-control information and the dispensing of contraceptives. The second amended section 237 of the Criminal Code, thereby making therapeutic abortions more accessible.

oral contraceptives, the condom or diaphragm in conjunction with a spermaticide or the IUCD. This is consistent use as *reported* by the woman.[2] Psychological accessibility was defined as the individual's ability to apply an effective method of birth control to her own need to control fertility. This requires that the woman must, firstly, recognize the need, that is the risk of pregnancy as a consequence of sexual intercourse, and secondly, employ an effective method of contraception to avoid pregnancy. This executive function requires motivation, which in turn is largely related to the woman's feelings about her own sexuality and the resolution of sexual conflict and identity formation. In other words, the woman who feels guilty about her sexual behaviour, unsure of herself as an autonomous individual who is separate from her parents and sexual partner, is unlikely to demonstrate a high level of psychological accessibility to contraception.

Four hypotheses were tested. The first hypothesis was that knowledge alone is the least effective variable influencing the use of effective contraception. The second was that the non-availability of services has a detrimental effect on contraceptive use but is not significantly correlated to the use of contraceptive methods. The third hypothesis was that psychological accessibility is the greatest single factor related to the use of effective contraception, and fourth, that as a group, adolescents have less knowledge of birth-control methods and services and a lower psychological accessibility to effective contraceptive practice than do older women.

Method

Ideally, when studying the variables associated with the non-use or misuse of contraceptives, control groups of both successful contraceptors, that is non-pregnant women, and unsuccessful contraceptors, that is, the women who are pregnant not by choice, should be utilized. Unfortunately, the tasks of identifying such populations and making them available for investigation are both major undertakings. Because of the unique problems inherent in exploring such intimate information, it would have involved considerable expenditure of time, manpower and funds. Given these constraints, the sample population was limited to all women who as a result of contraceptive failure (where ''failure'' referred to method, service or human failure) were referred to the Reproductive Regulation Clinic between January and December 1975, for termination of pregnancy. The sample size was 107. The sampling was divided into three groups, one of which reportedly utilized an effective method of birth control, a second group of users of ineffective methods, and a third group of non-users. There were no exclusion criteria excepting sexual assault, and no patient was so characterized.

---

[2]Since our sample all experienced contraceptive failure, whether method or human failure, we assume that even those ''effective contraceptors'' as defined above (i.e., users of effective methods) did *not* always take the pill as prescribed or always use the combined method of condom or diaphragm and spermaticide.

The chief research instrument was a questionnaire incorporating a standardized series of questions related to demographic data and a further battery of questions developed for use in this study by the Field Survey Unit, McMaster University. The questionnaire was pre-coded and pretested. A checklist consisting of 40 statements requiring the subjects' rating of concern vis-à-vis each statement was utilized, along with several miscellaneous questions, to identify the third variable, psychological accessibility.

Data were collected by the clinical social worker administering a questionnaire and completing an assessment interview. At the beginning of the clinical interview, the patient's informed consent and the research methodology were obtained and clarified respectively. Confidentiality was highlighted. A structured interview was not utilized.

The questionnaire was administered as follows: the patient was given a blank copy of the schedule and was requested to follow along as the interviewer read each question and recorded verbatim the response. The checklist at the end of the interview schedule was given to the respondent to complete after brief instructions were given by the interviewer. The checklist was also personally administered when language was a problem.

Further information was derived from the clinical assessment which focused on the decision-making process with regard to becoming pregnant and requesting termination. These data were analysed separately due to their subjective nature. The interviewer, following completion of the clinical assessment, but prior to the questionnaire completion, scored the patient on nine variables along a continuum of 1 to 5, where 1 suggested no evidence of the process and 5 suggested extreme evidence of the process. Factor analysis is not available on information contained in the clinical assessment as the tool was used only in the sense of reliability / validity testing for use in subsequent studies.

All data were analysed with the assistance of the Field Survey Unit in the McMaster Health Sciences Centre.

Findings

Demographic features of the study population are markedly similar to those reported by Dauber et al. (1972). The following characteristics are worth highlighting:

74 per cent were between the ages of 16 and 24 years;

67 per cent were Canadian citizens;

80 per cent described themselves as "not regular (church) attenders," even though 88 per cent described themselves as Roman Catholic (18 per cent) or Protestant (70 per cent);

82 per cent were "alone" vis-à-vis civil status; that is, they did not live with the sexual partner at the time of conception either within legal or common-law marriages;

93 per cent had advanced beyond grade school and 46 per cent had completed

secondary school (this distribution may be slightly elevated because of the Clinic's location on the university campus);

70 per cent were in the $15,000 income bracket;

66 per cent were financially dependent on their sexual partners, parents or an outside source;

77 per cent described themselves as being in a continuing relationship with the sexual partner, while 16 per cent described the relationship as casual.

Contraceptive Use

Approximately two-thirds (64 per cent) of the sample stated that they were using some form of contraception when they became pregnant. However, when asked to specify the method used at the time of conception, only 15 per cent reported using an effective method of contraception such as the pill or an IUD. A full 39 per cent were using methods of lesser effectiveness: 20 per cent condoms, 14 per cent rhythm method and 5 per cent "whatever."

The non-use of contraception or the use of methods of lesser effectiveness characterized 75 per cent of this study population. These results are consistent with those of studies by Dauber, Zalar and Goldstein in which 63 per cent and 71 per cent in two separate studies, failed to use effective contraceptive methods, and with Grauer's sample at The Jewish General Hospital in Montreal in which 41 per cent used nothing to prevent pregnancy (Grauer, 1972).

Equally interesting, when asked what methods were ever used, 55 per cent of the subjects had at one time used oral contraceptives: that is 49/59 women stopped using this highly effective method, but did not stop the coital activity which placed them at risk. In addition, no subject reported using the highly effective combined methods of condom and spermaticide. Given that these combined methods are the only effective method not requiring the collaboration of the medical profession and therefore, generally more available, its absence is significant.

Knowledge

A knowledge score was obtained by using Tietze's "Ranking of Contraceptive Methods by Levels of Effectiveness," (one point is awarded for each method *plus* one point for accuracy of effectiveness within a variance of one) (Tietze, 1970). The low knowledge range in this study is 2 to 7 and the high between 8 to 16.

Two-thirds (65 per cent) of the sample were characterized as having a high knowledge score and 35 per cent as low knowledge, suggesting a relatively enlightened population. However, when knowledge is related to use, the results are less positive. Even though two-thirds of the sample were indeed knowledgeable, 80 per cent of these women were either using ineffective or no birth control at the time of conception. The remaining one-third with a low knowledge score generated 95 per cent of poor and non-users (S. .0002). The results demonstrate that a high knowledge score increases the likelihood that some method of contraception will be used but it does not assure usage of an effective method, thus supporting the first hypothesis (S. .04).

A few miscellaneous findings: knowledge showed no significant correlation to any of the demographic features of the population, with the exception of age (S. .08). As one would expect, knowledge tends to accumulate as age increases and this indeed appears to be true in this sample. However, when we held knowledge constant, the use of some/any method of contraception increased as *age* increased regardless of the deficient knowledge base, suggesting that age may be a more significant determinant of contraceptive behaviour than knowledge.

Only 11 per cent of the sample knew of the combined method of condom or diaphragm plus spermaticide; all such women were highly knowledgeable (S. .0001). Finally, the sample accurately assessed their own knowledge when asked if they thought they had enough information to prevent pregnancy. There was a positive correlation at .0003 level of significance. Those lacking knowledge were aware of this deficiency.

Availability of Services

The series of questions related to the perceived availability of services indicated that 90 per cent of the sample knew where to obtain contraceptives, and 86 per cent knew how to make contact with the service. Even though the data revealed that only 39 per cent actually contacted these facilities, only 5 per cent of the study population cited inaccessibility to services as a reason for non-use of contraception. These findings support the second hypothesis, that non-availability of services is not a significant variable in the use of contraception. Another noteworthy finding of the study is that, of the 39 per cent of the sample who did contact family planning services, 28 per cent felt that their request was "put off," and 40 per cent wished there had been more discussion. When the remaining 60 per cent were asked about reasons for not contacting a birth-control service, 11 per cent said they anticipated a negative response and a further 25 per cent cited concerns regarding their feelings about their own sexuality as a deterrent. Clearly these later responses point to both psychological inaccessibility and the desperately poor reputation of health professionals in providing contraceptive counselling and services.

Psychological Accessibility

Factor analysis was done on the information gathered from the self-administered checklist to provide data on this last variable. The analysis tended to identify two clusters or fields of response. These responses reflect subjects' characteristics descriptively catergorized as "self-directed" and "other-directed" concerns.

The findings show that "other-directed" women tended not to contact birth-control services (S. .06) and that those subjects scoring high on the "self-directed" scales tended to use more effective methods (S. .06). The

Table 11–1

Self-Directed	Other-Directed
1. Less dependence on family.	1. More dependence on family.
2. More liberal attitudes towards intercourse.	2. Less liberal attitudes towards intercourse.
3. More likely to contact birth-control resource.	3. Less likely to contact birth-control resource.
4. More likely to use better methods.	4. Less likely to use better methods.
5. More tendency to use BCP.	5. Less tendency to use BCP.
6. Less likely to cite negative response from service as a reason for non-use.	6. More likely to cite negative response from service as a reason for non-use.
7. Less likely to use denial as a reason for non-use.	7. More likely to use denial as a reason for non-use.

correlations were not conclusive but did begin to offer some explanation for this knowledgeable group of women not protecting themselves from unwanted pregnancy.

In addition to the factor analysis data, there was further evidence of psychological barriers to contraception offered by the subjects themselves, in response to questions asking for *their own reasons* for not using birth control. Fully 56 per cent of the non-users gave *denial* of sexual activity or general *neglect* as their reason. Secondly, of the 23 women citing denial or neglect, more than one-half were financially dependent on their family. Self-supporting and agency-supported individuals showed a better use pattern than those financially dependent on their family or sexual partner (S. .03).

Summary

Figures 1 through 3 summarize the correlations between the three variables:

(i) knowledge and use.
(ii) psychological accessibility and use.
(iii) perceived availability of birth-control services and use.

Figure 1

Knowledge/Use

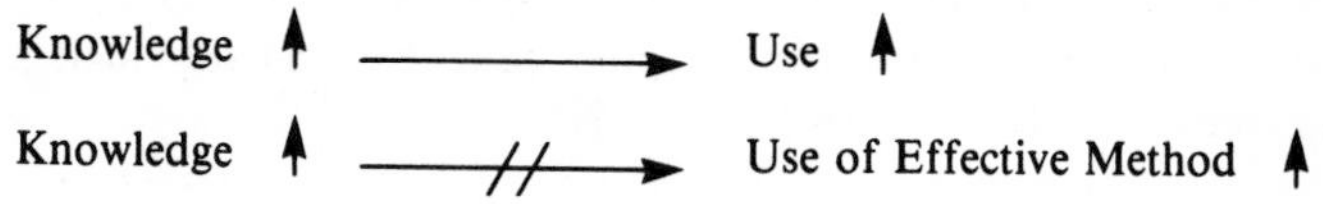

Knowledge ↑ ⟶ Use ↑

Knowledge ↑ ⟶//⟶ Use of Effective Method ↑

Figure 2

Psychological Access / Use

Psychological Access ↑ ⟶ Use ↑

Psychological Access ↑ ⟶ Use of Effective Method ↑

Figure 3

Availability / Use

Availability ↑ —//→ Use ↑

Receptiveness of Service ⟶ Use ↑

—//→ is not correlated to ↑ as variable increases

Discussion

This study refutes the simplistic view that lack of factual information is the singular cause of unwanted pregnancy, reduces the enthusiasm for the endless cloning of family planning services, and wearies the technocrat in search of the perfect contraceptive.

Emerging from this study is the suggestion that the psychological accessibility to employ already available methods and services may be a function of the acceptance and internalization by a woman of the recreational and relational aspects of intercourse, in addition to the traditional procreational role of coitus.

Conclusions

The paramount importance of ready access to family-planning services and the availability of safe, reversible, affordable birth-control methods notwithstanding, psychological accessibility to these resources emerges from this study as a key determinant of successful fertility control. Adolescents seem doubly disadvantaged, by their deficient information base for methods and services, and their poorly developed sense of control over their sexual and reproductive capacity. Health-care services and family-life education for this group particularly, must clearly focus more on the conflicts inherent in the process of developing a positive sense of identity and sexuality, and less on the "plumbing." Furthermore, professionals must strive to improve their own reputation as facilitators of effective contraceptive practices and providers of birth control services.

Suggestions for Further Study

Phase II, III, and IV studies, still on the drawing board, will explore the relationship between sexual and reproductive literacy, and the successful/unsuccessful setting and meeting of reproductive goals. Locus of control studies, as well as problem-solving skills in lifestyle areas will also be explored.

Acknowledgments

The willing and kind co-operation of the Reproductive Regulation Clinic Staff and the Staff of Ward 4B at the Medical Centre is gratefully acknowledged. The tireless work of Chris Lowry, Social Worker to the Clinic, is recognized and deeply appreciated.

References

Dauber, B., M. Zalar, and P. Goldstein. "Abortion Counselling and Behavioural Change." *Family Planning Perspective*, April 1972.

Grauer, H. "A Study of Contraception as Related to Unwanted Pregnancy." *Canadian Medical Association Journal* 197, October 21, 1972, pp. 739–41.

Tietze, C. "Ranking of Contraceptive Methods by Levels of Effectiveness." *American Association Planned Parenthood*, April 1970.

12

Psychological Factors and Unwanted Pregnancy

Keith Ian Pearce

This chapter deals with the efforts made in Calgary to explore some of the etiological factors involved in the production of unwanted pregnancies, particularly with a view to embarking upon more definitive preventive programs.

The Foothills Hospital is the principal teaching hospital of the Faculty of Medicine at the University of Calgary in Alberta. It is one of two hospitals in the city which carry out the majority of therapeutic abortions in Calgary, and its Therapeutic Abortion Committee has existed in one form or another since shortly after the opening of the hospital in 1966. Indeed, the Criminal Code amendment merely changed the number of procedures carried out at the hospital and the constitution of the Therapeutic Abortion Committee. Since the changes in the Criminal Code, and up until 1978, the demand for therapeutic abortions rose steadily, reaching proportions which were beginning to have an impact on the availability of other surgical resources in the hospital. Accordingly, the Medical Advisory Committee, on the advice of the Director of the Department of Obstetrics and Gynecology, placed a numerical limit of 35 cases a week on the number of abortions carried out at the hospital. The Therapeutic Abortion Committee has never been happy with this arrangement, particularly as the method of allocating this scarce resource has not been based upon patient need. The result of this change has been the direction of an increasing number of abortion candidates to the United States, and the tendency for waiting lists to build up, with a resultant higher proportion of late terminations with their accompanying increase in morbidity.

Thus, over the past two years approximately 1,750 abortions were performed annually. Each patient was required to complete certain paper and pencil tests prior to an interview with the nurse counsellor. One test (the Minnesota Multiphasic Personality Inventory or MMPI) was intended to identify patients who may be in some sort of psychiatric difficulty. The Cornell Medical Index was used as a type of functional inquiry with the expectation that unanticipated physical problems might be identified, and the third test, the Social History

Questionnaire, was intended to identify any social problems which would require some sort of consideration or intervention. The interview with the nurse counsellor was intended to review this material, answer the patient's questions and explore the reasons for contraceptive failure. The interview with the nurse counsellor served in addition to bring to the attention of the Committee at its weekly meeting, those patients that might require their particular attention. When problems that were remediable were identified the chairman of the Committee would write to the individual or institution concerned.

At the time of writing this chapter, modifications in this procedure are contemplated. More simple psychological screening tests are being considered; the social history is being reviewed because parts are not relevant to this particular procedure and additional efforts in respect of contraceptive counselling are being sought.

To the best of our knowledge such extensive data collection is not routinely available in other centres, and accordingly, careful analysis of it began in 1976 when 1,296 consecutive therapeutic abortions were reviewed and a report prepared for the Board of the Foothills Hospital. Although the data have been collected, unfortunately the resources to analyse them completely have not been available and accordingly, subsequent analyses were more limited and directed themselves to specific issues.

Since the first report was prepared, the policy of the Therapeutic Abortion Committee has been increasingly directed toward issues of prevention (see Figure 12–1) which in turn has led to an attempt to explore some of the causes of unwanted pregnancy.

Anyone who has worked in this area will have met, many times, the young woman who, distraught with an unwanted pregnancy, is questioned as to whether or not she used contraceptives. She tearfully will report that she did not and on further questioning will admit that she realized she was taking a risk. However, the inevitable phrase eventually slips out: "I didn't think it would happen to me." To label such comments and behaviour as "irresponsible" explains nothing, yet clearly there resides within this enigmatic term the ultimate explanation of many unwanted pregnancies. What constitutes an adequate definition of unwanted pregnancy is a matter for discussion (Pohlman, 1969; Miller, 1974). However, for the purpose of our work in Calgary we have defined an unwanted pregnancy in terms of the woman carrying the pregnancy making a fully informed decision to seek a therapeutic abortion. Until the Cobliner et al. paper in 1973, a review of the literature reveals a general acceptance by various authors of some sort of unconscious psychodynamic motivation in acquiring an unwanted pregnancy. Without bothering to review this literature in detail (see Meyers, 1976 for a review) it is reasonable to comment that while unconscious psychodynamic motivation may be an important contributing factor in some unwanted pregnancies, as a general explanation it is inadequate and in any case, was based upon a literature which had the most shaky scientific foundation.

Figure 12-1
Unwanted Pregnancy

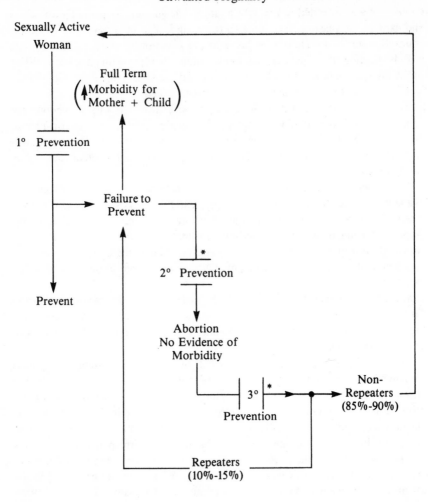

1°   Prevention — Community Responsibility
2°
3° } Prevention — Proposed Level of Foothills Hospital Intervention*

While some more recent authors, notably Abernethy (1973; 1974; 1975) have attempted to correct some of the deficiencies in design, the work still lacks sufficient rigour as to be generally acceptable.

It was Cobliner et al. (1973), who pointed out that in addition to lack of knowledge or insufficient access to contraceptive assistance there could well be operating a factor of psychological maturity. The same hypothesis is similarly proposed by Cvetkovich et al. (1975), apparently independently. That is, not having reached the formal operational stage of thinking (using the developmental theory of Piaget) the woman is unable to put into practice or apply in a mature fashion what she may know about contraception. To briefly summarize the relevant parts of Piaget's developmental theory one can say that the fully mature adult individual functions at the formal operational level of thinking, that is to say he or she is able to contemplate a problem and the relevant factors, perceive the likely outcome of alternative courses of action and then embark upon the most appropriate course of action, that is, to not only make but also *act* upon well-informed consideration of all the relevant factors (Sinclair, 1974). The stage of development which immediately precedes this final level of maturation is known as the concrete operational level and is characterized by the ability to conceptualize a problem and even to an extent to reason through the alternatives of the outcomes of different courses of action. However, in the last analysis the conclusions reached to not modify the individual's behaviour and therefore he or she is seen to be acting in an "irresponsible" or "immature" fashion.

It is clear that the chronological age at which maturing individuals move from one level of thinking to another varies enormously, indeed some never reach the formal operational level of thinking (Piaget, 1972; 1974). It has also been observed by Piaget (1972) that it is not unknown for individuals to function at the formal operational level in some areas of their life (for example, skilled craftsmen) and only at a concrete operational level in other areas. Stones (1966) also pointed out "adolescents and adults will revert to simpler modes of reasoning when faced with an entirely new situation." Thus, although there may well be a general relationship between chronological age and responsible sexuality other variables are clearly at work, one of these being the level of cognitive development achieved by the individual. Unfortunately, simple tests of developmental level do not exist in a manner which can be applied in group or near-group settings, and much of our work has been hampered by this inadequacy. However, what evidence we have accumulated does seem to support this hypothesis.

Thus, in examining the issue of unwanted pregnancy one is directed to two principal variables: the sexual and contraceptive knowledge available to the individual, and the level of cognitive development which would enable her to use this in order to avoid unwanted pregnancy. Other variables clearly operate; for example, there is a chance failure rate associated with all contraceptive methods and there are chance sexual encounters (for example rape) which would not normally be contemplated by a woman. However, while recognizing these two other factors one must also accept that they are relatively uncommon and account for a small proportion of the variability which determines the presence of an unwanted pregnancy.

Simple demographic data strongly suggest that a factor of "immaturity" operates. In a consecutive series of 1,296 unwanted pregnancies the simple plotting of age against number of candidates reveals a curve (see Figure 12–2) in which incidence climbs with age, peaking around 19 years of age, more or less

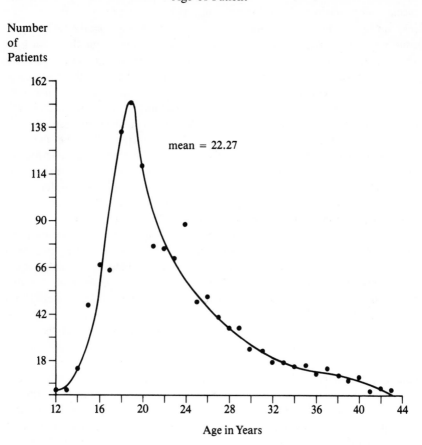

Figure 12-2
Age of Patient

plateaus and then declines fairly sharply after the age of 26. A number of factors lead to the decline in age incidence after 26, for example, the probable increase in wantedness of pregnancies due to marriage, the diminishing frequency of sexual relations and the increasing probability of the use of more reliable forms of contraception such as tubal ligation or vasectomy. Between the ages of 19 and 26 a number of factors are operating to confound any interpretation of the data such as a high frequency of sexual relations and an increase in the number of separations and divorces, while below the age of 19 factors such as ignorance and immaturity operate with declining frequency as the young woman increases in age. With a view to trying to separate some of these effects, a logarithmic conversion of the age distribution was made and is shown in Figure 12–3. The curve up to the age of 19 can be interpreted as part of a normal distribution which in turn suggests that the majority of young women have achieved maturity and / or well-informed status by around the age of 26. The linear regression after

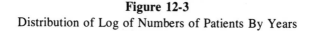

Figure 12-3

Distribution of Log of Numbers of Patients By Years

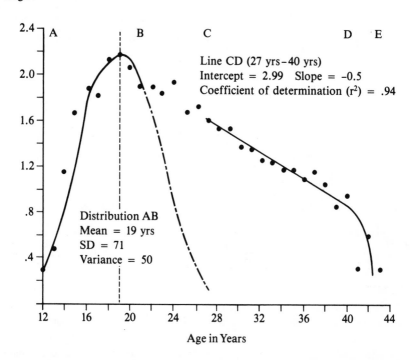

Log N

Line CD (27 yrs – 40 yrs)
Intercept = 2.99   Slope = –0.5
Coefficient of determination (r^2) = .94

Distribution AB
Mean = 19 yrs
SD = 71
Variance = 50

Age in Years

the age of 26 strongly suggests that factors other than immaturity, unavailability or ignorance are operating. Thus these data do appear to be at least compatible with the hypothesis that in the younger age groups, factors of immaturity, unavailability and ignorance are operating.

If we now turn to the MMPI data (see Table 12-1 and Table 12-2) Table 12-1 indicates that the majority of patients during the period under study completed

Table 12–1

MMPI RESULTS

Not done*	118 = 9%	*Not done, questionnaire	
Not valid	13 = 1%	lost or ruined	45
Normal	778 = 60%	Not done for cultural	
		or language reasons	73
Abnormal			118
(at least			
one scale			
> 70)	387 = 30%		

Table 12–2

MMPI RESULTS
ABNORMAL FINDINGS

	Hs(1)	D(2)	Hy(3)	Pd(4)	Mi(5)	Pa(6)	Pt(7)	Sc(8)	Ma(9)	Sl(0)
	1-0-8	2-0-41	3-0-15	4-0-69	5-0-10	6-0-3	7-0-3	8-0-6	9-0-43	
	1-2-2	2-1-1	3-1-6	4-1-2		6-2-2	7-1-1	8-1-2	9-2-1	
	1-3-6	2-3-6	3-2-4	4-2-9		6-4-3	7-2-1	8-2-5	9-4-11	
		2-4-12	3-4-3	4-3-5		6-7-1	7-8-4	8-3-2	9-5-3	
		2-6-3	3-6-1	4-5-1		6-8-5		8-4-7	9-8-9	
		2-7-10	3-7-2	4-6-9		6-9-2		8-6-4		
		2-8-2	3-8-1	4-7-2				8-7-3		
		2-9-2		4-8-19				8-9-8		
				4-9-6						
TOTAL	16	77	32	122	10	16	9	37	67	0

the MMPI and the principal reason for not completing an MMPI was invariably a problem of cultural relevance or language. A small proportion of native Indian applicants were culturally so different as to render the MMPI inappropriate, and a similar small proportion of recent immigrants with insufficient English were also excluded. Aside from this small proportion of cases, the patients who completed the test produced a reliable response in a majority of cases.

Reference to Table 12–2 reveals the majority of significant psychopathology as detected by the MMPI lies within three major areas, with the principal elevation on the D-scale, on the Pd scale, or on the Ma scale. Those familiar with interpretation of the MMPI will recognize that elevations on the Pd and the Ma scale are associated with psychopathic deviance. However, an important caution must be exercised and that is to recognize that such elevations are "normal" in adolescents, and it is not appropriate to make such a strict interpretation. Recently, corrections to the scoring methods applied to adolescents have been recommended. However we were not aware of these at the time that the series was collected. Thus, it is not appropriate to perceive these young women as "psychopaths," but rather as individuals who have failed so far to achieve complete maturity. Since one aspect of maturity may be the shift from the concrete operational level of thinking to the formal operational level of thinking, these data are consistent with our hypothesis concerning this as a factor in producing unwanted pregnancy.

An important aspect of our preventive endeavours in Calgary has been to embark upon a survey of school children which specifically examines sexual and

Table 12-3

ABORTION PATIENTS, MARITAL STATUS AND PREVIOUS ABORTIONS BY AGE

Age	18 and under (N = 50) N	%	19 – 21 (N = 59) N	%	22 – 25 (N = 48) N	%	26 – 39 (N = 46) N	%	Total
Marital Status									
Single	48	96	51	86.4	35	72.9	18	39.1	
Previous Abortions	5		10		12		5		
Married	—		2	3.4	6	12.5	15	32.6	
Previous Abortions	—		—		—		3		
Separated	—		3	5.1	3	6.3	4	8.7	
Previous Abortions	—		—		—		1		
Widowed	—		1	1.7	1	2.1	—		
Previous Abortions	—		—		—		—		
Divorced	—		2	3.4	3	6.3	5	10.9	
Previous Abortions	—		—		2		2		
Common Law (Living with boyfriend)	2	4	—		—		4	8.7	
Previous Abortions	2*		—		—		—		
Total N for Age Group	50		59		48		46		203
Total N & % Previous									
Abortion for Age Groups	7	(14%)	10	(19.6%)	14	(29.2%)	12	(23.9%)	43
N & % All Groups	50	(24.6%)	59	(29.1%)	48	(23.7%)	46	(22.7%)	100
N & % Previous Abortions All Groups	7	(3.5%)	10	(4.9%)	14	(6.9%)	12	(5.9%)	43 (21.2%)

*One subject had two previous abortions.

contraceptive knowledge, sexual attitude, and a factor which can be interpreted as psychological maturity. Once the survey had been carried out we decided to apply the sexual and contraceptive knowledge questionnaire to 203 consecutive therapeutic abortion candidates whose general characteristics are described in Tables 12–3, 12–4, 12–5 and 12–6. There was a 100 per cent compliance and their sexual and contraceptive knowledge scores are described in Tables 12–7 and 12–8.

Table 12–4

ABORTION PATIENTS' AGE DISTRIBUTION

	Age	N		%		
	14	1		0.5		
	15	6		2.9		Previous
96% single	16	8		3.9		Abortions
	17	15	Total	7.4		14%
	18	20	50	9.8	24.6%	
	19	19		9.4		Previous
86.4% single	20	17	Total	8.4		Abortions
	21	23	59	11.3	29.1%	19.6%
	22	15		7.4		
	23	13		6.4		Previous
72.9% single	24	11	Total	5.4		Abortions
	25	9	48	4.4	23.7%	29.2%
	26	7		3.5		
	27	7		3.5		
	28	5		2.5		
	29	5		2.5		
	30	4		2.0		
	31	2		1.0		
39.1% single	32	1		0.5		
32.6% married	33	3		1.5		
	34	5		2.5		Previous
	35	—		—		Abortions
	36	4		2.0		23.9%
	37	2		1.0		
	38	—	Total	—		
	39	1	46	0.5	22.7%	
Totals		203		100.2	100.1%	

	N	%	
All	152	74.9%	single
	23	11.3%	married
	10	4.9%	separated
	2	1.0%	widowed
	10	4.9%	divorced
	6	3.0%	common law (living with boyfriend)

Table 12–5

ABORTION PATIENTS' REASONS FOR NOT USING CONTRACEPTIVES DURING *FIRST* EXPERIENCE WITH INTERCOURSE

104 patients gave 113 reasons.

REASONS	FREQUENCY	
	N	%
1. Spontaneous, unplanned experience	41	36.3
2. Lack of knowledge of contraceptives	35	31.0
3. Contraceptives not available	18	15.9
Afraid to ask for them — 6		
Afraid to go to physician — 5		
Did not know where to get them — 3		
No way to get them — 1		
Did not want to go to doctor — 1		
Had none — 2		
4. Attitude to issue	8	7.1
Don't know why — 1		
Did not think of it — 1		
Careless, carefree — 2		
Just did not — 2		
Did not want to — 1		
Did not think about getting pregnant — 1		
5. Wanted to get pregnant	5	4.4
6. Intercourse forced or rape	5	4.4
7. Was already "pregnant"	1	0.9
Total	113	100.0

In order to provide some sort of comparison data we secured a sample of 25 female medical students from the three years of the undergraduate medical program at the University of Calgary (see Table 12–9). Clearly, the test requires standardization and considerable work in order to improve its discriminatory powers. Nonetheless the lowest scores are obtained in the youngest students, the highest scores between the ages of 22 to 25 years, and there is a noticeable slight falling off in the older age group which probably reflects a different level of knowledge in an older generation that matured before the "sexual revolution." Table 12–10 shows the number and percentage of abortion candidates who used contraceptives during their first and their most recent coital experience. During their first coital experience approximately half used no method at all, but this is age related with the percentage rising to 60 per cent in the 18-years-old and under. A similar result is found in relation to their most recent coital experience with the age difference being as expected less noticeable.

Table 12–11 which shows frequency of contraceptive use by major age groups reflects the same age difference with the younger age groups taking the greater risk.

Table 12–6

REASONS GIVEN BY ABORTION PATIENTS FOR NOT USING CONTRACEPTIVES AT *MOST RECENT* EXPERIENCE WITH INTERCOURSE

90 patients gave reasons.

REASON	FREQUENCY	
	N	%
1. Already pregnant	32	35.6
2. Spontaneous unplanned experience	16	17.8
3. Went off pill — 12		
Forgot to take pill — 2	14	15.6
4. Did not think I would get pregnant	8	8.9
5. Afraid to ask for contraceptives	5	5.6
6. Out of supplies or in process		
of getting them	4	4.4
7. Failure surgical sterilization		
Male — 2, female — 1	3	3.3
8. Other — first time — 2		
— wanted to get pregnant — 2		
— made a mistake — 1		
— did not know — 1		
— stupidity — 1		
— never used — 1	8	8.9
Total	90	100.1

Table 12–7

REPRODUCTION TEST

(MAXIMUM SCORE 12)

	N	X	SD	Range
Abortion Patients				
18 years and under	50	6.2	2.24	1 – 10
19 – 21 years	59	6.2	2.16	1 – 10
22 – 25 years	48	7.35	2.38	1 – 11
26 – 39 years	46	6.39	2.16	1 – 10
Total	203			
Female Medical				
Students	25	9.32	1.314	6 – 12

Table 12–8

CONTRACEPTIVE TEST

(MAXIMUM SCORE 19)

	N	X	SD	Range
Abortion Patients				
18 years and under	50	8.4	3.37	0 – 15
19 – 21 years	59	9.9	2.77	3 – 14
22 – 25 years	48	10.6	2.56	4 – 16
26 – 39 years	46	10.02	2.97	2 – 13
Total	203			
Female Medical				
Students	25	12.56	2.179	9 – 16

Table 12–9

FEMALE MEDICAL STUDENTS

REPRODUCTION TEST SCORE (MAXIMUM SCORE = 12)

	N	X	SD	Range
All Students	25	9.32	1.314	6 – 12
1st year	12	8.92	1.240	6 – 11
2nd year	3	9.0	1.0	8 – 10
3rd year	1	9.0	—	—
Not Known	9	10.0	1.414	7 – 12

CONTRACEPTION TEST SCORE (MAXIMUM SCORE = 19)

	N	X	SD	Range
All students	25	12.56	1.938	8 – 16
1st year	12	12.58	2.109	8 – 15
2nd year	3	13.0	1.0	12 – 14
3rd year	1	13.0	—	—
Not known	9	12.33	2.179	9 – 16

Table 12–10

NUMBER AND PERCENT ABORTION PATIENTS USING CONTRACEPTIVES AT FIRST AND MOST RECENT COITAL EXPERIENCE BY AGE GROUPS

AGE GROUPS		COITAL EXPERIENCE												
		FIRST CONTRACEPTIVES USED						MOST RECENT CONTRACEPTIVES USED						
		Yes		No		No Response		Yes		No		No Response		
	N	N	%	N	%	N	%	N	%	N	%	N	%	
18 years and under	50	19	38.0	31	62.0	-	-	19	38.0	28	56.0	3	6.0	
19 – 21 years	59	29	49.2	30	50.9	-	-	36	51.0	23	39.0	-	-	
22 – 25 years	48	27	56.3	18	37.5	3	6.3	24	50.0	22	45.8	2	4.2	
26 – 39 years	46	21	45.7	22	47.8	3	6.5	23	50.0	22	47.8	1	2.2	
All Groups Total	203	96	47.3	101	49.8	6	3.0	102	50.2	95	46.8	6	3.0	

Table 12–11

FREQUENCY OF CONTRACEPTIVE USE BY ABORTION PATIENTS FROM FIRST COITAL EXPERIENCE TO MOST RECENT ONE BY AGE GROUPS

Frequency of Contraceptive Use	AGE GROUPS									
	18 years and under (N=50)		19–21 years (N=59)		22–25 years (N=48)		26–39 years (N=46)		All Groups (N=203)	
	N	%	N	%	N	%	N	%	N	%
Not at all	16	32.0	6	10.2	2	4.2	5	10.9	29	14.3
Some of the time	6	12.0	7	11.9	3	6.3	3	6.5	19	9.4
Most of the time	17	34.0	30	50.9	26	54.2	22	47.8	95	46.8
Every time	6	12.0	16	27.1	16	33.3	13	28.3	51	25.1
No response	5	10.0	—		1	2.1	3	6.5	9	4.4

Frequency of Contraceptive Use by Age $x^2 = 25.178$, d.f. = 9, p < .01.
(Frequency of contraceptive use is associated with age).

Table 12–12

FREQUENCY OF INTERCOURSE ABORTION PATIENTS BY AGE GROUP

Frequency of Intercourse	Age Groups									
	18 years and under (N=50)		19 – 21 years (N=59)		22 – 25 years (N=48)		26 – 39 years (N=46)		All Groups (N=203)	
	N	%	N	%	N	%	N	%	N	%
Less than once a month	11	22.0	12	20.3	7	14.6	6	13.0	36	17.7
Once a month	6	12.0	6	10.2	4	8.3	6	13.0	22	10.8
Every two weeks	7	14.0	5	8.5	8	16.7	8	17.4	28	13.8
Once a week	13	26.0	18	30.5	9	18.8	9	19.6	49	24.1
More than once a week	10	20.0	17	28.8	18	37.5	14	30.4	59	29.1
No response	3	6.0	1	1.7	2	4.2	3	6.5	9	4.4

Frequency of intercourse by age $x^2 = 8.654$, d.f. = 12, not significant.

On the other hand Table 12–12 shows that frequency of intercourse does not exhibit a similar age relationship.

Tables 12–13 and 12–14 show the contraceptive methods used (when one was used) at the first and most recent coital experiences. Again one sees the tendency for the younger age group to use the less reliable forms of contraception. Clearly, a great deal remains to be done in terms of refining these data, particularly in terms of refining the tools available for obtaining them. However, it is clear that the information is compatible with the hypothesis that cognitive knowledge and psychological maturity are important factors in producing unwanted pregnancies.

Table 12–13

CONTRACEPTIVES USED BY ABORTION PATIENTS DURING FIRST COITAL EXPERIENCE BY AGE GROUPS

Contraceptives used					Age Groups					
	18 years and under (N=19)		19 – 21 years (N=29)		22 – 25 years (N=27)		26 – 39 years (N=21)		All Groups (N=96)	
	N	%	N	%	N	%	N	%	N	%
A. Condom	10	52.6	12	41.4	7	25.9	2	9.5	31	32.3
B. Foam, cream or jelly	—	—	—	—	1	3.7	4	19.1	5	5.2
C. Diaphragm										
D. IUD coil	—	—	1	3.5	—	—	3	14.3	4	4.2
E. Pill	6	31.6	10	34.5	13	48.2	6	28.6	35	36.5
F. Washed self off after	—	—	—	—	—	—	—	—	—	—
G. Rhythm method	1	5.3	—	—	1	3.7	1	4.8	3	3.1
H. Withdrawal	2	10.5	4	13.8	4	14.8	2	9.5	12	12.5
I. Some combination of above	—	—	2*	6.9	1†	3.7	3‡	14.3	6	6.3

*I = A + E, H + other unstated.
†I = E + H
‡I = A + B, A + C, A + E, B + C

As tentative conclusions which might be valuable in attempts to combat the high incidence of unwanted pregnancy it is appropriate to point out that sexual and contraceptive knowledge are limited and not freely available. Even if steps were taken to correct this element, problems of maturity which reflect on the individual's ability to make use of the knowledge she has will continue to be a problem, which can only be tackled by attempting to foster changes in attitude towards responsible sexuality. Indeed, in attempting to limit the numbers of unwanted pregnancies, one sees very clearly the need to face the same problems which have bedevilled all those attempts to use education as a preventive tool in modifying an individual's lifestyle. The problems faced by professionals wishing to reduce the incidence of unwanted pregnancy are not very different from those faced by their colleagues attempting to combat smoking or obesity.

Table 12–14

CONTRACEPTIVES USED BY ABORTION PATIENTS DURING MOST RECENT
COITAL EXPERIENCE BY AGE GROUPS

Contraceptives		Age Groups							
	18 years and under (N=19)		19 – 21 years (N=36)		22 – 25 years (N=24)		26 – 39 years (N=23)		All Groups (N=102)
	N	%	N	%	N	%	N	%	N	%
A. Condom	6	31.6	7	19.4	7	29.2	6	26.1	26	25.5
B. Foam	—	—	3	8.3	1	4.2	3	13.0	7	6.9
C. Diaphragm	—	—	2	5.6	—	—	—	—	2	2.0
D. IUD coil	1	5.3	5	13.9	—	—	2	8.7	8	7.8
E. Pill	5	26.3	8	22.2	10	41.7	2	8.7	25	24.5
F. Washed self off after	—	—	—	—	—	—	—	—	—	—
G. Rhythm method	1	5.3	—	—	1	4.2	2	8.7	4	3.9
H. Withdrawal	3	15.8	4	11.1	4	16.7	3	13.0	14	13.7
I. Some combination of above	3*	15.8	7†	19.4	1‡	4.2	5§	21.7	16	15.7

*I = A + E; A + G; A + F + G
†I = A + B; A + E; A + B + G; A + D + E; B + C; D + E; G + H.
‡I = G + H
§I = A + B; A + B + G; A + E + H; plus two unreported.

References

Abernethy, Virginia. "The Abortion Constellation: Early History and Present Relationships." *Archives of General Psychiatry* 29(1973):346–50.

Abernethy, Virginia. "Illegitimate Conception Among Teenagers." *American Journal of Public Health* 64(1974):662–65.

Abernethy, Virginia, Donna Robbins, George L. Abernethy, Henry Grunebaum and Justin L. Weiss. "Identification of Women at Risk for Unwanted Pregnancy." *American Journal of Psychiatry* 132(1975):1027–31.

Cobliner, W. Godfrey, Harold Schulman and Seymour L. Romney. "The Termination of Adolescent Out of Wedlock Pregnancies and Prospects for Their Primary Prevention." *American Journal of Obstetrics and Gynecology* 115(1973):432–44.

Cvetkovich, George, Barbara Grote, Ann Bjorseth and Julia Sarkissian. "On the Psychology of Adolescents' Use of Contraceptives." *The Journal of Sex Research* 11(1975):256–70.

Meyers, Marlene O.S. *"Logical Thought and Sexual Knowledge as Dimensions in Unwanted Pregnancy.* M.Sc. Thesis, The University of Calgary, 1976.

Miller, Warren B. "Relationship Between the Intendedness of Conception and the Wantedness of Pregnancy." *Journal of Nervous and Mental Diseases* 159(1974):396-406.

Piaget, Jean. "The Theory of Stages in Cognitive Development." In *Critical Features of Piaget's Theory of the Development of Thought*, edited by Frank B. Murray. New York: MSS Information Corporation, 1974, pp. 116-26.

Piaget, Jean. "Intellectual Evolution from Adolescence to Adulthood." *Human Development* 15(1972):1-12.

Pohlman, Edward. *The Psychology of Birth Planning*. Cambridge: Schentman Publishing Company, 1969.

Sinclair, Hermine. "Piaget's Theory of Development: The Main Stages." In *Critical Features of Piaget's Theory of the Development of Thought*, edited by Frank B. Murray. New York: MSS Information Corporation, 1974, pp. 68-78.

Stones, E. *An Introduction to Educational Psychology*. London: Methuen and Company Limited, 1966.

13

Repeaters: Different or Unlucky?*

Charlene Berger
Dolores Gold
Peter Gillett
David Andres
and
Robert Kinch

The rate of repeat abortions in 1977 in Canada was 11 per cent, with the figure varying greatly from province to province. Quebec has the highest number of repeat abortions, with 18 per cent of the reported abortions being obtained by women who have had at least one previous induced abortion (Statistics Canada, 1979). By comparison, figures for 1977 in the United States indicated that 22 per cent of the abortions reported were repeats (Center for Disease Control, 1979).

Earlier explanations of multiple abortions emphasized psychopathological variables which unconsciously motivated women to seek pregnancy and abortion (David, 1972; Fischer, 1974). Other explanations, although less psychoanalytically oriented, still linked repeat abortions to poorer personality adjustment (Jacobsson, von Schoultz and Solheim, 1976; Robert, 1972; Rovinsky, 1972). Other authors have expressed concern that some women are using abortion as a replacement for regularly practised contraception (Szabady and Klinger, 1972). The use of abortion as a substitute for contraception would create many problems, as abortion is expensive in terms of health-care costs and also presents increased risks to the health of the woman (Schneider and Thompson, 1976). Furthermore, repeat abortion may have negative implications for subsequent fertility and obstetrical performance.† In addition, many health-care personnel

*This research was funded by team grants from Health and Welfare, Family Planning Division, Canada and from Ministère des Affaires Sociales, Québec. In addition, the first author was supported by a Bourse de l'Enseignement Superieur from the Quebec Government.
†"Post-Abortion Effects," *Female Health Topics and Diagnostics Reporter,* 2(6), 1979, p. 1.
"Repeat Abortions Increase Risk," *International Family Planning Perspectives and Digest,* 4(4), 1978, pp. 24–125.

report that working in abortion clinics is stressful and is exacerbated by exposure to repeat abortions.*

Tietze has presented a statistical approach emphasizing that due to the technological limitations of contraceptives, a considerable number of repeat abortions are expected to occur, even among well-motivated women (1974, 1978). Based on his model, Tietze predicts that between 18 per cent and 75 per cent of contracepting women will have a repeat abortion within 10 years of their initial procedure, depending upon the use-effectiveness of the contraceptive method employed and age-related fertility.

The question still remains whether there are psychological or demographic characteristics that differentiate women who elect a repeat abortion from women who have an initial abortion. In other words, are repeat and initial aborters identical, with the exception that the former are further ahead in a sequence of contraception with its inevitable degree of failure? This paper will deal with whether or not women who request either a repeat or an initial abortion differ from each other in demographic, social, or psychological characteristics. Some of the data collected during a four-year study on abortion and contraception conducted at the Montreal General Hospital (MGH) will be presented to answer this question.

At the MGH, the abortion law is interpreted liberally and access to abortion is virtually unrestricted. As the majority of all hospital abortions in Quebec have been performed at this unit, women come from all parts of the province for the procedure. To ensure a representative sample of patients over a prolonged period of time, those women seeking abortions during three predetermined pregnancy termination sessions per week were approached to co-operate in the investigation. Thus a total of 643 women were asked to participate in the investigation, and of these 96 per cent agreed. A total of 578 women answered the interview and questionnaires, thus resulting in a usable sample of 90 per cent of all women whose co-operation was requested. This number represented 15 per cent of all women seeking early first trimester abortions during the period June 1977 through May 1978.

A structured 10-minute interview obtained demographic and background information about the woman, her partner, her past use of contraception, and her feelings about her decision to abort. Immediately after the interview, the subjects completed a test battery composed of a personality inventory and attitude scales which required approximately 45 minutes. The patients were reassured that their decision concerning participation in the study and their specific responses to the questionnaires would in no way influence their obtaining an abortion. The questionnaire battery was composed of standardized measures used in previous research which have been described elsewhere (Berger, 1978). Subsequent to the test administration, the patients underwent their abortion and contraceptive counselling, and abortion procedure.

---

*"Panel Discusses Problems of Repeat Abortion," *Female Health Topics and Diagnostics Reporter*, 2(6), 1979, p. 1.

Table 13–1

SELECTED CHARACTERISTICS OF ABORTION PATIENTS FOR MONTREAL
GENERAL HOSPITAL, QUEBEC, AND CANADA

		Montreal General Hospital*	Quebec†	Canada†
Age <20		20%	20%	31%
20–30		62	53	49
>30		18	26	19
Marital Status				
Never Married		64%	59%	60%
Ever Married		36	42	40
Number of Miscarriages	0	94%	89	91
	1	5	8	5
	≥2	1	3	1
	Unknown	—	—	2
Previous Induced Abortions	0	79%	83%	86%
	1	15	14	10
	2	5	2	1
	>2	1	1	—
	Unknown	—	—	3
Length of Gestation	<9 weeks	49%	40%	24%
	≥9 weeks	51	60	76

*The Montreal General Hospital sample includes only early first-trimester abortion patients.
†Statistics Canada, 1979 data include women obtaining abortions in hospitals by all abortion methods.

The results of the study will be examined to answer two questions. Firstly, we will determine how representative our sample of early abortion patients is to women who obtain abortions provincially and nationally. Secondly, we will compare our subsamples of initial and repeat abortion patients with each other to ascertain if there are differentiating characteristics.

Table 13–1 presents the data for our patients and the limited data available for the larger sample of all abortion patients in Quebec and Canada (Statistics Canada, 1979). Both the MGH and the Quebec samples are somewhat older than the Canadian sample, which contains more teenagers. Otherwise, the three samples appear relatively comparable. Of our sample of abortion patients, 21.6 per cent were returning for a repeat abortion. Of these 125 women, 71 per cent, 22 per cent, and 5 per cent had had one, two, or more than two previous abortions, respectively. The interval since the last previous abortion ranged from two months to 14 years, with 3.3 years being the average interval since the last abortion. The average length of gestation for the whole sample was 8.05 weeks pregnant, with a tendency for the repeaters to obtain an abortion earlier.

Table 13-2

DISTRIBUTION FOR SELECTED CHARACTERISTICS
OF INITIAL AND REPEAT ABORTERS

Characteristic	Initials N=453	Repeaters N=125	Significance
	%	%	
Age			
<20	23	8	$x^2=28.85$, df=2,
20–30	63	60	$p<.0001$
>30	14	32	
Education			
≤12	52	42	$x^2=4.26$, df=1,
>12	48	58	$p<.05$
*Socioeconomic Status**			
Middle Class	30	40	$x^2=5.04$, df=2,
Working Class	23	19	$p<.10$
Unemployed†	47	41	
Marital Status			
Never Married	67	52	$x^2=7.95$, df=1,
Ever Married	33	48	$p<.005$
Primary Language			
English	39	49	$x^2=4.32$, df=2,
French	53	44	p is NS
Other	8	7	
Religious Affiliation			
Catholic	68	57	$x^2=6.87$, df=4,
Protestant	17	20	p is NS
Jewish	3	4	
Other	5	7	
None	6	11	
Religiosity			
Weak	48	52	$x^2=1.60$, df=2,
Moderate	27	22	p is NS
Strong	25	26	
Children			
None	68	54	$x^2=7.92$, df=1,
One or Some	32	46	$p<.005$
Number of Miscarriages			
None	93	95	$x^2=2.9$, df=1,
One or Some	7	5	p is NS

*Assessed by the Blishen Socioeconomic Index.
†Includes students and housewives.

Table 13-3

PREVIOUS CONTRACEPTIVE PRACTICES
OF INITIAL AND REPEAT ABORTERS

		Initials $N=453$	Repeaters $N=125$	Significance
		%	%	
Ever Used Contraception				
	No	11	2	$x^2=9.54$, df=1,
	Yes	89	98	$p<.005$
Ever Used Pill				
	No	36	13	$x^2=23.17$ df=1
	Yes	64	87	$p<.0001$
Ever Used IUD				
	No	84	70	$x^2=11.61$, df=1
	Yes	16	30	$p<.001$
Ever Used Diaphragm				
	No	95	77	$x^2=35.58$, df=1,
	Yes	5	23	$p<.0001$.
Ever Used Foam				
	No	88	78	$x^2=7.16$, df=1,
	Yes	12	22	$p<.01$
Ever Used Condom				
	No	59	46	$x^2=6.55$, df=1,
	Yes	41	54	$p<.01$
Ever Used Withdrawal				
	No	71	64	$x^2=1.86$, df=1,
	Yes	29	36	p is NS
Ever Used Rhythm				
	No	70	63	$x^2=1.66$, df=1,
	Yes	30	37	p is NS

Table 13-2 presents the demographic data for the samples of initial and repeat patients. The repeaters are older than the initials. In accordance with this age difference, the repeaters are better educated, tend to score higher on the Blishen Socioeconomic Index (Blishen, 1967), are more likely to be or have been married, and to have had children. The two groups of women do not differ in language affiliation, religious classification, or intensity of religious beliefs.

The initials and repeaters differ in their history of contraceptive usage, with more repeaters having used birth control in the past (Table 13-3). Specifically, the repeaters are more likely than the initials to have ever used the more reliable methods, the pill and IUD, as well as the diaphragm, foam, and condoms. The

Table 13–4

CONTRACEPTIVE PRACTICES OF INITIALS AND REPEATERS
DURING MONTH OF CONCEPTION

	Initials	Repeaters	Significance
	%	%	
Less than 20-years-old	N=105	N=10	
Noncontracepting	68	70	$x^2=.01$, df=1,
Contracepting	32	30	p is NS
20–30-years-old	N=284	N=75	
Noncontracepting	53	51	$x^2=.07$, df=1,
Contracepting	47	49	p is NS
Greater than 30-years-old	N=64	N=40	
Noncontracepting	45	35	$x^2=.70$, df=1,
Contracepting	55	65	p is NS
All ages	N=453	N=125	
Noncontracepting	55	47	$x^2=2.34$, df=1,
Contracepting	45	53	p is NS

Table 13–5

COMPARISON OF REPEAT AND INITIAL ABORTERS ACCORDING TO METHOD
OF CONTRACEPTION USED DURING THE MONTH OF CONCEPTION

	Initials	Repeaters	Significance
	%	%	
Less than 20-years-old	N=34	N=3	
Pill, IUD	6	0	$x^2=8.0$, df=2,
Condom, Diaphragm, Foam	41	67	p is NS
Withdrawal, Rhythm	53	33	
20 –30-years-old	N=133	N=37	
Pill, IUD	29	22	$x^2=1.26$, df=2,
Condom, Diaphragm, Foam	37	46	p is NS
Withdrawal, Rhythm	34	32	
Greater than 30-years-old	N=33	N=24	
Pill, IUD	18	4	$x^2=4.73$, df=2,
Condom, Diaphragm, Foam	36	63	$p<.10$
Withdrawal, Rhythm	46	33	
All Ages	N=200	N=64	
Pill, IUD	24	14	$x^2=5.40$, df=2,
Condom, Diaphragm, Foam	38	53	$p<.10$
Withdrawal, Rhythm	39	33	

groups do not differ in their past use of the least effective methods, rhythm and withdrawal. There is no difference in the proportions of repeaters and initials who were using contraception at the time of conception. This finding holds true for women at all age levels, that is, below 20, 20 to 30, and over 30 (Table 13–4). When only the women who used contraception during the month of conception are examined, we find that the initials and repeaters differ somewhat in their choice of contraceptive methods (Table 13–5). For the repeaters, the preferred methods are the diaphragm, condom, and foam, followed by rhythm and withdrawal. For the initials, the preferred methods are rhythm and withdrawal, followed by diaphragm, condom and foam. The least-used methods for both were the pill and IUD.

The reasons given by the nonusers for not using contraception do not differ from the initials and repeaters. The majority of the reasons given form four categories. The most frequently given reasons, 38 per cent, involve lack of information or erroneous beliefs, for example, they did not know how to use birth control or felt they were safe. The second most commonly given category of reasons, 28 per cent, involves lack of planning, and being in situations where birth control was not immediately available. The side effects of birth control methods are given as a reason for their nonuse by 23 per cent, while 9 per cent stated that their partner objected to or claimed responsibility for birth control. Only five women from the total sample initially wanted to get pregnant and then changed their minds.

The data describing the woman's relationship with her partner reveal very few differences between the initials and repeaters. Both groups of women are equally likely to be involved in a relationship, to be cohabiting, to have relationships of similar length, to have conceived by their partner as opposed to by another, and to have told their partner about their pregnancy. There are no differences in the partner's reactions to the pregnancy with over 50 per cent of the partners of both groups of women perceived as reacting negatively. Also over 75 per cent of the partners of the repeaters and the initials were perceived as being favourable to the decision to abort.

However, three variables are found to differentiate the repeaters' relationships from the initials. More of the repeaters made the decision to have an abortion alone, without consulting their partner. This is in agreement with the finding that the repeaters describe their relationship as being less satisfactory than do the initials. The only other variable that differs for the two groups of women, is frequency of intercourse, with the repeaters reporting an average frequency of 11.4 times in the month in which they conceived compared to the initials' average of 8.7 times. This higher rate is found for all three age levels.

The two groups of women are very similar in their anticipation of and reaction to the abortion. Over 90 per cent of both groups anticipated having little difficulty in obtaining an abortion and over 70 per cent feel positively about their decision to abort. Only 4 per cent of the women express misgivings about their decision. There are no differences in the women's behaviour in the procedure and recovery rooms as rated by trained observers. Immediately following the abortion, over 86 per cent of the women rate themselves as feeling relieved.

The last data to be reported from the interview concern the women's future contraceptive plans. More initials plan to have children in the future than do the repeaters. More than 95 per cent of all the women plan to use birth control in the future, with over 75 per cent opting to use the pill, IUD or sterilization. However, more of the initials than the repeaters are planning to use the more effective methods, the pill and IUD, while more repeaters are planning to use barrier methods than are the initials. Over 15 per cent of both groups are still undecided as to which contraceptive they will use after the procedure.

In addition, as reported elsewhere (Berger, 1978), the two groups did not differ on their attitudes towards egalitarian sex roles, sex in general, and contraception. Nor were there differences in physical complaints, emotional adjustment, and cognitive functioning as assessed by the personality measure. It is noteworthy that the repeaters did not show elevated distress patterns on scales measuring insomnia, perceptual distortion, neuroticism, impulsivity, mood fluctuation, and panic reaction, amongst others.

The results of our investigation do not support the contention that women who have repeat abortions have psychological or social characteristics that predispose them to have multiple abortions. Initial and repeat aborters are more similar than dissimilar. The major difference between the two appears to be that the repeaters are an older sample of women who are more experienced in the sexual, reproductive, and contraceptive domains.

Many people are interested in the question of whether having an abortion has an effect on subsequent use of contraception (Schneider and Thompson, 1976). The finding that repeaters have used birth control more extensively and are more likely to have used the more effective methods of contraception than the initials, does not confirm the fear that repeat abortion is used to replace contraception. Similar findings have also been reported by other studies (Brewer, 1976; Steinhoff, Smith, Palmore, Diamond and Chung, 1979; Kurstin and Oskamp, 1979). Any effect of prior abortion on subsequent birth-control use could also be positive, acting to facilitate more effective birth-control behaviour. At the time of the abortion, both initials and repeaters appear more motivated to not only use birth control, but also plan to use the more effective methods. It is currently impossible to determine if abortion leads to improved birth-control use or has no effect. Such a question cannot be answered by retrospective data based solely on abortion patients. Instead, data should be collected in a prospective study examining the subsequent birth-control behaviour of all initial aborters, that is, those women who contracept or not, who become pregnant or not, and who have an abortion or not. Only those initial aborters who have not been successful in avoiding pregnancy and who choose to abort come to the notice of the abortion researcher, and therefore, conclusions cannot be drawn about the effects of an abortion on the use of birth control for the whole population of initial aborters.

In view of the greater contraceptive experience of the repeaters, the finding that they were no more likely than the initials to be using birth control at the time of conception, appears puzzling at first. The repeaters had had more experience with the pill and IUD, both of which are associated with side effects of varying degrees of intensity. Since 23 per cent of the noncontracepting women reported side effects as their reason for not using birth control, it is possible that the repeaters had switched from the pill and IUD to diaphragm, foam, and condom or had stopped contracepting, due to their experiencing unacceptable side effects of the more effective methods. On the basis of his review of the literature, Bracken (1977) also speculated that repeaters are more likely to experience side effects.

There is no evidence indicating that repeaters are more likely to be involved in brief liaisons; both groups are equally likely to be having serious, lengthy relationships. However, repeaters are more likely to describe their relationships as less satisfactory than the initials. The variable of quality of the woman's relationship with her partner has been found to differentiate repeaters from initials in other studies (Bracken, Hachamovitch and Grossman, 1972; Steinhoff et al., 1979; Szabady and Klinger, 1972). The findings that the repeaters experience less satisfactory relationships, are older, and are more likely to have a higher frequency of intercourse but at the same time are not more likely to have used birth control at the time of conception, suggest various hypotheses. It has been found that more effective use of birth control is associated with higher rates of intercourse (Bracken et al., 1972; Westoff and Ryder, 1977; Vincent and Stelling, 1973), with more serious relationships (Bracken et al., 1972; Fujita, Wagner and Pion, 1971; Reiss, Banwart and Foreman, 1975), and with increasing age (Westoff and Ryder, 1977). In addition, an inverse association has been found between the power of the woman relative to her partner in sexual matters and rate of unprotected coitus (Jorgenson, King and Torrey, 1980). In view of these data, it is clear that some of our repeaters exhibit an atypical pattern where an older woman, seriously involved in a lengthy relationship with a high rate of intercourse, is not using effective birth control procedures. This suggests the possibility that a causal link exists between unsatisfactory relationships and inadequate use of birth control, for whatever reasons, and consequently, greater risk of undesired pregnancy.

On the other hand, it is possible that the poorer quality relationship is not necessarily associated with ineffective or nonuse of birth control, but rather, is associated only with the decision to abort. It could be that women, who are in an unsatisfactory relationship, who have had one abortion, and who become unintentionally pregnant again, are more likely to abort. Similar women who are in a satisfactory relationship may be more likely to carry their pregnancy to term. Thus, the difference in quality of relationship that has been found in this and other studies, may not be due to situational characteristics that lead to higher risks of undesired pregnancy, but again may be due to self-selection which leads to a sample of repeat abortion patients that are not representative of all women confronted with undesired pregnancies. Obviously, neither of these speculations can be rejected on the basis of the present data and should be examined in further research. It is also important to emphasize that a higher rate of intercourse leads to a greater risk of pregnancy; consequently, this is another factor that should be taken into account in future studies.

Our results do not support the hypothesis that repeaters are more distressed by the abortion procedure (Adler, 1976); the repeaters' expectations of, motivations for, and reactions to the abortion are similar to those of the initials. Some possible benefits of having had a prior abortion might be indicated by the fact that the repeaters tend to come earlier for their abortion. The finding that a sizable minority of abortion patients still have indefinite contraceptive plans at the time of the abortion reveals a need for specific birth-control counselling for these women. Specialized counselling should be devised to capitalize on the high level of motivation demonstrated by the women on the day of the procedure.

The results of this study clearly support Tietze's thesis (1974, 1978) that substantial numbers of repeat abortions can be predicted to occur in well-motivated, contracepting women. Whether a woman is having a first or later abortion does not appear to be linked strongly to her psychological or demographic characteristics, with the exception of age. The role that the woman's relationship with her sexual partner plays as a factor in the events associated with the abortion should be examined. If this variable is causally linked with undesired pregnancy, counselling programs could be established that would enable the woman to handle her interpersonal relationship in a manner more satisfactory to herself.

While the initial-repeater distinction may have little theoretical or practical importance, the variable of whether a woman is contracepting or not appears to be of more interest (Berger, 1978). Attempts to differentiate contraceptors from noncontraceptors on various cognitive, attitude, and personality variables, as well as situational and relationship variables, have met with some success (Mindick and Oskamp, 1979; Gold and Berger, 1980). The payoffs from studies of contraceptors and noncontraceptors are likely to be greater for both theory and practice than those from attempts to differentiate women who have repeat abortions.

References

Adler, N.E. "Sample Attrition in Studies of Psychosocial Sequelae of Abortion: How Great a Problem?" *Journal of Applied Social Psychology* 6(1976):240–59.

Berger, C. "Psychological Characteristics of Anglophone and Francophone Initial and Repeat Aborters and Contraceptors." Ph.D. Dissertation, Concordia University, 1978.

Blishen, B. "A Socioeconomic Index for Occupations in Canada." *Canadian Review of Sociology and Anthropology* 4(1967):41–53.

Bracken, M.B. "Psychosomatic Aspects of Abortion: Implications for Counselling." *Journal of Reproductive Medicine* 19(1977):265–72.

Bracken, M.B., M. Hachamovitch, and G. Grossman. "Correlates of Repeat Induced Abortions." *Obstetrics & Gynecology* 40(1972):816–25.

Brewer, C. "Third Time Unlucky: A Study of Women Who Have Three or More Legal Abortions." *Journal of Biosocial Medicine* 1(1977):99–105.

Center for Disease Control: Abortion Surveillance, 1977. U.S. Department of Health, Education and Welfare, Atlanta, 1979.

David, H.P. "Abortion in Psychological Perspective." *American Journal of Orthopsychiatry* 42(1972):61–68.

Fischer, N. "Multiple Induced Abortions: A Psychoanalytic Case Study." *Journal of the American Psychoanalytic Association* 22(1974):394–407.

Fujita, B.N., N.H. Wagner, and R.J. Pion. "Contraceptive Use among Single College Students: A Preliminary Report." *American Journal of Obstetrics & Gynecology* 109(1971):787–93.

Gold, D. and Berger, C. "The Influence of Psychological Factors on Male Contraceptive Behavior." Manuscript submitted for publication, 1980.

Jacobsson, L., B. von Schoultz, and F. Solheim. "Repeat Aborters — A Social-Psychiatric Comparison." *Social Psychiatry* 11(1976):75–86.

Jorgenson, S.R., S.L. King, and B.A. Torrey. "Dyadic and Social Network Influences on Adolescent Exposure to Pregnancy Risk." *Journal of Marriage and the Family*. 42(1980):141–55.

Kurstin, C. and Oskamp, S. *Contracepting Behavior after Abortion*. Paper presented at the American Psychological Association Meeting, New York City, 1979.

Mindick, B., and S. Oskamp. "Longitudinal Predictive Research: An Approach to Methodological Problems in Studying Contraception." *Journal of Population* 2(1979):259–76.

Reiss, I.L., A. Banwart, and H. Foreman, "Premarital Contraceptive Usage: A Study and some Theoretical Exploration." *Journal of Marriage and the Family* 37(1975):619–30.

Robert, A.L. "Aspects Psychologiques de l'Interruption Répétée de Grossesse." *Sexologie* 2(1972):45–48.

Rovinsky, J.J. "Abortion Recidivism: A Problem in Preventive Medicine." *Journal of Obstetrics & Gynecology* 39(1972):649–59.

Schneider, S.M., and D.S. Thompson. "Repeat Aborters." *American Journal of Obstetrics & Gynecology* 44(1976):316–20.

Statistics Canada. *Therapeutic Abortions, 1977*. Health Division, Ottawa, 1979.

Steinhoff, P.G., R.G. Smith, J.A. Palmore, M. Diamond, and C.S. Chung. "Women who Obtain Repeat Abortions: A Study Based on Record Linkage." *Family Planning Perspectives* 11(1979):30–38.

Szabady, E., and A. Klinger, "Pilot Surveys of Repeated Abortion Seeking." *International Mental Health Research Newsletter* 14(1972):6–9.

Tietze, C. "The Problem of Repeat Abortions." *Family Planning Perspectives* 6(1974):148–50.

Tietze, C. "Repeat Abortions — Why More?" *Family Planning Perspectives* 10(1978):286–88.

Vincent, M.S., and F.H. Stelling, "A Survey of Contraceptive Practices and Attitudes of Unwed College Students." *Journal of American College Health Association* 21(1973):257–63.

Westoff, C.F., and N. Ryder, *The Contraceptive Revolution*. Princeton, New Jersey: Princeton University Press, 1977.

Part 4

Options For The Future

Introduction

While abortion has been practised for centuries it has only recently become an agonizing social issue. Admittedly, the prevention of unwanted pregnancies to achieve reduction in the abortion incidence is the preferred goal of any society. Most governments have relied almost exclusively on mass dissemination of contraceptive education and services to sexually active couples as an answer to unintended pregnancies. But these solutions have not been able to make a significant impact on the problem. Once the technology is in place and the system of delivering is mapped out, a more serious problem to be faced is the task of effecting an attitudinal change among sexually active people so that they develop a degree of rationality in their sexual behaviour. Never before has there been such a wide acceptance of non-generative sex. Current sexual norms tend not only to permit free and open expression of sexual feelings but also encourage their fullest realization. In this climate the task of preventing unwanted pregnancies seems difficult, if not impossible. It is feared that a woman faced with a problem pregnancy does not find alternatives to abortion which appear viable and perhaps this situation will remain so for some time to come.

The four papers in this section, although not theoretically correlated, examine the central issues relevant to the general concern of future outlook for abortion and the prospects for the reduction in its demand if not elimination.

David did a comprehensive review of the current status of legal abortion in 140 countries, its worldwide prevalence, and the demographic characteristics of abortion seekers. The author observes that despite considerable achievements in liberalizing abortion laws, several inequities exist in terms of its accessibility. The demographic characteristics of women seeking abortion are largely influenced by social attitudes towards premarital sex and pregnancy, the normative age at first marriage and the availability of contraceptive and abortion services. Consistent with the observations made in Part 4, the author reports a growing incidence of repeat abortions, particularly in North America, and warns that their rates will continue to rise for some years. Worldwide abortion mortality and morbidity of induced abortion, nevertheless, have considerably declined mainly because of the widespread trend toward earlier abortions. The author believes that a woman who does not wish to continue her pregnancy should get "sympathetic legal, social and medical support for her decision."

The issue of abortion is inseparable from the question of sexual behaviour, and many fears regarding the breakdown in the family and responsible sexual behaviour are attributed to abortion. However, Diamond found no evidence in his data from Hawaii and Canada that the availability of abortion influences age at first coitus, the marital status of aborting women, the ratio of women seeking pregnancy termination, the level of contraceptive practice or the rates of illegitimacy. The author concluded that "indeed several changes in these behaviours have been noted over time but basically these seem continuations of long term trends rather than marked divergences in behaviour."

Contraceptive instructions may improve knowledge, but not necessarily ensure acceptance of contraceptive means. This is one of the conclusions reached by Sachdev (Chapter 16). The author reviewed an extensive literature on the determinants of contraception and concluded that a host of interacting motivational, attitudinal, psychological and interpersonal factors contribute to effective contraceptive activity. Based on a variety of data pertaining to the contraceptive dossiers of young people, the prevalence of their sexual activity, the current status of contraceptive research and the demographic profile of Canadian population, the author foresees that the incidence of unintended pregnancies will continue to show an upward trend. As a consequence, the demand for abortion will not fall in the near future; in fact, it may rise among the teenagers.

Rodman's paper concludes this section by making us aware that any attempts at developing a satisfactory abortion policy are likely to be frustrated by multiple moral ambiguities and normative vagueness. He is, however, optimistic that in view of the developments in medical technology, post-coital methods of contraception and in embryology, a resolution of the arguments by the pro-choice and pro-life groups and the controversy surrounding private morality is very likely to emerge in most countries of the world. It is suggested that future legislation on abortion will reflect a more liberal compromising public stance, allowing abortions within specified gestational limits.

14

Worldwide Abortion Trends*

Henry P. David

Introduction

More is known about the epidemiology of induced abortion than about any other surgical procedure (Cates, Gold, and Salik, 1979; Grimes and Cates, 1979). No elective procedure has evoked as much public debate, generated such ethical and moral controversy, or received greater attention from the media and the public (David, 1978).

It is the purpose of this paper to consider worldwide abortion trends, offering overviews of the current legal situation and incidence of legal abortion, demographic characteristics of abortion clients, determinants of abortion-seeking behaviour and repeat abortions, psychological sequelae, late abortions, consequences of denied abortions, and service-provider influences. Specific information on Canada is presented in the tables.

Legislative Trends

As of January 1980, the worldwide legal status of abortion ranges from complete prohibition, to elective abortion at the request of the woman in the first trimester of pregnancy. Table 14–1 presents the current legal status of abortion in 140 countries, organized according to four major categories of abortion availability. Presently, about two-thirds of the world's population live under conditions of liberal legislation, mostly in Asia, North America, and Europe. While considerable advances have been made in liberalizing abortion, legal authorization of elective abortion does not guarantee that abortion is equally available to every woman requesting termination of an unwanted pregnancy. Serious problems remain in implementing existing legislation. For example, in some developing countries such as India and Zambia, pregnancy termination resources are limited, and many women are unaware of their location or legality. In some developed nations, such as France, the Federal Republic of Germany, and Italy,

*Paper prepared for presentation at the 4th International Meeting on Fertility Control, Genoa, Italy, March 6–8, 1980. I am pleased to acknowledge the considerable contribution of Dr. Christopher Tietze but am solely responsible for the contents of this paper.

Table 14–1

LEGAL STATUS OF ABORTION BY GROUNDS JANUARY 1980: 140 COUNTRIES

Illegal No indications allowed in legislation N=24	*Restrictive* Narrow, life-threatening only N=38	*Conditional* Broad health, eugenic and juridical indications N=46	*Elective* On request or for social indications in first trimester N=32
Belgium	Afghanistan	Albania	Austria
Burundi	Bahrain	Algeria	Bulgaria
Central African Republic	Bangladesh	Argentina	China
Colombia	Benin	Australia	Cuba
Dominican Republic	Botswana	Bahamas	Cyprus
Gabon	Burma	Barbados	Czechoslovakia
Haiti	Chad	Bolivia	Denmark
Indonesia	Chile	Brazil	Finland
Mali	Guatamala	Cameroon	France
Malta	Iraq	Canada	German Democratic Republic
Mauritania	Ireland	Congo	German Federal Republic
Monaco	Ivory Coast	Costa Rica	Hong Kong
Mongolia	Kenya	Ecuador	Hungary
Niger	Kuwait	Egypt	Iceland
Panama	Laos	El Salvador	India
Philippines	Lebanon	Ethiopia	Iran
Portugal	Lesotho	Fiji	Italy
Rwanda	Libya	Gambia	Japan
Seychelles	Madagascar	Ghana	Korea (N)
Somalia	Malawi	Greece	Norway
Spain	Mauritius	Grenada	Poland
Tonga	Nauru	Guinea	Romania
Western Samoa	Nicaragua	Guyana	Singapore
Zaire	Nigeria	Honduras	Sweden
	Pakistan	Israel	Switzerland
	Paraguay	Jamaica	Tunisia
	Saudi Arabia	Jordan	U.S.S.R.
	Senegal	Korea (S)	United Kingdom
	Sierra Leone	Liberia	U.S.A.
	Sri Lanka	Luxembourg	Viet Nam
	Sudan	Malaysia	Yugoslavia
	Syria	Mexico	Zambia
	Togo	Morocco	
	United Arab Emirate	Nepal	
	Uruguay	Netherlands	
	Venezuela	New Zealand	
	Yemen (N)	Papua/New Guinea	
	Yemen (S)	Peru	
		South Africa	
		Swaziland	
		Tanzania	
		Trinidad and Tobago	
		Turkey	
		Uganda	
		Zimbabwe	

Sources: Official Gazettes, *International Digest of Health Legislation*, Law Files of the Population Council, the Transnational Family Research Institute, the

women who want abortions still face considerable obstacles. Conservative attitudes among physicians and hospital administrators have curtailed full implementation of the law, especially for economically disadvantaged women. In the United States, translating an acknowledged constitutional right into free choice and equal accessibility to available services, regardless of economic circumstances, often involves overcoming substantial medical, social, and bureaucratic barriers (AGI, 1979; Callahan, 1979).

The other third of the world's population lives in countries (mostly in Central and South America, Africa, and a few in Europe) where abortion is either completely illegal or permitted only on strictly defined grounds to protect the woman's life or health (Cook and Dickens, 1978; Tietze and Lewit, 1978; Tietze, 1979a; David, 1980). For example, in the Caribbean and Latin America, Cuba is the only country where abortion is widely available without cost to the woman during the first trimester (David, 1979b). In many other countries where abortion is technically illegal, as in the Netherlands and in Taiwan, statutes are only loosely enforced. Some abortions on medical grounds are probably tolerated in all countries with restrictive legislation. Authorities seldom interfere in the absence of public complaints.

In retrospect, it is apparent that during the last quarter century a social revolution has occurred in the realm of abortion legislation. In 1954 abortion was illegal in all countries of the world with the exception of Iceland, Denmark, Sweden, and Japan. In subsequent years more than 30 countries changed their formerly restrictive laws or policies to permit abortion on request or on a broad range of social indications. The relaxation of abortion laws in diverse countries with different sociocultural heritages can be traced to three interrelated reasons: (a) general recognition of the threat of illegal abortion to public health, (b) support for women's rights to terminate an unwanted pregnancy under safe conditions at an early state of gestation, and (c) provision of equal access to abortion for rich and poor women alike (Tietze, 1979b). Social and technological changes, coupled with the increasingly vocal demands of well-organized women and their male supporters, could no longer be resisted by reluctant legislatures (Dellapenna, 1979).

During the same period, concern about low birth rates induced Bulgaria, Czechoslovakia, Hungary, and Romania to modify their liberal legislation as part of well-organized pronatalist efforts (David and McIntyre, 1980). New Zealand and Israel became the only Western democracies to succumb to conservative pressures, returning to a more restrictive legislative stance. In several other European countries with low birth rates, abortion at the request of the pregnant woman, or on broadly interpreted sociomedical or socioeconomic indications, exists side by side with pronatalist population policies. In only a few lands (e.g., Singapore and Tunisia) was abortion legalized expressly to limit population growth and enhance socioeconomic development.

In countries where restrictions on abortion are enforced (e.g., Portugal and Spain), women have not been deterred from seeking illegal terminations of unwanted pregnancies. Throughout recorded history women have resorted to abortion regardless of moral or legal sanctions and often at considerable physical or psychological risk and cost. The limited impact of reimposing restrictive legislation is illustrated by the Romanian experience. Following the unexpected and abrupt restriction of access to legal abortion in 1966, abortion-related deaths rose seven-fold in the subsequent decade, largely due to a resurgence of illegal abortions performed by untrained practitioners in poorly-equipped facilities (David and McIntyre, 1980).

In the long run, the most difficult struggle may be to change social attitudes. As long as significant segments of the population oppose both abortion and freer access to contraception — which would reduce the need for abortion — termination of unwanted pregnancies will continue to involve humiliating restrictions for economically disadvantaged women.

Incidence Worldwide

The total number of pregnancies terminated each year by induced abortion throughout the world is not known and perhaps never will be. According to available estimates and surveys conducted by the International Planned Parenthood Federation (1974, 1978) in 180 countries, about one pregnancy is deliberately terminated for every three live births, totalling approximately 55 million abortions per year or 34 million not counting the People's Republic of China. These estimates must be regarded with considerable caution since they combine information from countries where abortion is legal and reliably reported with estimates from countries which do not report abortion data (e.g., China and the U.S.S.R.) or where induced abortion remains illegal, as in many developing countries of Africa and Latin America. No reliable method has yet been devised to estimate the incidence of illegal abortions (Tietze, 1979a). While there is little doubt that desperate women will resort to abortion no matter what the legal circumstances or risks to well-being, the frequently quoted statement that induced abortion is the world's leading method of fertility regulation has no basis in verifiable fact and is almost surely wrong (Berelson, Mauldin, and Segal, 1979).

The numbers of legal abortions, abortion rates per 1,000 women 15 to 44 years of age, and abortion ratios per 1,000 live births six months later for countries reporting such data are compiled for selected years in Table 14–2. The highest abortion rate is reported from Bulgaria (68.3) followed by Cuba (52.1) and Hungary (39.2). In the United Kingdom and in the countries of northern Europe numbers of legal abortions and abortion rates appear to have stabilized; some declined following a period of fairly rapid increase. Abortion numbers are still rising in the United States but at a much slower rate. Stationary or declining rates of legal abortions are reported from eastern Europe.

Table 14–2

NUMBER OF LEGAL ABORTIONS, ABORTION RATES, AND ABORTION
RATIOS: SELECTED AREAS AND YEARS

Country and year	Number of abortions	Abortion rate per 1,000 women 15–44	Abortion ratio per 1,000 live births
Bulgaria			
1973	115,400	61.2	799
1974	125,000	66.4	851
1975	123,700	65.8	854
1976	121,100	64.5	854
1977	122,900	65.6	884
1978	127,800	68.3	—
Canada			
1973	43,200	8.8	127
1974	48,200	9.6	136
1975	49,300	9.5	133
1976	54,500	10.3	151
1977	57,600	10.6	—
1978	62,300	11.3	—
Cuba			
1973	112,100	60.3	523
1974	131,500	69.5	664
1975	126,100	65.3	662
1976	121,400	61.0	681
1977	114,800	55.9	724
1978	110,400	52.1	—
Czechoslovakia			
1973	81,200	25.9	280
1974	83,100	26.4	286
1975	81,700	25.9	298
1976	84,600	26.8	294
1977	89,000	27.9	318
1978	92,500	28.9	—
Denmark			
1973	16,500	16.2	233
1974	24,900	24.2	345
1975	27,900	27.0	402
1976	26,800	25.8	428
1977	25,700	24.4	413
1978	23,700	22.3	—

Table 14–2 (Cont'd)

NUMBER OF LEGAL ABORTIONS, ABORTION RATES, AND ABORTION
RATIOS: SELECTED AREAS AND YEARS

Country and year	Number of abortions	Abortion rate per 1,000 women 15–44	Abortion ratio per 1,000 live births
England and Wales (residents)			
1973	110,600	11.7	170
1974	109,400	11.6	175
1975	106,200	11.2	179
1976	101,900	10.6	180
1977	102,700	10.6	179
1978	112,100	11.4	—
Finland			
1973	23,400	22.4	388
1974	22,800	21.8	362
1975	21,500	20.4	316
1976	19,800	18.6	300
1977	17,800	16.7	277
1978	16,900	16.0	—
France			
1976	134,200	12.3	183
1977	151,500	13.7	203
1978	148,400	13.3	—
German Democratic Republic			
1973	110,800	32.2	619
1974	99,700	28.8	553
1975	87,800	25.2	468
1976	81,900	23.3	392
1977	78,000	22.0	—
German Federal Republic			
1977	54,300	4.3	94
1978	73,500	5.7	—
Hungary			
1973	169,600	73.5	1,024
1974	102,000	44.3	514
1975	96,200	41.9	515
1976	94,700	41.5	520
1977	89,100	39.2	—

Table 14–2 (Cont'd)

NUMBER OF LEGAL ABORTIONS, ABORTION RATES, AND ABORTION RATIOS: SELECTED AREAS AND YEARS

Country and year	Number of abortions	Abortion rate per 1,000 women 15–44	Abortion ratio per 1,000 live births
India			
1973	24,300	0.2	1.1
1974	44,900	0.4	1.9
1975	97,700	0.8	4.1
1976	214,000	1.7	8.8
1977	278,000	2.2	11.0
Japan			
1973	700,500	26.3	340
1974	679,800	25.5	346
1975	671,600	25.2	353
1976	664,100	24.9	372
1977	641,200	24.1	354
1978	618,000	23.3	—
Norway			
1973	13,700	18.1	226
1974	15,200	19.8	263
1975	15,100	19.7	277
1976	14,800	19.0	275
1977	15,000	19.7	—
Poland			
1973	138,600	18.0	227
1974	142,400	18.2	225
1975	138,600	17.5	215
Scotland			
1973	7,500	7.4	104
1974	7,600	7.4	110
1975	7,300	7.1	108
1976	7,200	6.9	116
1977	7,300	6.9	—
Singapore			
1975	12,900	23.5	319
1976	15,500	27.5	371
1977	16,400	28.4	—

Table 14–2 (Cont'd)

NUMBER OF LEGAL ABORTIONS, ABORTION RATES, AND ABORTION
RATIOS: SELECTED AREAS AND YEARS

Country and year	Number of abortions	Abortion rate per 1,000 women 15–44	Abortion ratio per 1,000 live births
Sweden			
1973	26,000	16.3	237
1974	30,600	19.2	284
1975	32,500	20.2	325
1976	32,400	20.0	334
1977	31,500	19.3	333
1978	31,900	19.4	—
Tunisia Public Sector			
1973	6,500	5.0	34
1974	12,400	10.9	63
1975	16,000	13.7	78
1976	20,300	16.8	98
1977	21,200	16.8	—
United States			
1973	744,600	16.6	239
1974	898,600	19.6	282
1975	1,034,200	22.1	331
1976	1,179,300	24.5	361
1977	1,320,300	26.9	400

Note: Reporting incomplete from France, German Federal Republic, India, Japan, and Poland.
Source: Tietze, 1979a with subsequent data also kindly provided by C. Tietze, December 1979.

Demographic Characteristics of Abortion Clients

Among the major demographic characteristics related to abortion-seeking behaviour are the woman's age, the number of prior births, and her marital status. As shown in Table 14–3, there are wide variations among countries reporting such data. The proportion of women under 20 years of age, of women without prior births, and of unmarried (mostly single) women is high in the United States, Canada, Great Britain, and Sweden. In recent years, the United States has reported the highest proportion of teenagers and unmarried women among all women obtaining pregnancy terminations (CDC, 1979; Tietze, 1979a).

Conversely, the proportion of older, parous, and married women is high in Tunisia, India, Japan, Czechoslovakia, and Hungary. Intermediate positions are represented by Denmark, Finland, the German Federal Republic, and Singapore. These patterns tend to reflect differences in adolescent sexual activity, societal disapproval of premarital pregnancies and births, the customary age at first marriage, and differences in the availability and accessibility of contraceptive and abortion services (Tietze, 1979a, 1979b).

Determinants of Abortion-Seeking Behaviour

While abortion occurs among nearly all social and economic strata of society, lack of access to modern contraceptives appears to be the major determinant for seeking terminations of unwanted pregnancies (PCC, 1979). Most women at risk of unwanted pregnancy reside in developing countries where commercial and public health networks for the delivery of family planning services are weak. In developed countries, including those where abortion is legal, adolescent and low income couples appear to have the most difficulty in obtaining contraceptives.

Table 14–3

PER CENT DISTRIBUTION OF LEGAL ABORTIONS BY WOMAN'S AGE, PRIOR BIRTHS, AND MARITAL STATUS: SELECTED COUNTRIES, LATEST AVAILABLE YEARS

Countries	Year(s)	Woman's Age 19 or less	Woman's Age 20 or more	Prior Births none	Prior Births one or more	Marital Status unmarried	Marital Status married
Canada	1977	30.8	69.2	60.3	39.7	69.9	30.1
Czechoslovakia	1978	5.6	94.4	11.6	88.4	19.9	80.1
Denmark	1978	18.9	71.9	36.0	64.0	54.6	45.4
England and Wales	1977	27.9	72.1	51.8	48.2	61.2	38.8
Finland	1978	22.1	77.9	*46.3	*53.7	62.6	37.4
France	1977	12.2	87.8	NA	NA	42.2	57.8
German Democratic Republic	1976	13.5	86.5	NA	NA	NA	NA
German Federal Republic	1978	13.0	87.0	38.3	61.7	41.1	58.9
Hungary	1977	10.7	89.3	22.8	77.2	30.3	69.7
India	1972/5	NA	NA	11.1	88.9	7.2	92.8
Japan	1978	2.5	97.5	NA	NA	NA	NA
Scotland	1977	29.1	70.9	47.6	52.4	60.5	39.5
Singapore	1977	8.1	91.9	26.5	73.5	NA	NA
Sweden	1978	19.6	80.4	40.7	59.3	NA	NA
Tunisia	1976	2.1	97.9	5.4	94.6	NA	NA
United States	1977	31.3	68.7	50.2	49.8	77.2	22.8

*1976
NA = Not Available
Sources: Governmental reports, some of which were provided by C. Tietze, December 1979.

Inconsistent contraceptive use is another major determinant, especially for those (often young) couples who practise contraception only sporadically or find presently available contraceptive methods inconvenient. Sexually active adolescents are in particular need of practical information on how contraception works, and how to practice it effectively during this period of high fertility risk.

While not a major determinant worldwide, contraceptive failure is a significant motivating factor among couples determined to avoid unwanted births. Human error in contraceptive practice, coupled with contraceptive failure, will probably continue to account for 5 per cent to 10 per cent of all abortions.

Changes in personal circumstances occasionally lead to abortion when, as a result of family crisis, desertion, or widowhood, a wanted pregnancy becomes unwanted. In countries where consensual unions or male migration are common, women suddenly abandoned and already caring for several other children may feel compelled to avoid another birth at all costs.

Amniocentesis after the sixteenth week of pregnancy is an increasingly important determinant of abortion in highly developed countries. Most couples who learn about fetal defects decided on abortion. Pregnant women exposed to rubella, x-rays, toxic chemicals or harmful drugs may automatically choose abortion rather than risk fetal abnormality (PCC, 1979).

Repeat Abortions

One of the most sensitive subtopics within the emotionally laden issue of abortion is the rise in the incidence of repeated abortion. Some abortion counsellors are disappointed when a client returns for another abortion. Certain social scientists may worry about "neurotic recidivism," and responsible policy makers become concerned about the opinion of those citizens for whom abortion is morally unacceptable except as a backup measure for contraceptive failure.

The proportion of repeat abortions, experienced as a percentage of all abortions, has increased most rapidly in those countries, such as the United States, where restrictive abortion laws and practices have only recently been replaced by relatively easier access to pregnancy termination. For example, in the United States the proportion of repeat abortions rose from about 12 per cent of all reported abortions in 1973 to 24 per cent in 1977 and probably continued to rise somewhat in 1978 (Tietze, 1978; CDC, 1979; Forrest et al., 1979). The U.S. rate of repeat abortions per 1,000 women aged 15 to 44 who had a prior abortion was 70.3 in 1976 compared with a first abortion rate of 20.5 per 1,000 women without prior abortions (Tietze & Jain, 1978). In Denmark, which liberalized its abortion legislation in the same year as the United States, a gradual increase in the repeat abortion ratio has also been observed (Denmark, 1978). In Hungary, however, which legalized abortion in 1956, the proportion of repeat abortions reached a plateau by the late 1960s (Hungary, 1969; Tietze, 1979a). All such data must be considered cautiously since women's responses to questions about repeat abortion are notoriously subject to error, selective forgetting, and deliberate denial, regardless of the legal status of abortion (Hogue, 1975; Tietze, 1979a).

At least five factors combine to place women who have had at least one abortion at greater risk for a repeat abortion compared to women who have not had a prior termination (Tietze, 1978). First is the factor of age. Among women who have had at least one abortion there are greater proportions in the sexually most active prime reproductive ages (20–29 years) and lower percentages of teenagers and older women compared to the pool of women without prior abortion experience. Secondly, it can be assumed that nearly all women who had abortions were sexually active and probably resumed sexual activity after their abortions. Thirdly, all women with abortion experience were able to conceive compared to the 40 per cent of all women aged 15 to 44 without abortion experience who were unable to conceive, had undergone surgical sterilization, were married to vasectomized men, or were not sexually active. Fourthly, women who had one abortion are likely to resort to another to avoid a future birth whereas women at risk of having a first abortion probably include a substantial number who would not choose to terminate an unintended conception. Finally, there is a very small group of women who consciously prefer to rely on abortion rather than on contraception, plus a larger number who find it difficult to practise contraceptive vigilance consistently and effectively. These women are at high risk for both first and repeated abortions (Tietze, 1978).

In sum, an increasing proportion of repeat abortions among all legal abortions and a repeat abortion rate substantially higher than a first abortion rate can be expected for a number of years after abortion has been legalized, as the pool of

Table 14–4

DEATH-TO-CASE RATE FOR LEGAL ABORTIONS BY WEEKS OF GESTATION,
UNITED STATES, 1972–1977

Weeks of Gestation	Deaths	Cases*	Rate†	Relative Risk‡
≤8	12	2,600,000	0.5	1.0
9–10	23	1,648,000	1.4	2.8
11–12	20	865,000	2.3	4.6
13–15	19	274,000	6.9	13.8
16–20	43	316,000	13.6	27.2
≥21	12	61,000	19.7	39.4
Total	129	5,764,000	2.2	

*Alan Guttmacher Institute estimate.
†Deaths per 100,000 abortions.
‡Based on index rate for ≤8 menstrual weeks' gestation of 0.6 per 100,000 abortions.
Sources: Center for Disease Control, *Abortion Surveillance 1977* and C. Tietze, December 1979.

women at risk for repeat abortion continues to rise to an eventual plateau. This phenomenon should not be interpreted as a decrease in the practice of contraception or motivational deficiencies. Indeed, after considering all the factors already mentioned, plus a certain amount of unavoidable contraceptive failure, Tietze (1978) concludes that "a substantial majority" of women after experiencing their first abortion "did in fact practice contraception with a high degree of consistency and success." This finding has been substantiated by more recent studies (e.g., Howe, Kaplan, and English, 1979; Shepard and Bracken, 1979).

Psychological Sequelae

Of all the complications of abortion, psychological sequelae are the most difficult to assess (Potts, Diggory, and Peel, 1977). Many psychological and psychiatric studies on alleged sequelae of abortion consist of impressionistic case reports, often without even rudimentary methodological concerns. Under more carefully controlled conditions, the Joint Program for the Study of Abortion noted 16 major psychiatric complications among 72,988 legal abortions during 1970 to 1971 in the United States, or a rate of two admissions to psychiatric hospital per 10,000 abortions (Tietze and Lewit, 1972). A prospective study of post-abortion psychosis in the Midlands region of the United Kingdom found an incidence of three per 10,000 abortions compared with a postpartum psychosis rate of 17 per 10,000 deliveries (Brewer, 1977).

Assuming that psychiatric or psychological morbidity is a real and measurable phenomenon, the explanation for the wide range of opinions still expressed in the psychiatric literature and in public debates may well lie in the inadequacy of much of the published work, including (a) overemphasis on clinical case histories that ignore the large majority of aborting women who never seek post-operative psychiatric consultation, (b) the lack of psychological assessment prior to the unwanted pregnancy or abortion, and (c) the absence of standardized follow-up procedures and anchored psychiatric diagnoses. Unless the pre-abortion psychiatric condition of the woman is examined it is impossible to draw conclusions concerning the post-abortion condition presumed to be caused by the procedure. Such an effort is currently in progress in Denmark, where the unique population registration system makes it feasible to compare the incidence of post-abortion hospitalization for mental disorder with postpartum admissions to psychiatric hospitals, while also controlling for prior mental disorder, age, and parity (David, 1979a).

Review of the diverse literature leads to the conclusion that legal abortion induced in the first trimester does not carry a significant risk of psychiatric trauma. Whatever psychological risk exists is less than that associated with carrying a pregnancy to term. In those rare instances where post-abortion psychiatric disturbances appear, they are more likely to relate to the degree of adjustment existing before the pregnancy than to the abortion procedure (Belsey et al., 1977). Feelings of guilt and depression, when noted, are usually mild and transitory. For the vast majority of women abortion engenders a sense of relief and often represents successful coping with a personal crisis and social stress.

Late Abortions

As indicated in Table 14–5, the last few years have seen a shift from later to earlier abortions in most countries for which data are available (Tietze, 1979a). Few abortions are performed anywhere at more than 20 weeks gestation, even when legally permitted. For example, 0.9 per cent of all legal abortions in the United States were in this category and 0.4 per cent in the United Kingdom (CDC, 1979; Registrar General, 1973).

Recent findings confirm that the highest proportion of delayed abortion occurs among educationally and economically deprived women, especially those under 20 years of age. Most often, such women are single, experiencing their first pregnancy. Social environmental reasons for delaying the abortion decision include lack of information on availability or location of services, financial difficulties, bureaucratic or service-provider bias, parental consent requirements, and inaccurate medical and/or clinical diagnosis. Personal psychological conflicts leading to delay include ambivalence about the abortion decision, hesitation or fear to confide in partner or parents, a history of irregular menstrual periods, and late recognition or denial of pregnancy.

The worldwide trend toward earlier terminations of unwanted pregnancies contributes significantly to the continuing reduction of mortality associated with legal abortions. In the United States only abortions at 16 or more weeks' gestation were more dangerous than childbirth in the period 1972 to 1977. The situation was probably similar in other countries for which age-specific risks cannot be computed, owing to the relatively small numbers of legal abortions and associated deaths (Tietze, 1979a, 1979b).

Service-Provider Influences

The attitudes of medical and allied health personnel are central to the equitable provision of abortion services. As "gate keepers" they often control access to abortion and effective implementation of the law and a woman's decision (David, 1978).

For many physicians and nurses, abortion represents an ethical and moral dilemma, posing conflicts between a personal commitment to save lives and the woman's decision to terminate her unwanted pregnancy (e.g., Nathanson and Becker, 1977). Conditions of practice, perceptions of professional roles, and the woman's economic status are often interrelated. Historically, women with greater economic resources have had far fewer difficulties in obtaining abortions from qualified physicians than have economically disadvantaged women, whether the abortion sought was legal or illegal. Inequity is increased when

Table 14–5

PER CENT DISTRIBUTION OF LEGAL ABORTIONS BY WEEKS OF GESTATION:
SELECTED COUNTRIES AND YEARS

Country and year	8 weeks or less	9–12 weeks	13–15 weeks	17 weeks or more
Canada				
1974	20.8	58.0	14.6	6.6
1977	23.8	60.4	11.0	4.8
1978	24.7	59.9	11.1	4.3
Czechoslovakia				
1973	61.3	38.1	0.5	0.1
1976	58.5	41.0	0.4	0.1
1978	56.6	42.9	0.4	0.1
England and Wales				
1968	12.7	49.3	27.2	10.8
1970	13.6	57.7	23.1	5.6
1972	18.7	60.9	17.2	3.2
1974	23.7	59.1	14.2	3.0
1975	24.4	58.2	14.1	3.3
1977	25.5	58.1	13.0	3.4
Finland				
1974	29.5	59.3	9.9	1.3
France				
1976	53.4	45.0	1.4	0.2
German Federal Republic				
1978	6.8	76.5	15.8	0.9
Hungary				
1972	75.9	23.6	0.4	0.1
1975	70.6	28.6	0.6	0.2
1977	69.2	30.0	0.5	0.3
Sweden				
1968	3.7	39.2	35.4	21.7
1970	5.8	53.7	27.9	12.6
1972	8.9	64.5	19.5	7.1
1974	18.6	68.1	9.9	3.4
1976	37.6	56.0	4.8	1.6
1977	40.7	53.3	4.3	1.7
United States				
1973	38.2	47.3	8.0	6.5
1974	44.4	43.6	6.6	5.4
1975	46.5	42.7	6.0	4.8
1976	47.5	42.8	5.5	4.2
1977	50.0	41.1	5.2	3.7

Source: Tietze, 1969a with subsequent data also kindly provided by C. Tietze, December 1979.

private prejudice is permitted to become public policy because physicians and hospital administrators refuse to perform or permit legal abortions.

In some respects the process of obtaining an abortion differs markedly from traditional medical practice. Women wishing to terminate an unwanted pregnancy are usually "healthy" and seldom in need of medical diagnosis or medical treatment of a medically identified disease. Some physicians are prepared to perform abortions to save a woman's physical health, but not to preserve the economic well-being of her family (Potts, 1979). Women requesting implementation of their abortion decision do so because their pregnant condition is personally aversive or perceived to be socially stigmatizing (Adler, 1979a, 1979b). The role conflict between serving as a medical implementor of a woman's decision and the more traditional orientation of medical decision-maker is perhaps a greater divisive influence in the abortion debate than are more widely discussed moral and ethical issues.

Concluding Note

After presenting a brief overview of the current legal situation in 140 countries I end this paper with the recognition that the personal decision to terminate an unwanted pregnancy or to carry to term is seldom easy and often agonizing. Perhaps the time has come to view legal abortion less in terms of negative sequelae and more in terms of successful coping behaviour. Unintended conception and unwanted pregnancy create personal stress which each woman should be free to resolve within a reasonable period of time and with sympathetic legal, social, and medical support for her decision.

References

Adler, N.E. "Abortion: A Social-psychological Perspective." *Journal of Social Issues* 35(1979):100–119.

Adler, N.E. "Psychosocial Issues of Therapeutic Abortion." In *Psychosomatic Obstetrics and Gynecology*, edited by D. Youngs and A. Ehrhardt. New York: Appleton-Century-Crofts, 1979b, pp. 159–77.

Alan Guttmacher Institute. *Abortions and the Poor: Private Morality, Public Responsibility*. New York: Author, 1979.

Belsey, E.M., H.S. Greer, S. Lal, S.C. Lewis, and R.W. Beard. "Predictive Factors in Emotional Response to Abortion: King's Termination Study." *Social Science and Medicine* 11(1977):71–82.

Brewer, C. "Incidence of Post-abortion Psychosis: A Prospective Study." *British Medical Journal* 60 59(1977):476–77.

Berelson, B., P. Mauldin and S. Segal. *Population: Current Status and Policy Options*. New York: Population Council, Center for Policy Studies, Working Papers, 1979, No. 44.

Callahan, D. "Abortion and Government Policy." *Family Planning Perspectives* 11(1979):275–79.

Cates, W., Jr., J. Gold, and R. Selik. "Regulation of Abortion Services — For Better or Worse." *The New England Journal of Medicine* 301(1979):720–23.

Center for Disease Control. *Abortion Surveillance, 1977*. Atlanta: Author, 1979.

Cook, R.J., and B.M. Dickens. "A Decade of International Change in Abortion Law, 1967–1977." *American Journal of Public Health* 68(1978):637–44.

David, H.P. "Unwanted Pregnancies: Costs and Alternatives." In *Demographic and Social Aspects of Population Growth*, edited by C.F. Westoff and P. Parke, Jr. Vol. 1 of the Commission on Population Growth and the American Future Research Reports. Washington: US Government Printing Office, 1972a, 439–466.

David, H.P. "Abortion in Psychosocial Perspective." *American Journal of Orthopsychiatry* 42(1972b):61–68.

David, H.P. "Abortion: A Continuing Debate." *Family Planning Perspectives* 10(1978):313, 316.

David, H.P. "Postpartum and Post-abortion Psychotic Reactions: An Overview." *Population and Environmental Psychology Newsletter*, January 1979a.

David, H.P. "Notes from Cuba." *Abortion Research Notes* 8, Nos. 1 and 2, 1979b.

David, H.P. "International Abortion Legislation and Practices in Historical Perspective." Unpublished paper, 1980.

David, H.P., Z. Matejcek, Z. Dytrych, V. Schüller, and H.L. Friedman. "Developmental Consequences of Unwanted Pregnancies: Studies from Sweden and Czechoslovakia." *Basic Problems in Cross-cultural Psychology*, edited by Y.H. Poortinga. Amsterdam: Swets and Zeitlinger, 1977, 184–89.

David, H.P. "Psychosocial Studies of Abortion in the United States." In *Abortion in Psychosocial Perspective: Trends in Transnational Research*, edited by H.P. David, H.L. Friedman, J. v.d. Tak, and M.J. Sevilla. New York: Springer Publishing Co., 1978, pp. 77–115.

David, H.P., and R.J. McIntyre, R.J. *Reproductive Behavior: Central and Eastern European Experience*. New York: Springer Publishing Co., forthcoming.

Dellapenna, J.W. "The History of Abortion: Technology, Morality, and the Law." *University of Pittsburgh Law Review* 40(1979):359–428.

Denmark/National Health Service. *Statistics on Legal Abortion, 1977 and Earlier Years*. Copenhagen: Author, 1978.

Dytrych, Z., Z. Matejcek, and V. Schüller. "Children Born to Women Denied Abortion in Czechoslovakia. In *Abortion in Psychosocial Perspective: Trends in Transnational Research*, edited by H.P. David, H.L. Friedman, J. v.d. Tak, and M.J. Sevilla. New York: Springer Publishing Co., 1978, 201–224.

Forrest, J.D., C. Tietze, and E. Sullivan. "Abortion in the United States, 1976–1977." *Family Planning Perspectives* 10(1978):271–79.

Hass, P.H. "Maternal Role Incompatibility and Fertility in Urban Latin America." *Journal of Social Issues* 28(1972):111–127.

Hogue, C. "Low Birth Weight Subsequent to Induced Abortion: A Historical Prospective Study of 948 Women in Skopje, Yugoslavia." *American Journal of Obstetrics and Gynecology* 123(1975):675–81.

Howe, B., H.R. Kaplan, and C. English. "Repeat Abortions: Blaming the Victims." *American Journal of Public Health* 69(1979):1242–46.

Hungary/Central Statistical Office. *Survey Techniques in Fertility and Family Research: Experience in Hungary.* Budapest: Author, 1969.

International Planned Parenthood Federation. *Survey of World Needs in Population.* London: Author, 1974.

International Planned Parenthood Federation. "Unmet Needs." *People* 5(3)(1978):25–32.

Matejcek, Z., Z. Dytrych, and V. Schüller. "Children from Unwanted Pregnancies." *Acta Psychiatrica Scandinavica* 57(1978):67–90.

Matejcek, Z., Z. Dytrych, and V. Schüller. "The Prague Study of Children Born from Unwanted Pregnancies." *International Journal of Mental Health* 7(1979a):63–77.

Matejcek, Z., Z. Dytrych, and V. Schüller. "Follow-up Study of Children Born from Unwanted Pregnancies." Unpublished paper, 1979b.

Miller, W.B. "The Intendedness and Wantedness of the First Child." In *The First Child and Family Formation*, edited by W.B. Miller and C.F. Newman. Chapel Hill: Carolina Population Center, 1978, 209–43.

Nathanson, C.A., and M.H. Becker. "The Influence of Physicians' Attitudes on Abortion Performance, Patient Management and Professional Fees." *Family Planning Perspectives* 9(1977):158–63.

Pohlman, E.W. *The Psychology of Birth Planning.* Cambridge, MA: Schenkman, 1969.

Population Crisis Committee. "World Population Trends." *Population*, 1979, No. 9.

Potts, M.B. "Perspectives on Fertility Control." *International Journal of Gynaecology and Obstetrics* 16(1979):449–55.

Potts, M.B., D. Diggory, J. Peel *Abortion.* Cambridge: Cambridge University Press, 1977.

Registrar General. *Supplement on Abortion.* London: HM Stationary Office, 1973.

Shepard, M.J., and M.B. Bracken. "Contraceptive Practice and Repeat Induced Abortion: An Epidemiological Investigation." *Journal of Biosocial Science* 11(1979):289–02.

Tietze, C. "Repeat Abortions — Why More?" *Family Planning Perspectives* 10(1978):286–88.

Tietze. C. *Induced Abortion: 1979.* 3rd ed. New York: Population Council, 1979a.

Tietze, C. "Legal Abortion in the World Today." In *Pregnancy Termination: Procedures, Safety, and New Developments*, edited by G.I. Zatuchini, J.J. Sciarra, and J.J. Speidel. Hagerstown: Harper and Row, 1979b, 406–15.

Tietze, C., and A.K. Jain. "The Mathematics of Repeat Abortion: Explaining the Increase." *Studies in Family Planning* 9(1978):294–99.

Tietze, C., and S. Lewit. "Joint Program for the Study of Abortion: Early Medical Complications of Legal Abortion." *Studies in Family Planning* 3(1972):97–122.

Tietze, C., and S. Lewit. "The Universal Practice." *People* 5(2)(1978):4–7.

United Nations Fund for Population Activities. *Survey of Laws on Fertility Control*, edited by J. Stepan. New York: UNFPA, 1979.

15

Abortion and Sexual Behaviour

Milton Diamond

Invariably, many who consider abortion an issue as well as a procedure link it to questions of sexual behaviour. To the so-called right-to-life advocates, the link is given a negative value. The charges are made, for example, that: "easy abortion leads to increased promiscuity"; "easy abortion reduces respect for life or maternal love"; "available abortions lead to reduced contraceptive use"; or "legalized abortion fosters the dissolution of the family." The clear implication of all these charges is that legal and available abortions encourage socially disapproved behaviours. For those who defend a woman's right to choose, abortion is seen as an additional and necessary means to help in the solution of social problems: "legal abortion decreases economic discrimination"; "legal abortion reduces the birth of unwanted, unloved and abused children"; "the legalization of abortion allows women to better control their family size and help solidify the planned family"; "legal abortion aids in population control and fosters an improved quality of life for all" (Steinhoff and Diamond, 1977).

In essence, both sides stress different aspects of abortion and make assertions for which unfortunately there is no direct evidence. At best, some correlations exist but cause-and-effect studies are non-existent. Indeed, all investigators interested in the social forces attendant on reproduction and population question two basic types of relationships between sexuality and abortion. The first asks how the legalization of abortion affects sexual expression; for example, are people more promiscuous because abortion is legal, and are people now less concerned with contraceptives? The second asks the reverse type of question. For example, is a rise in sexual permissiveness leading to an increase in abortion, and does this reflect less concern for human life or relations? Much research and writing has attempted to analyse these relationships.

This chapter will briefly review some available data and information about abortion and sexual behaviour and see how the claims of both sides meet. Since the United States and Canada share much the same religious, regional, economic, and cultural heritage, the ethical issues, attitudes and concerns involved in this discussion are in many ways similar for both countries.

Background

Consideration of reproductive functions has been tied to concern with sexual expression in all cultures. On some levels, the ties are understandable even if indirect. Puberty and menstruation have long been recognized as affording a reproductive capacity and a marked spurt in sexual interest. Societies were generally sexually more restrictive if they valued strict attention to lineage for social, political, economic or religious reasons. If a daughter or son had political, social, or economic value as a future husband or wife, or might be a liability, free choice in sexual expression or marital partners was curtailed. In few societies were, or are, sexual partners available without concern for recording parentage. In more permissive societies, in contrast, sexual liaison might occur without social disapproval. And children, if and when they occurred, might be accepted without adverse stigmas. In ancient Hawaii, as in many Polynesian societies, a knowledge of lineage was important among the Alii (royalty) and progeny might be cause for strong dispute, and even infanticide, but among commoners, all children were assured of a welcome; illegitimacy was not a Hawaiian concept. But in neither restrictive nor permissive societies was sexuality necessarily seen as a question of sin or morality; it was more a question of propriety, expectations, economics or politics.

Ancient Judaism, while advocating a pronatalist reproductive philosophy, simultaneously encouraged sexual expression to solidify the marriage relationship. Sex for pleasure was advocated as long as it was within marriage and for its enhancement. Moreover, it was specifically recognized that sexual desires of women were natural and to be expected (Feldman, 1974). The sexual desires of men were recognized by implication. This Hebraic, pronatalist, promarital sexual philosophy was in marked contrast to the Christianity which developed from it.

As Christianity began to take hold in the West, it competed not only with Judaism, but with religions that ranged from ascetic to sensual (Bullough, 1976; Karlen, 1971). From this competition, there emerged during the Middle Ages a dominant Christian view that not only made chastity a moral ideal but linked it with the concept of reproduction as the only justification for sexual activity (Cole, 1966). And women were to be ever virginal in mind (if not in body), their prime goal to be mothers. This is the pronatalist, antisexual thesis. Many early Christian writers made pleasure-seeking synonymous with paganism. This philosophy has as its legacy a belief that continues to taint sexual expression, contraception and abortion in contemporary Christian society. The legacy is the belief that sexual activity for pleasure is immoral, and the only legitimate ''purpose'' for coitus is reproduction.

Tied to the concern with lineage, pronatalism, and the attendant moral concept that sexual expression is only permissible for procreation within marriage is the negative outlook of society toward illegitimacy. Abortion is one way of avoiding illegitimacy and its sequelae. This avoidance is seen as a social good by those "pro-choice" and a social evil by those "pro-life." The theoretical linkage to sexual behaviour is that avoidance of the fear and/or pain of the social concomitants of an illegitimate birth will supposedly release people from sexual restraints. One anti-abortion spokesperson predicted general sexual license and moral decay would accompany legal abortion. She saw strong anti-abortion laws as a desired deterrent to sexual expression:

> our youth are deprived of inner resources and spiritual power that strengthens them against the onslaughts of sexual passion . . . legalized abortion will lead our youth down the path to shame and sorrow . . . in the height of strong passion, when both are about to yield to the complete act of love, the one single thought (not the most noble motivation) comes: "I might become pregnant" . . . and either the boy or the girl puts on the brake. . . . (Madden, 1969)

Such feelings are still voiced today, and not only by laymen. Imber (1979), for example, reinterprets the contention of Potts, Diggory and Peel (1977) that women seek abortion as a sign of responsibility. He claims the sign is one of irresponsibility. Imber comments on ". . . the authors' unwillingness to consider that the routinization of abortion practice, at least in American Society, coincides with a cultural abandonment of all ideals concerning sexual responsibility."

Some Evidence

To shed light on these questions concerning the legalization of abortion, it is convenient to consider some available evidence from both Hawaii and Canada. Hawaii is in many ways similar to portions of Canada in regard to abortion. Both regions have a polyglot, multiracial, and plural but basically Christian religious population, and in both geopolitical areas abortion has been legalized for a decade or more, in Canada since 1969 and in Hawaii since 1970. In contrast, the United States as a whole has legalized abortion only since 1973 and its availability has been geographically spotty. In many regions of the United States, access to legal abortion is still sufficiently hampered by legal and medical manoeuvres, or the absence of abortion facilities, so as to be nonexistent (Seims, 1980). In contrast, abortions in Hawaii are available to all; state funds will pay the expenses of women needing financial assistance. This allows Hawaii to provide data for a total population where abortion is probably more available than anywhere else in the Western world, providing a sort of marker. In all other Western countries, abortion requires the approval of physicians, and the woman must justify the procedure to a medical or bureaucratic committee. No such review is required in Hawaii. The insular nature of Hawaii also allows for a closer inspection of its population.

Our group* has been studying pregnancy, birth control and abortion in Hawaii since the law went into effect. The geography, population and research design are such that fairly comprehensive and detailed data on social, reproductive and demographic parameters for the years 1970 to 1973 are available for analysis; less detailed but additional data are available prior to 1970 and from 1974 to 1978.

The detailed Hawaiian data are from a large sample of women giving birth and woman having abortions in all hospitals in Hawaii during the 1970 to 1973 study period. The data were accumulated from hospital charts and self-administered questionnaires. These data provide information not only of the women's reproductive history, but also of her attitudes and practices in regard to sexual behaviour, birth-control usage, and pregnancy, maternity and abortion decisions. The data from 1974 to 1978 are from hospital records alone and thus less informative.

From this large pool of women, special groups (conception cohorts) have been especially studied. These conception cohorts theoretically include all those women who conceived at the same time — selected two-month periods — and thus were making their sexual-reproductive decisions at about the same time, while influenced by similar large social forces, whatever events were prevalent subsequent to passage of the present abortion law (see Diamond et al., 1973; and Smith et al., 1976, for a detailed description of cohort construction). Other data are from standard sources such as the Hawaii Department of Health Statistical Reports. The Canadian data are mainly from Statistics Canada and Schwenger (1974). Data from Hawaii will be presented first and then the data available from Canada and elsewhere will be considered.

Age of First Coitus

It had been hypothesized that the availability of legal abortion might encourage coitus in those who otherwise would refrain from such. Data for our total population (Table 5–1) do not show a significant or rapid decrease in age of first coitus linked to the availability of legalized abortion. The ten years prior to legalization of abortion saw a slow but steady decrease in age of first coitus. This continued so that the mean age of first coitus was about 19 when the legalization of abortion occurred in Hawaii in 1970. Following the law change, this age decreased slightly but remained relatively stable for the subsequent three years.

It was seen consistently that those women choosing abortion were younger at

*Collection of the data reported here was a collaborative effort of the Pregnancy, Birth Control and Abortion Study of the University of Hawaii. Principal Collaborators were Milton Diamond, Professor of Anatomy and Reproductive Biology, School of Medicine; Patricia G. Steinhoff, Professor of Sociology; Roy G. Smith, Professor of Maternal and Child Health, School of Public Health; James A. Palmore, Professor of Sociology and Assistant Director East-West Population Institute. Financial support was largely provided by the National Institutes of Child Health and Human Development and the Ford Foundation.

Table 15-1

MEAN AGE FIRST COITUS (Year)
Cohorts 1970–1973

	7–8/1970	4–5/1971	1–/1972	9–10/1972	Mean
Women Aborting	18.7	18.2	18.2	18.0	18.3
Women Delivering	19.3	19.2	19.3	19.0	19.2

Quartiles (3-month intervals) Total Population

	3–1970	4–1970	1–1971	2–1971	3–1971	4–1971	1–1972	2–1972	3–1972	4–1972	1–1973
Women Aborting	18.6	18.4	18.3	18.2	17.9	18.1	17.9	18.5	17.9	18.6	18.0
Women Delivering	19.5	20.4	—	19.1	—	—	18.9	—	—	19.3	—

first coitus than those choosing maternity, but the difference between the two groups was small and remained about the same over three years of observation. The age difference between the two groups is not unexpected since youthfulness is a very common motivation for abortion.

The age of first coitus for Hawaiian women during the years 1974 to 1978 is not known. No national or comparable provincial data are available for Canada.* Small scale regional studies of sexuality in Canada are available and the data are not organized to obtain comparable figures. Nevertheless, they seem to indicate approximately the same mean age for first coitus, 18 to 19 in 1974 to 1975, and allowing for some variation between the two groups, show an increasing trend to premarital coitus among anglophones and francophones (e.g., Hobart, 1976; Pool and Pool, 1978). Some investigators feel the changes in the late 1970s in Canada are particularly dramatic. Edward S. Herold of the Department of Family Studies of the University of Guelph (personal communication) finds a marked decrease in the mean age of first coitus and incidence of the population engaging in premarital coitus. Similarly, in the United States as a whole during the period from 1971 to 1976, a probability sample of unmarried women 15 to 19 years of age found a decrease in the mean age of first coitus from 19-plus to between 18 and 19 (Kantner and Zelnik, 1972; Zelnik and Kantner, 1977).

Partner

Concern exists that legalized abortion would alter the relationship between men and women and more permissive or promiscuous sexual interchanges would result. It was evident that those women becoming pregnant and aborting in 1974 or 1975 were less, not more, likely to be single than those pregnant in 1970 (Table 15–2). However, by 1977, these figures reversed themselves so that the woman having an abortion was more likely to be single. Among those women who elected to carry the pregnancy to term after abortion became legal, most were married but increasingly were likely to be single (Table 15–2). Over the years therefore, proportionately more pregnant women in Hawaii were single regardless of whether they chose to abort or deliver (Table 15–2).

In Canada following the legalization of abortion, no significant change was apparent in the marital status of those women delivering; from 1968 to the mid-1970s, approximately 9 per cent of all deliveries were to single women (Table 15–3). Among those women electing abortion, more were likely to be single as the procedure became established (Table 15–3).

Our data and that of others (e.g., Kantner and Zelnik, 1972; see Diamond and Karlen, 1980) indicate that by and large the relationships involved are stable. Premarital coitus is most often with the intended spouse.

---

*A survey of sexual matters by the Royal Commission on Abortion was conducted in 1976. It gathered data using Gallup services but did not question women younger than 18 years of age.

Table 15–2

HAWAII BIRTHS AND ABORTIONS 1968–1978

	1968	1969	1970	1971	1972	1973	1974	1975	1976	1977	1978
Total Population:											
Civilian	677,400	701,800	714,771	746,600	768,800	783,041	792,281	809,600	830,600	834,900	840,093
Births: Total	14,641	15,721	16,508	15,874	15,438	15,373	15,528	15,777	16,414	16,983	16,762
Birth Rate/1000 pop.	21.6	22.4	23.1	21.3	20.1	19.6	19.6	19.5	19.8	20.3	20.0
% Births to Singles	9.5%	9.5%	9.6%	8.8%	9.3%	10.4%	10.9%	12.3%	12.5%	14.3%	16.0%
% Births to Marrieds	90.5%	90.4%	90.4%	91.2%	90.7%	89.6%	89.2%	87.7%	87.5%	85.7%	84.0%
Abortions: Total	—	—	2,863*	4,268	4,501	4,486	4,027	4,545	5,163	5,249	6,014
Abortion Rate/100 live births	—	—	17.3	26.9	29.3	29.2	26.0	28.8	31.5	30.9	35.9
% Abortions to Singles†	—	—	63.9%	63.0%	63.0%	62.7%	61.4%	60.9%	62.1%	64.7%	67.2%
% Abortions to Marrieds	—	—	36.1%	37.0%	37.0%	37.3%	38.6%	39.1%	37.8%	35.3%	32.8%

*Abortion not available whole year.
†Includes women reported as separated, divorced or widowed; common law marriage is not recognized in Hawaii.

Table 15-3

CANADA BIRTHS AND ABORTIONS
1968-1978

	1968	1969	1970	1971	1972	1973	1974	1975	1976	1977	1978
Births: Total	364,310	369,647	371,988	362,187	347,319	343,373	345,645	358,621	364,630	360,340	—
Rate/1000 pop.	17.6	17.6	17.9	16.8	15.7	15.5	15.4	15.7	15.8	15.5	—
Fertility Rate/ 1,000 15–44	75.8	72.5	71.7	70.5	67.7	—	—	—	—	—	—
% Births to Singles	9.0	9.2	9.6	9.0	9.0	9.0	—	—	—	—	—
% Births to Married	91.0	90.8	90.4	91.0	91.0	91.0	—	—	—	—	—
Abortions: Total	—	4,378*	11,152	30,923	38,853	43,201	48,136	49,311	54,478	57,131	62,290
Rate/100 live births	—	1.2	3.0	8.6	11.2	12.6	13.9	13.8	14.9	15.3	17.4
Rate/1,000 pop. 15–44	—	.85	2.1	6.6	8.2	8.8	9.5	9.5	10.3	10.6	11.3
% Abortions to Singles	—	—	—	—	—	—	—	—	58%	60%	61%
% Abortions to Married	—	—	—	—	—	—	—	—	31%	29%	27%
Other†	—	—	—	—	—	—	—	—	11%	11%	11%

*Abortion not available whole year.
†Includes common law marriages.

Contraception

The hypothesis exists that legalized abortion would decrease the use of contraceptives and increase the chance of pregnancy. Data from our cohort sample in Hawaii (Table 15–4) do not support this thesis. Regrettably, even when a pregnancy was not desired, coitus was still often unprotected, but no more so in 1973 than in 1970 when abortion was first legalized. In fact, among women who claimed coitus occurred unexpectedly, a trend was seen to a greater likelihood of their using contraception in 1973 than in 1970. For these cohorts, two-thirds of their unplanned pregnancies occurred while using a birth-control method. Particularly notable, however, is that a significant increase was seen in the proportion of women choosing abortion if the pregnancy occurred despite the use of birth-control methods.

It should be kept in mind that a large majority of women use contraceptives effectively and never appear in any abortion or pregnancy study. For the United States as a whole, a dramatic increase in contraceptive use has been reported between the years of 1971 and 1976; a national probability sample among unmarried teenagers found an increase of 53 per cent for whites and 76 per cent for blacks in contraceptive usage (Zelnik and Kantner, 1977). The figures for older women are markedly higher.

In Canada, adequate data over time on contraceptive practices for a provincial or national sample are not available.

Review of several additional studies is pertinent to this discussion. Fordney-Settlage, Baroff and Cooper (1973) found that by the time most women in their sample sought contraceptives, they were already sexually active. And, several studies have reported that increased contraceptive use tends to correlate with increased coital frequency but not an increase in number of partners (Freedman, 1979; Garris, Steckler and McIntire, 1976; Reichelt, 1978). Furthermore, data from those Hawaiian women who had second or third abortions during the study period lend no support to the contention that women

Table 15–4

POPULATION PERCENTAGE USING BIRTH CONTROL AT CONCEPTION
PREGNANCY UNPLANNED (COHORTS) HAWAII CONCEPTION DATES

	7–8/1970	4–5/1971	1–2/1972	8–9/1972	Mean
Total N=	(1,465)	(2,533)	(3,016)	(2,662)	(9,675)
Coitus Expected	65.5	65.9	66.1	65.7	65.8
Coitus Unexpected	3.0	4.5	8.6	10.2	6.8

POPULATION PERCENTAGE OF WOMEN WHO USED BIRTH CONTROL
DECIDING TO ABORT

Total Population	29.8	38.6	41.4	43.8	38.3

substitute abortion for contraception. Their use of contraceptives was in keeping with that of their peers. Their incidence of pregnancy was as low as can be expected, given the shortcomings of currently available contraceptives and their use (Steinhoff, Smith, Palmore, Diamond and Chung, 1979). Few Hawaiian women depend upon abortion as a primary method of birth control.

Pregnancy Decision

After an initial adjustment to legalized abortion during the first year among our cohort sample, the ratio of pregnant women choosing to abort, for any reason, remained about the same for the years 1971 to 1973; between 1 of 4 and 1 of 5 pregnancies were aborted (Table 15–5). Among the total population, this ratio and the attendant abortion rate per 100 live births showed a slow but steady rise until 1978 when a marked increase was seen (Table 15–6). The reason for the sharp increase is not known. Among our cohorts, it was apparent that among women who became pregnant despite the use of some birth control method, a gradual but steady increase was noted in the proportion that chose to abort; between 1970 and 1973, the incidence rose from 29.8 per cent to 43.8 per cent (Table 15–4). Available data also indicate that the Hawaiian birth rate remained about the same for the years 1967 through 1978 despite a *peak* in 1970, the year abortion was legalized (Table 15–2).

In Canada (Table 15–3), the birth rate dipped from 17.6 per 1,000 population in 1968 and 1969 prior to abortion legalization to 15.7 in 1972. This dip in birth rate is particularly noticeable if calculated per 1,000 women aged 15 to 49 rather than for the total population, from 75.8 in 1968 to 67.7 in 1972 (Statistics Canada; Schwenger, 1974). From 1972 until 1977, the Canadian birth rate remained fairly stable. In contrast, the gross abortion rate after the first two years has increased slowly and continually, from 8.6 in 1971 to 17.4 in 1978. The abortion rate in Canada and Hawaii run parallel with each other but the Canadian

Table 15–5

PERCENTAGE OF PREGNANT WOMEN DECIDING TO ABORT OR DELIVER: HAWAII

COHORTS (Conception Dates)

	7–8/1970	4–5/1971	1–2/1972	8–9/1972	Mean
Women Aborting	19.0	23.1	23.8	22.9	22.7
Women Delivering	81.0	76.9	76.2	77.1	77.3
Abortion Rate / 100 deliveries	23.4	30.1	31.3	29.7	28.6
Ratio	1 : 4.3	1 : 3.3	1 : 3.2	1 : 3.4	3.6

Table 15-6

PROPORTION (%) OF PREGNANT WOMEN DECIDING TO ABORT OR DELIVER — HAWAII
TOTAL PREGNANT POPULATION 1970 TO 1978

	1970	1971	1972	1973	1974	1975	1976	1977	1978	Mean
Women Aborting	2,863	4,268	4,655	4,486	4,027	4,545	5,163	5,249	6,014	4,586
%	14.8	21.2	23.2	23.1	21.1	22.4	23.9	23.6	26.4	22.2
Women Delivering	16,508	15,874	15,438	15,373	15,543	15,777	16,414	16,983	16,762	16,075
%	85.2	78.8	76.8	76.9	79.9	77.6	76.1	76.4	73.6	77.9
Abortion Rate per 100 live deliveries	17.3	26.9	30.2	29.2	25.9	28.8	31.5	30.9	35.9	28.5
Ratio aborting/ deliveries	5.8	3.7	3.3	3.3	3.8	3.5	3.2	3.2	2.8	3.6
Total Pregnancies	19,371	20,142	20,093	19,999	19,701	20,322	21,577	22,232	22,776	20,660

rate is about half that of Hawaii. This is probably due in part to the greater restrictions on abortion in Canada and its relative unavailability in some areas.

While no woman becomes pregnant in order to have an abortion, many women do become pregnant in order to be mothers. However, circumstances often change between the time a decision is made to conceive and when the pregnancy comes to term. The magnitude of the change may be sufficient to convince a pregnant woman she no longer wants to maintain the pregnancy. With the possibility to legally abort, it might be asked how frequently does such a change occur. Data from our study indicate that women who chose to become pregnant did not elect to terminate the pregnancy with any greater frequency three years after the legalization of abortion than at the start; this recourse is taken in fewer than 2 per cent of planned pregnancies.

Illegitimacy

The availability of a legal abortion for an unplanned pregnancy would hypothetically lead to a decrease in illegitimate births. Data from our cohort sample show that when the Hawaiian population of women is considered, no trend in this direction is seen for the years 1971 to 1973 (Table 15–7). Slightly more than 1 of 10 births were illegitimate in 1970 (11.0 per cent) and this remained true through 1972. In 1973, slightly fewer than 1 of 10 births were illegitimate (9.8 per cent).

Inspection of total State of Hawaii data from 1968 to 1978 (Table 15–2) reveals that 9.5 per cent of births were illegitimate in 1968 and 1969, the two years preceding legalization of abortion. This percentage remained fairly constant despite the legalization of abortion in 1970 for the following years 1971 and 1972. From 1973, the illegitimacy rate rose steadily, to 16 per cent of births in 1978. During this same period, the overall birth rate has remained fairly constant (Table 15–2).

From the data available, the Canadian illegitimacy rate seemed to parallel the Hawaiian rate (Table 15–3). Approximately 9 per cent of Canadian births were illegitimate prior to, during and following the legalization of abortion (Schwenger, 1974).

In Hawaii, the percentage of abortions performed on single women has risen during the past several years from what had been a fairly stable rate; from the low 60s to 67.2 per cent in 1978 (Table 15–2). In Canada, the data available again seem to parallel our findings (Table 15–3).

Data of illegal abortions are scanty, but one old large-scale study in the United States indicated that women seeking the procedure were most often likely to be married rather than single (Gebhard, Pomeroy, Martin and Christenson, 1958). Regrettably, data for the intervening years, from the mid-1950s to 1970, are not available, so the shift in marital status may not be attributable to a change in law.

Table 15–7

MARITAL STATUS AT DELIVERY
COHORTS-HAWAII

Delivery Dates

	4–5/1971	1–2/1972	10–11/1972	5–6/1973	Mean
Single (%)	11.0	11.3	11.3	9.8	10.9
Married (%)	87.7	87.4	87.9	89.8	88.2
Separated/Divorced/ Widowed	1.3	1.3	0.8	0.4	1.0

Summary and Conclusions

During the last ten years, the years during which abortion has been legal in Canada and Hawaii, changes in some reproductive behaviours have occurred and indeed greater changes may yet appear. It is clear, however, that most of the changes are gradual, not precipitous or dramatic. And, most changes such as the lowering of age of first coitus and the increase in contraceptive use are continuations of long-standing trends. In specific regard to abortion, those women electing the procedure the years immediately following legalization seemed essentially similar to those who elected the procedure initially. They were not significantly younger than before, used contraceptives about as before, elected abortion for unwanted pregnancies as before and were no more nor less likely to have illegitimate children. Canadian and Hawaiian birth rates, while surely declining, have done so fairly slowly since the legalization of abortion.

Several years after abortion became legal, various factors under study did change. Most notably, the women becoming pregnant were more likely to be single than they were in the past. Of these women, more chose (surprisingly) to deliver rather than abort, but many more pregnant single women also chose to terminate their pregnancies than previously.

It appears that if a marked shift in reproductive behaviour continues to develop, it is likely to be for primary reasons other than a change in law. This may reflect the complexity of our society's behaviours and our society's ways of dealing with pregnant women and mothers as well as its ways of dealing with abortion. Of particular significance may be the economic, social and community support now offered by government and private institutions for these women and their families as well as the declining influence of religion and family sanctions.

An example from another time and place may be illustrative. Almost two centuries ago, France dramatically changed its old legal system and began living under the Napoleonic Code. This code allowed divorce and private consensual homosexual acts. Many people predicted an onslaught of family breakups and a rampage of open promiscuity and homosexuality. But relatively few people applied for divorce and most homosexuals kept their activities secret. Divorced people were still stigmatized and homosexuals were still harrassed by police and other citizens (Karlen, 1971). There is little evidence that the situation has yet changed markedly. Change of law does not necessarily change behaviour or attitude.

In regard to abortion, initially we probably did not see development of a new set of behaviours but rather witnessed a shift from patterns that were illegal and dangerous to those that are legal and safe (Diamond et al., 1972; Steinhoff and Diamond, 1977). The more recent situation may reflect attitudinal changes as to the acceptability of abortion as a solution to a problem with an unplanned and unwanted pregnancy. We are also simultaneously seeing changes in marital behaviours which may account for the reproductive trends seen. Marriage is no longer considered as significant a solution to illegitimacy as it was in the 1960s (Steinhoff, 1978; O'Connell and Moore, 1980). Also, marriages are occurring later, so more time is available for premarital relations. Cohabitation is now more accepted than it was in the past.

And, indeed, the data do indicate that some sexual behaviours are different now than they were ten years ago. Closer inspection of these data and additional data will tell us how different. It is likely however, that such behaviours, as the legalization of abortion itself, are only aspects of our cultures' adaptations to the changes in family ties and values, structures to personal behaviours, increasing social anonymity and perhaps individual and collective fatalism in view of world tensions. It is only future historians and social critics who will be able to accurately judge if these trends are permanent and whether or not they are positive.

It is thus not that abortion laws, or having abortion as an option, do not affect behaviour but rather that such behaviours, interact with social and psychological sanctions or support systems that are as strong or stronger in their influence than the force of law. It is possible that over time the transfer of reproductive control from law to choice will cause social changes we cannot as yet foresee. But the persistence of problems with willpower, the poor use and ineffectiveness of many contraceptives, illegitimacy and lack of fulfillment in eroticism and relationships suggests we need not more or stricter laws, but greater knowledge about sexuality and reproduction and more emotional comfort with the subject (Diamond and Karlen, 1980).

References

Bullough, Vern L. *Sexual Variance in Society and History*. New York: John Wiley, 1976.

Cole, William G. *Sex in Christianity and Psychoanalysis.* New York: Oxford University Press, 1966.

Diamond, Milton and Arno Karlen. *Sexual Decisions.* Boston: Little, Brown, 1980.

Diamond, Milton, Roy G. Smith, Patricia G. Steinhoff, and James A. Palmore. *Report to the Legislature, State of Hawaii: Abortion in Hawaii; the First Year.* Honolulu: State of Hawaii, 1972.

Diamond, Milton, G. Patricia Steinhoff, James A. Palmore, and Roy, G. Smith. "Sexuality, Birth Control and Abortion. A Decision Making Sequence." *Biosocial Science* 5(1973):347–61.

Feldman, David M. *Marital Relations, Birth Control and Abortion in Jewish Law.* New York: Schocken Books, 1974.

Fordney-Settlage, Diane S., S. Baroff, and D. Cooper. "Sexual Experience of Younger Teenage Girls Seeking Contraceptive Assistance for the First Time." *Family Planning Perspectives* 5(1973):223–26.

Freedman, Ronald. "Theories of Fertility Decline." *Social Forces* 58(1979):1–17.

Garris, Lorie, Allan Steckler, and John R. McIntire. "The Relationship Between Oral Contraceptives and Adolescent Sexual Behaviour." *J. Sex Research.* 12(1976):135–46.

Gebhard, Paul H., Wardell B. Pomeroy, Clyde Martin, and Cornelia V. Christenson, *Pregnancy, Birth Control and Abortion.* New York: Harper, 1958.

Herold, Edward, S. Personal Communication. Department of Family Studies, University of Guelph. Guelph, Ontario, 1980.

Hobart, Charles W. "Youth and Sex Expression." In *The Canadian Family,* edited by K. Ishwaren. Toronto: Holt, Rinehardt and Winston, 1976.

Imber, Jonathan B. "Sociology and Abortion: Legacies and Strategies." *Contemporary Sociology* 8(1979):825–86.

Kantner, John F. and Melvin Zelnik. "Contraception and Pregnancy." *Family Planning Perspectives* 5(1973):21–35.

Kantner, John F. and Melvin Zelnik. "Sexual Experience of Young Unmarried Women in the United States." *Family Planning Perspectives* 4(1972):9–18.

Karlen, Arno. *Sexuality and Homosexuality.* New York: Norton, 1971.

Madden, Gerri. *Testimony Quoted in Abortion Politics,* p. 112. Steinhoff, P.G. and Diamond M. Honolulu: University Press of Hawaii, 1969.

O'Connel, Martin and Maurice J. Moore. "The Legitimacy Status of First Births to U.S. Women Aged 15–24, 1939–1978." *Family Planning Perspectives* 12(1980):16–23, 25.

Pool, Janet Sceats and D. Ian Pool. *Contraception and Health Care Among Young Canadian Women.* Ottawa: Carleton University, Department of Sociology and Anthropology, 1978.

Potts, Malcolm, Peter Diggory, and John Peel. *Abortion.* New York: Cambridge University Press, 1977.

Reichelt, Paul A. "Changes in Sexual Behavior Among Unmarried Teenage Women Utilizing Oral Contraception." *J. of Population* 1(1978):57–68.

Schwenger, Cope W. "Abortion as a Public Health Problem and Community Health Measure." In *Family Planning in Canada*, edited by B. Schlesinger, pp. 240–51. Toronto: University of Toronto Press, 1974.

Seims, Sara. "Abortion Availability in the United States." *Family Planning Perspectives* 12(1980):88–101.

Smith, Roy G., Patricia G. Steinhoff, James A. Palmore, and Charlotte Payne. "The Utilization of Conception Cohorts for the Evaluation of Family Planning Programs." *Contraception* 13(1976):515–30.

Steinhoff, Patricia G., Roy G. Smith, James A. Palmore, Milton Diamond, and C.S. Chung. "Women Who Obtain Repeat Abortions: A Study Based on Record Linkage." *Family Planning Perspectives* 11(1979):30–38.

Steinhoff, Patricia G. and Milton, Diamond. *Abortion Politics*. Honolulu University Press of Hawaii, 1977.

Zelnik, Melvin and John F. Kantner. "Sexual Contraceptive Experience of Young Unmarried Women in the United States, 1976 and 1971." *Family Planning Perspectives* 9(1977):55–71.

16

Problems of Fertility Control Among Canadian Women

Paul Sachdev

In recent years the phenomenal rise in the rates of abortions and unwanted/unplanned pregnancies among Canadian women has been a cause for widespread public and professional concern. There is nothing new about abortions or unwanted pregnancies; they have been with us since the dawn of civilization. What is new is that despite our contraceptively sophisticated society, the prevention or at least reduction of unintended pregnancies among married and unmarried Canadian women has not been achieved. As a consequence, legal or illegal abortions continue to occur. It is evident from the data reported in this volume and elsewhere that the incidence of unwanted pregnancies and induced abortions is disturbingly high and embarrassingly troublesome for public health professionals and pregnancy counsellors.

National figures on the incidence of unplanned or unwanted pregnancies among Canadian married women are not available, but through extrapolation from the U.S. National Survey of Family Growth in 1973, it is estimated that they accounted for nearly 33 per cent of all live births between 1968 and 1973 (Weller and Hobbs, 1978). A few local studies confirm a high prevalence of unwanted pregnancies among married women. For example, sociological research at Laval University estimated that in certain regions of Quebec about two-thirds of the pregnancies were believed to have occurred when couples did not want them (Gourgues, 1974). Another Quebec study involving 376 couples who attended the "Centre de Consultation Conjugale of Quebec" reported the occurrence of one unplanned childbirth among 45 per cent of the couples and 67 per cent experienced two unplanned births (Lux, 1975).

A Toronto study based on 601 married women selected by stratified random sample in 1973/74 reported that 14.2 per cent of them did not want their last child (Osborn, 1975). Virginia Elahi noted in a Halifax survey that nearly 40 per cent of the women in the low and 25 per cent in the middle and high socio-economic groups had more living children than their desired family size (Elahi, 1973). In their study of 506 vasectomized men Grindstaff and Ebanks (1971) found that about 39 per cent of the total living children born to 489 couples were accidental.

Also, Scott and Stone (1973) report that of 197 consecutively delivered mothers at Grace Maternity Hospital in Halifax, Nova Scotia, 37 per cent of the married women did not want their current pregnancy. In a Vancouver study of 2,450 married women conducted by the United Community Services between 1971 and 1973 to determine family planning services need, it was found that 10 per cent of the families had five or more pregnancies and 7 per cent had six or more pregnancies which were unplanned (United Community Services, 1972).

The incidence of out-of-wedlock conceptions among unmarried women and particularly among teenagers has reached epidemic proportions, causing great public concern and debate. In contrast to the generally steady declining birth rates since 1958 the number of illegitimate births in Canada has climbed from 3.9 per cent in 1956 to about 12 per cent in 1978 of all live births, with some areas registering out-of-wedlock births as high as 24.8 (Yukon Territory) and 26.6 (N.W.T.) per 100 live births (Statistics Canada, 1979)*. In 1978, about 42.5 per cent of these births occurred to women under 20 years of age with some provinces reporting as high as 60 per cent (Vital Statistics, 1978). Stated differently, there are now twice as many babies born to unmarried women as there were a decade ago and more than half these mothers are teenagers. According to Planned Parenthood of Canada, more than 1,000 teenagers become pregnant every week in Canada (Bulletin, 1980). Interestingly, while the frequency of out-of-wedlock pregnancies is declining among older women, it continues to rise among teenagers (Addy, 1977; Bouma and Bouma, 1975).

Another indicator of the mounting incidence of out-of-wedlock pregnancies is reflected in the rising abortion rates. Many unwanted pregnancies which are not brought to term, are submitted to induced abortions each year. For Canada as a whole, the abortion rate (per 100 live births) rose from 11.2 per cent in 1970 to 18.1 per cent in 1979 with Ontario and British Columbia reporting close to one-and-a-half (25.4 per cent) to two times (34.2 per cent) respectively the national abortion rate. The single biggest annual increase in the abortion rate — occurred in 1971 when 30,923 pregnancies were terminated via therapeutic abortions. This represented an increase of 186.7 per cent over the previous year. According to the committee on the operation of the Abortion Law (1977) illegitimate births and therapeutic abortions combined constituted 1 out of 6 (17.8 per cent) of all deliveries during the period 1970–73.

A high proportion of these abortions are performed on young and unmarried women. For instance, approximately two-thirds (64.0 per cent) of all abortions performed in 1979 were experienced by unmarried women, with teenagers under 20 years constituting about one-third (30.5 per cent) of these women. Married

---

*There has been a continuous decline in fertility in Canada since 1957 as reflected in declining overall birth rate (per 1,000 population) which fell by more than 44.3 per cent between 1957 (28.5) and 1978 (15.3), and in the fertility rate which dropped more than 50 per cent between 1959 and 1976 from 3.9 to 1.8 children respectively per woman. (Statistics Canada, *Canada's Population: Demographic Perspectives*, Catalogue 98-802E, 1979.)

women accounted for one-quarter (24.7 per cent) among those who received therapeutic abortions in 1979 (Statistics Canada, 1980).

There is considerable evidence that a large proportion of young women engage in sexual activity without or with only minimal use of contraception. Several Canadian studies on teenage pregnancy and abortion consistently report complete absence of pregnancy control measures ranging from one-third to as much as two-thirds of sexually active women (Addy, 1973; Arnold et al., 1974; Canadian Facts, 1973; Elahi, 1973; Garrett, 1974; Grauer, 1975; Guyatt, 1974; Herold and Goodwin, 1980; Hunter, 1974; Kazanjian, 1973; Krishnamoni and Jain, 1979; Lipper et al., 1973; Meikle, 1974; Sachdev, forthcoming; Sullivan and Watt, 1975; Watt, 1974; Wolfish, 1971).

While infrequent use of preventive devices can admittedly expose a woman to the risk of impregnation, the choice of methods further influences the degree of risk involved in sexual experience. The studies reveal that the most common methods employed by unmarried women are condom and withdrawal, putting the onus on the man to keep them from getting pregnant (Canadian Facts, 1973; Guyatt, 1974; Herold and Goodwin, 1980; Hunter, 1974; Meikle, 1974; Sachdev, forthcoming; The Regina Family Planning Clinic Study, 1975). A significant number rely on the least effective methods — rhythm, withdrawal, douche (Hunter, 1974; Kazanjian, 1973; Krishnamoni and Jain, 1979; Sachdev, forthcoming; The Regina Family Planning Clinic Study, 1975). These findings are consistent with those reported by Kantner and Zelnik (1972) in their U.S. national probability sample of 4,240 never-married women 15 to 19 years of age. The authors observed that only about one-fifth of them employed contraception "every time" they had sex and about 42 to 60 per cent of females of both races relied on male methods of contraception.

Contrary to the commonly held assumption that the erratic and non-contraceptive behaviour of unmarried women stems from their lack of knowledge about modern methods of birth control, research studies note unequivocally that a very large majority — anywhere from 75 to 94 per cent of the samples studied — claimed familiarity with many of the contraceptive methods and their use (Canadian Facts, 1973; Guyatt, 1974; Krishnamoni and Jain, 1979; Lipper et al., 1973; Munz et al., 1976; Pool and Pool, 1978; Sachdev, forthcoming).

The question frequently asked is why so many women do not use adequate contraceptive measures to ensure protection against a pregnancy they do not want? The literature on unwed motherhood is unanimous that an unwanted pregnancy poses serious social and economic hardships to a young woman and precipitates a wide spectrum of emotional and psychological difficulties, threatening both her immediate and long-range interests. While physical sequalae to abortions are very limited and the adverse psychological after-effects are generally mild to moderate according to the more recent follow-up studies, the decision to abort remains an agonizing and distressing experience for many women (Bracken, 1978; Freeman, 1978; Illsley and Hall, 1976; Sachdev, forthcoming).

By far the most recurring explanation the women give for their erratic use or failure to use contraception is their belief that pregnancy would not happen to them. Stated among other reasons are that contraceptives interfere with spontaneity of sexual relations, induce emotional and moral ambivalence, imply admission of intent and consequently carry reputational and self-definitional implications. A few eschew contraception in order to consciously choose impregnation and motherhood (Cobliner et al., 1973; Freeman, 1977; Kantner and Zelnik, 1972; Mudd et al., 1978; Nadelson et al., 1980; Ryan and Sweeney, 1980; Sachdev, forthcoming; Shah et al., 1975).

A number of researchers question the validity of these reasons, which they contend are relevant in so far as they explain these women's contraceptive behaviour at their conscious or cognitive plane. As these researchers rely upon a psychodynamic perspective, they interpret the discrepancy between a woman's intent to avoid pregnancy and her erratic or non-contraceptive behaviour in terms of some purposeful unconscious motives or what Lehfeldt calls "willful exposure to pregnancy" (Clothier, 1943; Gottschalk et al., 1964; Kasanin and Handshin, 1941; Kravitz et al., 1966; Lehfeldt, 1970; Polak and Friedman, 1969; Roberts, 1966; Thomas, 1967; Young, 1954). These theorists assert that when a woman engages in a sexual act without adequate protective measures she tends to block out the consequences in order to fulfill her deep emotional and psychological needs.

Interestingly, the psychodynamic explanation of out-of-wedlock pregnancies which was advanced more than two decades ago persisted throughout the 1970s and it continues to influence professionals' orientations today (Abernethy and Abernethy, 1974; Abernethy, 1974; Benedek, 1970; Brandt et al., 1978; Coe and Blum, 1972; Ford et al., 1971; Kane et al., 1973; Kane et al., 1974; Kane and Lechenbruch, 1973; Kimball, 1970; Moore and Caldwell, 1976; Nadelson et al., 1980; Pannor, 1971; Perez-Reyes and Falk, 1973; Ryan and Sweeny, 1980).

However, there are researchers who reject the psychodynamic explanation and view the phenomenon of out-of-wedlock pregnancy as an unanticipated consequence of sexual activity. (Cole et al., 1975; Furstenberg, 1971; Furstenberg, 1976; Jaffee and Polgar, 1968; Rains, 1971). They argue that barring a few women who consciously or subconsciously have a prior commitment to pregnancy, a large majority of these conceptions are accidents which may be considerably reduced through information about and wide availability of contraceptive means. Their premise is based on the contention that society's structural arrangements can present to a woman realistic external barriers preventing her from effective utilization of contraceptive means. Some of these obstacles are age, marital status, confidential consultation, embarrassment, and attitudinal and information conditions.

However, there is a degree of unanimity among experts that mere availability of information and access to contraceptive technology will not ensure its effective utilization (Abernethy, 1973; Abernethy and Abernethy, 1974; Brandt et al., 1978; Chilman, 1978; Freeman et al., 1980; Hansson et al., 1979; Kane et al., 1973; Kane and Lachenbruch, 1973; Reiss et al., 1978; Thompson, 1975; Zelnik and Kantner, 1978). They cite as an example the large number of unwanted pregnancies among Canadian married women who do not face the same paradoxical circumstances and structural obstacles as do the young unmarried women. These pregnancies result from married couples' failure to use or irregular and inappropriate use of birth-control devices. Some studies report that as many as two-thirds of these couples attempt no contraception during the sex act even though they want to forestall further pregnancies (Arnold et al., 1974; Elahi, 1973; Grauer, 1975; Greenglass, 1974; Hepworth, 1975; Kazanjian, 1973). In the Metropolitan Toronto study, Osborn (1975) observed that 57 per cent of the sample analysed were "irregular" in their use of contraception. An attitude survey of 673 married people in St. John's, Newfoundland done by the Family Planning Association of Newfoundland and Labrador (1975) revealed that although 93 per cent of them were aware of the pill, only 38.5 per cent were currently using any method of birth control. Consistent with these findings, Janet Pool (1975) found in a study of 802 randomly selected French and English ever-married subjects living in low-density housing units in Ottawa that although 97.1 per cent of them knew at least one method of birth control, the proportion ever using any method was much less than that. The most startling conclusion of the Toronto General Hospital study involving 928 abortion women was cited by the authors in these words: "A more difficult statistic to explain is that 68 per cent of the married women engaged in unprotected intercourse" (Sullivan and Watt, 1975).

In an effort to identify factors underlying effective contraception, Reuben Hill and his associates as early as 1958 stressed the significance of human and psychological variables (e.g., acceptability of contraceptive means and positive interaction between sexual partners) in addition to the knowledge about and the ready availability of contraceptive means. Rainwater (1960) investigated the decision-making patterns involved in contraceptive practices of working-class couples living in Chicago and Cincinnati. Like Reuben Hill et al., he too concluded that the dynamics of effective contraception rest upon the user's psychological receptivity to contraceptive devices and mutual support between sexual partners, among other vital conditions. The other determinants he suggested, include awareness of the need for fertility control, open communication and ability to regulate and plan sexual activity. Thus we see that effective contraception is a deliberate and co-operative act, and the supply of contraceptive methods is only one part in the implementation of this act. Rainwater observed, "it seems likely that failures at the interpersonal level are more common than technical failures in the use of appliances" (p. 21). The significance of dyadic communication, consultation and mutual co-operation in effective contraceptive activity was also stressed by Treffers (1968).

Whelpton and Kiser (1954) noted the importance of socio-economic factors in influencing fertility behaviour but stressed the significance of psychological variables in understanding the dynamics of the irregular use or non-use of contraception. Donald Bogue (1964) too, proposed a refreshing focus on interpersonal psychological factors for understanding and modifying fertility-control behaviour. In an extensive review of the family planning literature, Polhman (1968) emphasized psychological motivation for fertility control. Commenting on the reasons for misuse or rejection of contraception, Sandberg and Jacobs (1971) in their incisive and thought-provoking essay recognized the powerful influence of interpersonal and psychological forces on the acceptance and regularity of contraceptive use. The authors state:

> While many of the reasons for misuse or rejection of contraception are included within the commonly discussed areas of contraceptive knowledgeability, acceptability, availability, cost, religious proscription, etc., innumerable other reasons, principally in the psychological and interpersonal relationship realms, are also operative, consciously or unconsciously, in both partners. (p. 227)

Some researchers have attempted to correlate certain sexual life patterns of unmarried women with efficient contraception. They suggest that a positive self-image, an unequivocal attitude towards and acceptance of one's sexuality and a stable sexual relationship are highly conducive to the use of contraception by women. It is hypothesized that a woman with a positive self-image, that is, who feels attractive to males, expects a greater likelihood of being sexually involved and, therefore, is more inclined to prepare herself contraceptively (Abernethy, 1974; Reiss et al., 1975). Freeman (1977) defined self-image in terms of 42 personality attributes and found among her 148 abortion patients (mostly never-married) that the post-abortion contraceptive use was much higher among women with positive self-image (84 per cent) than those with negative self-image (43 per cent). Closely allied to the concept of self-image is the attitude towards one's sexuality. It is suggested that since the act of contraception is intimately linked with sexuality, and the use of most female-oriented contraceptive devices requires contact with their genitalia, women who accept their own sexuality are less likely to view sexual liaisons as resulting from unplanned and uncontrollable urges. As a consequence they are more likely to assume responsibility in contraception. It is the ambivalent woman who seeks to neutralize her family proscriptions by not thinking about contraceptives, which imply planning and preparedness (Brandt et al., 1978; Dembo and Lundell, 1979; Fisher, 1978; Furstenberg, 1971; Miller, 1976; Nadelson, 1974; Notman, 1975; Rains, 1971; Reiss et al., 1975). Non-use may also serve as a defence against guilt feelings induced by violation of personal and family sex norms (Monsour and Stewart, 1973; Rader et al., 1978).

The degree of dyadic commitment in a heterosexual relationship is cited in many studies as one of the principal determinants of whether and how often contraceptives will be used. The deeper the involvement the more likely it is that contraception will be practised (Anderson et al., 1978; Furstenberg, 1971; Kantner and Zelnik, 1972; Luker, 1975; Miller, 1976a; Reiss et al., 1975;

Sorensen, 1973). This relationship may be attributed to several intervening variables. For instance, with increased involvement, the communication between sexual partners progressively improves and becomes more open on sexual and contraceptive matters (Thompson, 1978). Deep involvement between partners also fosters mutual planning, and the male's readiness to assume responsibility in avoiding undesired pregnancy by either using a contraceptive himself or encouraging his partner to use one (Kirkendell, 1961). Studies have shown that encouragement by the male partner is a strong contributor to effective contraceptive use in young women (Cahn, 1978; Thompson, 1978; Venham, 1972). A recent study by Apkom et al. (1976) found that over three-quarters (77 per cent) of the women in a family planning clinic were supported by their boyfriends in seeking contraceptive services. Herold and Goodwin (1980), in their study of 486 single females aged 13 to 20, noted that 52 per cent of them indicated that they needed the support and encouragement of their boyfriends to initiate contraception.

A stable relationship also affords more opportunities for sexual liaisons which tend to occur in a regular and predictable fashion (Anderson et al., 1978; Kantner and Zelnik, 1972; Luker, 1975; Miller, 1976a; Sorensen, 1973; Spanier, 1976; Vincent and Stelling, 1973). These conditions allow the couple greater control over sex and make coitus-unrelated methods of contraception more acceptable. Furstenburg (1971) posits that in a casual relationship the man may not feel an obligation to prevent the consequence of unprotected sex and, therefore, may ignore the woman's request to practice contraception. But in a stable relationship her bargaining position is improved so that she is better able to ensure her male friend's compliance with her request to assume contraceptive responsibility.

Some researchers have studied comparable groups of pregnant and non-pregnant adolescent females and have identified the social mileu underlying contraceptive usage and out-of-wedlock pregnancy (Angrist, 1966; Brandt et al., 1978; Glass, 1972; Gottschalk et al., 1964; Kaats and Davis, 1970; Sarrel, 1969; Spanier, 1976; Thompson, 1978). They suggest that pregnant adolescents are more responsive to peer group influence in the establishment of their norms regarding contraceptive use and premarital pregnancy than to their religious teachings or parental guidance. Cahn (1978), in a sample of aborting and contracepting women, confirmed the hypothesis that females who avoided pregnancy received more influential information and support for their behaviour from their peers than did the aborters.

Several recent studies identify certain personality traits as determinants of effective contraceptive use. They posit that women who are impulsive and present-oriented (Bardwick, 1973; Cobliner et al., 1973; Furstenberg, 1971; Miller, 1976a; Miller, 1976b), dogmatic (Joe et al., 1979; Lundy, 1972; Miller, 1976a), and who characteristically tend to use denial and self-directed aggression have a low frequency of contraceptive use. It is hypothesized that impulsiveness and here-and-now gratification-seeking attitudes limit a woman's ability to achieve what Jean Piaget calls "operative thinking," which encourages anticipation of a sexual act, enables risk assessment and mobilization of efforts to prevent unwanted pregnancy. It is therefore not surprising to note that the practice of most forms of contraception rests on operative thinking. Similarly, dogmatic women are less favourable to sexual freedom and pleasure and, therefore, less favourable to contraception for coital relations.

Steinlauf (1979) holds that effective contraception is positively related to a woman's problem-solving skills and her belief in internal control. These traits are conceptually related to a sense of power and competence, and are similar to those observed by Bauman and Undry (1972), Fox (1975), Leach (1977), and McDonald (1970). According to these authors a feeling that life is controlled by external events leads to chance taking and infrequent contraception. Fisher (1978), Jaccard et al. (1976), and Smith (1978) claim that a woman's decision to contracept is largely influenced by (a) her perceptions of the necessity and consequences of behaviour, (b) her perceptions of what her significant others expect her to do, and (c) her motivation to conform to their expectations.

Thus, we see from the above discussion that in view of the currently available volitional contraceptive means, the act of contraception is highly complex, and its successful implementation is anchored in multiple human, interpersonal, psychosocial, attitudinal and technical factors which interact varyingly and uniquely for a given individual at a given time. The contraceptive behaviour is further complicated by the complex nature of sexual behaviour of young women. The literature points out that there has been an easier access in the past decade to contraceptive service and while more and improved birth-control instructions have improved information they have been less than successful in their impact on the burgeoning incidence of abortions and unintended births among young single Canadian women (Brandt et al., 1978; Dembo and Lundell, 1979; Freeman et al., 1980; Hansson et al., 1979; Klerman, 1980; Koadlow, 1978; Ryan and Sweeney, 1980; Scales, 1978). Statistics on repeat abortions among Canadian women provide strong testimony for this dilemma posed by the complex nature of contraceptive behaviour. There were, for instance, 17.9 per cent of the women in the 1976 national patient survey who had at least one abortion (Committee on the Operation of the Abortion Law, 1977). This was higher than the national abortion rate of 15.1 per cent of live births in that year. Over the four years between 1975 and 1978 the per cent of cases with at least one previous induced abortion increased by more than 53 per cent (Statistics Canada, 1978, p. 27). Recognizing the powerful influence of psychological and interpersonal factors on effective contraception, Rainwater (1960) commented, ". . . it becomes clear that instruction in techniques by physicians and clinics is not enough — the problem involves a host of social and psychological considerations." Kar (1971) reviewed the literature on the dynamics involved in the use of contraception and concluded:

> Literature suggests that probably the most significant determinants of the acceptance of contraception is neither innovation of modern birth control methods nor the proselytizing efforts by various family planning

organizations, but the initiative of individuals to control their own fertility" (p. 235).

There is, however, a trend towards an overall increase of contraceptive use among young people. Zelnik and Kantner (1977) in the U.S. National Survey found that during the period between 1971 and 1975, there were 53 per cent more unmarried teenagers among whites who used contraceptives during every sex act. There are no Canadian national data available but it seems likely that the receptivity of Canadian youth to contraception, like their counterparts in the U.S., has also increased in recent years. But the critical question in preventing undesired pregnancy is the consistency in contraceptive use. Studies show that the contraceptive profile among all ages remains highly sporadic for the majority of sexually active adolescents (Kantner and Zelnik, 1973; Zelnik and Kantner, 1977). Inconsistent and erratic contraceptive patterns are also observed among a large majority of Canadian young women who continue to depend on chance for pregnancy prevention (Garrett, 1974; Herold and Goodwin, 1980; Krishnamoni and Jain, 1979; Sachdev, forthcoming; Sullivan and Watt, 1975).

The only sure way to turn the rising tide of unwanted/unplanned conceptions is abstinence, an idea which is entirely far-fetched and impractical given today's liberal sexual attitudes among both women and men. On the contrary, the trends in the proportion of adolescents losing virginity have increased very sharply in the last decade both in Canada and the U.S. The only nation-wide data on the sexual behaviour of young Canadians were made available by the Committee on the Operation of the Abortion Law (1977). It reported that 40 per cent of the single males between 15 to 17 years had experienced coitus during 1976, the year of the survey and this proportion increased to 63.8 per cent for those 18 to 23 years. The proportion of single women between 15 to 23 years who had had coitus during the year of the survey was 36.1 per cent (pp. 329–31). The level of sexual activity reported in some of the regional Canadian surveys is higher than in the Committee Survey. For instance, Mann (1970) found that 37 per cent of all female university students at York University in Ontario were sexually active. Hobart (1972) studied the sexual attitudes and behaviour of randomly-selected students from anglophone and francophone Canadian universities and trade schools and found that 44 per cent of anglophone women were sexually experienced. Pool and Pool (1978) found in the Carleton University community sample of female students for the 1974/75 academic year that 62 per cent of the single students had had sexual experience. Another Ontario study of 486 single females aged 13 to 20 who were attending birth-control centres between 1976 and 1977 found that 50 per cent of them were sexually experienced (Herold and Goodwin, 1980). In a sample of 509 undergraduate students, 17 to 23 years at a Montreal University in 1973 Munz et al. (1976) found that 40.7 per cent of the females and 57.7 per cent of the males were non-virgins.

The trends in the rates of premarital intercourse in the U.S. parallel those in Canada. Zelnik and Kantner (1977), in their national survey of 15 to 19-year-old single females, found an increase of 43.9 per cent from 1971 to 1976 in unmarried white women who experienced coitus. Chilman (1978) reviewed several regional and national surveys on the sexual experience of unmarried women in the United States and concluded, "that between about 1967 and 1974, premarital intercourse rates for white females rose by about 300 per cent. . ." (p. 113).

Not only are adolescents engaging in sexual relations in higher proportion than ever but their initiation of sexual experiences is occurring at an earlier age. For instance, in the Carleton University Community survey 58 per cent of the females had experienced coitus between 15 and 17 years of age (Pool and Pool, 1978). In the Herold and Goodwin study, referred to above, 75 per cent of their sample had their first exposure to coitus at age 15 (Herold and Goodwin, 1980). In the U.S. too, by 1973 sexual experience was occurring at younger ages than in the past, with over one-fourth of white males and females experiencing their first coitus by age 15 or 16 (Finkel and Finkel, 1975; Jessor and Jessor, 1975; Kantner and Zelnik, 1972; Sorensen, 1973; Vener and Stewart, 1974; Vener et al., 1972).

Studies have shown that a large majority of these women — from 30 to 90 per cent — experience their initial coital event in the absence of contraception. The initial acts are unplanned, which precludes the possibility of making deliberate and rational planning for contraception (Anderson et al., 1978; Apkom et al., 1976; Bauman and Wilson, 1974; Bauman, 1971; Furstenberg, 1971; Herold and Goodwin, 1980; Miller, 1976a; Needle, 1975; Pool and Pool, 1978; Reichelt and Werley, 1975; Reiss, 1975; Settledge et al., 1973; Thompson, 1978; U.S. Dept. of HEW, 1976; Zelnik and Kantner, 1978). Chilman (1978) concluded on the basis of her extensive review of major U.S. studies that "only about 50 per cent of sexually active females studied between 1968 and 1974 said they used any form of contraceptive at their first intercourse" (p. 155). The analysis of the 1976 data from the National Survey of young women in the U.S. by Zabin et al. (1979) revealed that one-half of all first premarital teenage pregnancies occurred in the first six months of sexual experience. Thus, we see that the Canadian adolescent population at risk of undesired pregnancy remains substantially large.

The demographic profile of young Canadian women provides added reason for concern about their exposure to unintended pregnancies. As noted earlier, the overall fertility rate among Canadian women has been steadily declining since 1957. But this trend is not matched by a similar downward trend in the birth rate among single people in the population. For instance, the birth rate among the adolescent population between 15 and 24 years of age has increased in numbers and proportion from 16.2 per cent in 1961 to 21.6 per cent in 1976 of the total population. This represents an annual growth rate of more than 5 per cent, which is far above the annual growth rate of only 1.4 per cent for the population as a whole (Statistics Canada, 1979). And this age group is composed exclusively of single, never-married people. For instance, 78.9 per cent of young Canadians of both sexes (female 72 per cent), between 15 and 24 years of age were never-marrieds in 1978 (Statistics Canada, 1979b). Thus, even if the rate of sexual activity among young people remains unchanged, there will be a greater number reporting sexual relationships and thus be at risk of pregnancy.

To further confound the problem, the prospects of discovering an "ideal" contraceptive continues to elude scientists (Atkinson et al., 1980; Brenditt, 1980), and as long as the act of contraception involves individual motivation and efforts the likelihood of unwanted pregnancies occurring will remain high. As Sandberg and Jacob (1971) observe, even with the availability of an "ideal" contraceptive, "it is probably for reasons of psychology rather than technology that social systems which require or allow volitional and individually initiated contraceptive use as the sole method of population control will fail to accomplish that goal" (p. 227). Similar pessimism about the ability of currently available methods of contraception to prevent unwanted pregnancies among married couples was voiced by Westoff in his National Fertility Study (NFS) when he said, "the 1970 NFS showed that one-third of all couples using contraception to prevent an unwanted pregnancy fail over a five-year period; 14 per cent fail in one year's time, but 26 per cent fail in a year if their purpose is to postpone a wanted pregnancy" (Westoff, 1975: 114). In the U.S., Tietze recognizes the technological limitations of the modern methods of contraception and foresees a number of repeat abortions even among contraceptively highly motivated women. He predicts that between 18 to 75 per cent of contracepting women will experience repeat abortions sometime within ten years following their initial encounter, depending upon their age and the methods of contraception (Tietze, 1974, 1979).

There is a further possibility that more and more women who are users of contraceptive devices, will experience unwanted pregnancies. Widely publicized risks for the pill and IUD have led many women to reject these methods and to switch to traditional less effective methods of contraception. Undoubtedly, the coitus-related methods are not conducive to their acceptance and consistent long term use.

From the above it seems very likely that the coming years will witness an upward trend in the incidence of unwanted, unintended/unplanned pregnancies among Canadian women. Many of these women will depend on abortion — legal or illegal, controversial or not, ignominious or not — as a solution to their problem pregnancy, especially when adoption and a "quickie marriage" do not appear as viable alternatives for young women (Bluford and Peters, 1973; Bracken et al., 1978; Kerenyi et al., 1973; Sachdev, forthcoming; Smith, 1973).

References

Abernethy, Virginia. "The Abortion Constellation." *Archives of General Psychiatry* 29(1973):120–26.

Abernethy, Virginia. "Illegitimate Conception Among Teenagers." *American Journal of Public Health* 64(1974):662–65.

Abernethy, Virginia and Abernethy G. "Risk for Unwanted Pregnancy Among Mentally Ill Adolescent Girls." *American Journal of Orthopsychiatry* 44(1974):442–50.

Addy, C. *American and Canadian Studies of Adolescent Sexual Attitudes and Behavior: A Review of Selected Research Reports.* Paper presented at Symposium on Adolescent Sexuality, Regina, Saskatchewan, May 9, 1977.

Addy, Cenovia. "Trends in Family Planning." An address to the University of Saskatchewan, School of Social Work, November 21, 1973.

Akpom, C. Amechi, Kathy L. Akpom, and Marianne Davis. "Prior Sexual Behavior of Teenagers Attending Rap Sessions for the First Time." *Family Planning Perspective* 8(1976):203–206.

Anderson, P., K. McPherson, N. Beeching, J. Weinberg, and M. Vessey. "Sexual Behavior and Contraceptive Practice of Undergraduates at Oxford University." *Journal of Biosocial Science* 10(1978):277–86.

Angrist, S. "Communication About Birth Control: An Explanatory Study of Freshman Girls' Information and Attitudes." *Journal of Marriage and the Family* 28(1966):284–86.

Arnold, Robert, Cyril Greenland, and Marylen Wharf. *Family Planning in Hamilton:* Hamilton Planned Parenthood Society, 1974.

Atkinson, Linda S. "Prospects for Improved Contraception." *Family Planning Perspectives* 12(1980):173–92.

Bardwick, Judith M. "Psychodynamics of Contraception with Particular Reference to Rhythm." In *Proceedings of a Research Conference on Natural Family Planning*, edited by William A. Uricchio. Washington D.C.: The Human Life Foundation, 1973.

Bauman, Karl E. "Selected Aspects of the Contraceptive Practices of Unmarried University Students." *Medical Aspects of Human Sexuality* (August 1971):76–89.

Bauman, Karl E. and Richard Udry. "Powerlessness and Regularity of Contraction in an Urban Negro Male Sample: A Research Note." *Journal of Marriage and the Family* (February 1972):112–14.

Bauman, Karl E., and Robert R. Wilson. "Contraceptive Practices of White Unmarried University Students: The Significance of Four Years at One University." *American Journal of Obstetrics and Gynecology* 118(1974):190–204.

Benditt, John M. "Current Contraceptive Research." *Family Planning Perspectives* 12(1980):149–55.

Benedek, T. *Parenthood: Its Psychology and Psychopathology.* Boston: Little, Brown and Co., 1970.

Bishop, Mary F. "Voluntarism in Family Planning in Canada." In *Family Planning in Canada: A Source Book*, edited by Benjamin Schlesinger. Toronto: University of Toronto Press.

Bluford, Robert, and Robert E. Peters. *The Unwanted Pregnancy.* New York: Harper and Row, 1973.

Bogue, Donald. "The Demographic Break-through: From Projection to Control." *Population Index* 30(1964):449–54.

Bouma, Gary D., and Wilma J. Bouma. *Fertility Control: Canada's Lively Problem*. Don Mills: Longman Canada Limited, 1975.

Bracken, Michael B., L.V. Klerman, and M. Bracken. "Abortion, Adoption, or Motherhood: An Empirical Study of Decision-making During Pregnancy." *American Journal of Obstetrics and Gynecology* 130(1978):251–62.

Bracken, Michael B. "A Causal Model of Psychosomatic Reactions to Vacuum Aspiration." *Social Psychiatry* 13(1978):135–45.

Brandt, Carol L., Francis J. Kane, and Charles A. Moan. "Pregnant Adolescents: Some Psychosocial Factors." *Psychosomatics* 19(12)(1978):790–93.

Bulletin. *Planned Parenthood Federation of Canada*. Winter, 1980.

Cahn, Jerry. *'The Influence of Others on Teenagers' Use of Birth Control*. Unpublished doctoral dissertation. City University of New York, 1978.

Canadian Facts. *An Assessment of Mass Media Campaign for Family Planning*. Vol. 1–3, Toronto: Canadian Facts Co. Ltd., 1973.

Chilman, Catherine S. *Adolescent Sexuality in a Changing American Society: Social and Psychological Perspectives*. Washington, D.C.: U.S. Govt. Printing Office, 1978.

Clothier, Florence. "Psychological Implications of Unmarried Parenthood." *American Journal of Orthopsychiatry* 13(1943):531–49.

Cobliner, Godfrey W., Harold Schulman, and Seymour L. Romney. The Termination of Adolescent Out-of-Wedlock Pregnancies and the Prospects for Their Primary Prevention." *American Journal of Obstetrics and Gynecology* 115(1973):432–44.

Coe, Barbara B. and Myrtle Blum. "The Out-of-Wedlock Pregnancy: Six Years's Experience with a University Population." *Obstetrics and Gynecology* 40(1972):807–12.

Cole, J.B., F.C.L. Beighton, and Iver H. Jones. "Contraceptive Practice and Unplanned Pregnancy among Single University Students." *British Medical Journal* 4(1975):217–19.

Committee on the Operation of the Abortion Law. *Report of the Committee on the Operation of the Abortion Law*. Ottawa: Minister of Supply and Services, 1977.

Cvetkovich, George, Barbara Grote, James Lieberman, and Warren Miller. "Sex Role Development and Teenage Fertility-related Behavior." *Adolescence* 13(50)(1978):231–36.

Dembo, Myron H., and Beverly Lundell. "Factors Affecting Adolescent Contraceptive Practices: Implications for Sex Education." *Adolescence* 15(56)(1979):657–64.

Elahi, Virginia K. *A Family Planning Survey of Halifax*. Halifax: Dalhousie University, Department of Preventive Medicine, 1973.

Family Planning Association of Newfoundland and Labrador. *Attitudes Toward*

and Utilization of Family Planning Services in the City of St. John's.
Mimeographed, July, 1975.

Finkel, Madelon, and David Finkel. "Male Adolescent Contraceptive Utilization." *Adolescence* 13(51)(1978):443–51.

Fisher, William A. *Affective, Attitudinal, and Normative Determinants of Contraceptive Behavior Among University Men.* Unpublished doctoral dissertation, Purdue University, 1978.

Ford, Charles V., Pietro Castelnuovo-Tedesco, and Kahilila D. Long. "Abortion: Is it a Therapeutic Procedure in Psychiatry?" *Journal of American Medical Association* 218(1971):1173–78.

Fox, Greer. "Sex Role Attitudes as Predictors of Contraceptive Use." Paper presented at the Annual Meeting of the National Council on Family Relations, Salt Lake City, Utah, August 20–23, 1975.

Freeman, Ellen W. "Abortion: Subjective Attitudes and Feelings." *Family Planning Perspectives* 10(1978):150–55.

Freeman, Ellen W. "Influence of Personality Attributes on Abortion Experiences." *American Journal of Orthopsychiatry* 47(1977):503–13.

Freeman, Ellen W., and Karl Rickels. "Adolescent Contraceptive Use: Current Status of Practice and Research." *Obstetrics and Gynecology* 53(1979):388–94.

Freeman, Ellen W., Karl Rickels, George R. Huggins, Emily H. Mudd, Celso-Ramon Garcia, Hellen O. Dickens. "Adolescent Contraceptive Use: Comparisons of Male and Female Attitudes and Information." *American Journal of Public Health* 70(1980):790–97.

Furstenberg, Frank F. "Birth Control Experiences among Adolescents: The Process of Unplanned Parenthood." *Social Problems* 19(1971):192–203.

Furstenberg, Frank F. *Unplanned Parenthood: The Social Consequences of Teenage Childbearing.* New York: The Free Press, 1976.

Garrett, Nancy. "Choosing Contraception According to Need," in *Family Planning in Canada: A Source Book*, edited by Benjamin Schlesinger. Toronto: University of Toronto Press, 1974.

Glass, J.C. "Premarital Sexual Standards Among Church Youth Leaders: An Exploratory Study." *Journal for the Scientific Study of Religion* 11(1972):361–67.

Gottschalk, Louis A., J.L. Titchener, H.N. Piker, and S.S. Stewart. "Psychological Factors Associated with Pregnancy in Adolescent Girls: A Preliminary Report." *Journal of Nervous Mental Disease* 138(1964):524–34.

Gougues, Jules H. "Sexualité et Planification des Naissances en Milieu Défavorise Urbain Québécois." Mimeographed Report, 1974.

Grauer, H. "A Study of Contraception as Related to Unwanted Pregnancy." *Canadian Medical Association Journal* 107(1975):739–41.

Greenglass, Esther. "Attitudes Toward Abortion." In *Family Planning in*

Canada: A Source Book, edited by Benjamin Schlesinger. Toronto: University of Toronto Press, 1974.

Grindstaff, Carl F., and Edward G. Ebanks. "Vasectomy as a Birth Control Method." In *Population Issues in Canada*, edited by G. Grindstaff et al. Toronto: Holt, Rinehart and Winston, 1971.

Guyatt, Doris. "Family Planning and the Adolescent Girl." In *Family Planning in Canada: A Source Book*, edited by Benjamin Schlesinger. Toronto: University of Toronto Press, 1974.

Hansson, R.O., W.H. Jones, and Chernovetz, M.E. "Contraceptive Knowledge: Antecedents and Implications." *The Family Coordinator* 28(1979):29–34.

Henry, Sarah. "Unwanted Teenage Pregnancy: Its Causes and Remedies. *Canadian Medical Association Journal* 121(1979):489–90.

Hepworth, Philip H. *Family Planning and Abortion Services and Family Life Education Programs*. Vol. 5. (Ottawa: The Canadian Council on Social Development, 1975.

Herold, Edward S., and Marilyn S. Goodwin. "A Comparison of Younger and Older Adolescent Females Attending Birth Control Clinics." *Canadian Family Physician* 26(1980):687–94.

Hill, Reuben J. Stycos, Mayone Black, and W. Kurt. *The Family and Population Control: A Puerto Rican Experiment In Social Change*. Chapel Hill: University of North Carolina Press, 1959.

Hobart, Charles W. "Sexual Permissiveness in Young English and French Canadians." *Journal of Marriage and the Family*, (May 1972):292–303.

Hunter, Marlene E. "Applications for Abortion at a Community Hospital." *Canadian Medical Association Journal* 111(1974):1088–1092.

Illsley, R., and M.H. Hall. "Psychosocial Aspects of Abortion: A Review of the Issues and Needed Research." *Bull. WHO* 53(1976):83–90.

Jaccard, James J., and Andrew R. Davidson. "The Relation of Psychological, Social, and Economic Variables to Fertility-Related Decisions." *Demography* 13(1976):329–38.

Jaffee, Frederick and Steven Polgar. "Family Planning and Public Policy: Is the 'Culture of Poverty' the New Cop-out?" *Journal of Marriage and the Family* 30(1968):228–35.

Jessor, Shirely and Richard Jessor. "Transition from Virginity to Nonvirginity among Youth: A Social-psychological Study Over Time." *Developmental Psychology* 11(1975):473–84.

Joe, Victor C., R.N. Jones, A.S. Noel, and B. Roberts. "Birth Control Practices and Conservatism." *Journal of Personality Assessment* 43(1979):536–40.

Kaats, G.R., and K.E. Davis, "The Dynamics of Sexual Behavior of College Students." *Journal of Marriage and Family* 32(1970):390–99.

Kane, Francis J., Peter A. Lachenbruch, Morris A. Lipton, and D. Baram.

"Motivational Factors in Abortion Patients." *American Journal of Psychiatry* 130(1973):290–93.

Kane, Francis J., and Peter A. Lachenbruch. "Adolescent Pregnancy: A Study of Aborters and Non-aborters." *American Journal of Orthopsychiatry* 43(1973):796–803.

Kane, Francis J., C.A. Moan, and B. Bolling. "Motivating Factors in Pregnant Adolescents." *Diseases of Nervous System* 35(1974):131–34.

Kantner, John F. and Melvin Zelnik. "Sexual Experiences of Young Unmarried Women in the U.S." *Family Planning Perspective* 4(4)(1972):9–17.

Kantner, John F. and Melvin Zelnik. "Contraception and Pregnancy: Experience of Young Unmarried Women in the United States." *Family Planning Perspectives* 5(1973):21–35.

Kantner, John and Melvin Zelnik. "Sexuality, Contraception and Pregnancy Among Young Unwed Females in the United States." In *Demographic and Social Aspects of Population Growth*, edited by C.F. Westoff and R. Parke Jr. Washington, D.C.: Commission Research Reports, Vol. 1, 1973.

Kar, S.B. "Individual Aspirations Related to Early and Late Acceptance of Contraception." *The Journal of Social Psychology*, 83(1971):235–45.

Kasanin J., and Sieglinde Handshin. "Psychodynamic Factors in Illegitimacy." *American Journal of Orthopsychiatry* 41(1941):66–84.

Kazanjian, Arminee. "ACCRA: A Review of the First Two Years Research." Mimeographed, 1973.

Kerenyi, Thomas, E. Glascock, and M. Horowitz. "Reasons for Delayed Abortion: Results of Four Hundred Interviews." *American Journal of Obstetrics and Gynecology* 117(1973):299–311.

Kimball, Chase P. "Some Observations Regarding Unwanted Pregnancies and Therapeutic Abortions." *Obstetrics and Gynecology* 35(1970):293–96.

Kirkendall, Lester A. *Premarital Intercourse and Interpersonal Relationships*. New York: Julian Press, Inc., 1961.

Klerman, Lorraine V. "Adolescent Pregnancy: A New Look at a Continuing Problem." *American Journal of Public Health*, 70(1980):776–78.

Koadlow, Elsie. "Psychological Aspects." *Australian Family Physician* 7(1978):16–20.

Kravitz, Henry, Bernard Trossman, and B.R. Feldman. "Unwed Mothers: Practical and Theoretical Considerations." *Canadian Psychiatric Association*, 11(1966):456–63.

Krishnamoni, Devaki and S.C. Jain, "Termination of Pregnancy — The Last Resort." Paper Read at Annual Meeting of Canadian Psychiatric Association, Vancouver, B.C. September, 1979.

Leach J. "The Repeat Abortion Patient." *Family Planning Perspectives* 9(1977):37–42.

Lehfeldt, Hans. "Psychological Factors." In *Manual of Family Planning and Contraceptive Practice*, 2nd ed. edited by Mary S. Calderone. Baltimore: The Williams and Wilkins Co., 1970.

Lipper, Irene, H. Cvejic, B. Peter, and R.A. Kinch. "Abortion and the Pregnant

Teenagers." *Canadian Medical Association Journal* 109(1973):852–56.

Luker, Kristin. *Taking Chances: The Decision Not to Contracept.* Berkley: University of California Press, 1975.

Lundy, James R. "Some Personality Correlates of Contraceptive Use among Unmarried Female College Students." *The Journal of Psychology* 80(1972):9–14.

Lux, Andre. Personal communication, 1975.

MacDonald A. "Internal/External Locus of Control and the Practice of Birth Control." *Psychology Report* 27(1970):206–10.

Mann, W.E. "Sex at York University." In *The Underside of Toronto*, edited by W.E. Mann. Toronto: McClelland and Stewart, 1970.

Meikle, Stewart. "A Preliminary Analysis of Data Derived from the Calgary Birth Control Clinic." In *Family Planning and Abortion Services and Family Life Education Programs*, Vol. 5, edited by Philip H. Hepwarth. Ottawa: The Canadian Council on Social Development, 1975.

Miller, Warren B. "Sexual and Contraceptive Behavior in Young Unmarried Women." *Health Care for Women* 3(1976a):427–53.

Miller, Warren B. "Sexual and Contraceptive Behavior in Young Unmarried Women." *Primary Care*, 3(1970):427–53.

Miller, Warren B. "Some Psychological Factors Predictive of Undergraduates' Sexual and Contraceptive Behavior." Paper presented at the 84th Annual Convention of the American Association, Washington, D.C., September, 1977.

Monsour, Karen and Barbara Stewart. "Abortion and Sexual Behavior in College Women." *American Journal of Orthopsychiatry*, 43(1973):804–14.

Moore, K.A., and S.B. Caldwell. *Out-of-Wedlock Pregnancy and Child-bearing.* Washington, D.C.: The Urban Institute, 1976.

Mudd, Emily H., H.O. Dickens, C. Garcia, K. Rickel, E. Freeman, G. Hugging, and J. Logan. "Adolescent Health Services and Contraceptive Use." *American Journal of Orthopsychiatry* 48:495–504.

Munz, Diane, S. Carson, B. Brock, L. Bell, I. Kleinman, M. Robert, and J. Simon. "Contraceptive Knowledge and Practice among Undergraduates at a Canadian University." *American Journal of Obstetrics and Gynecology* 124(1976):499–503.

Nadelson, Carol. "Abortion Counselling: Focus on Adolescent Pregnancy." *Pediatrics* 54(1974):765–69.

Nadelson, Carol C., I. Malkah T. Notman, and Jean W. Gillon, "Sexual Knowledge and Attitudes of Adolescents: Relationship to Contraceptive Use." *Obstetrics and Gynecology* 55(1980):340–45.

Needle, Richard H. "The Relationship between First Sexual Intercourse and Ways of Handling Contraception among College Students." *Journal of American College Health Association* 24(1975):106–111.

Notman, Malkak T. "Teenage Pregnancy: The Non-use of Contraception." *Psychiatric Opinion* 12(1975):23–27.

Osborn, R.W. Private communication from Dr. R.W. Osborn, Department of

Preventive Medicine, University of Toronto, dated August 13, 1975.

Pannor, Reuben. *The Unwed Father — New Approach to Helping Unmarried Young Parents*. New York: Springer Publishing Company, 1971.

Perez-Reyes, Maria G., and Ruth Falk. "Follow-up after Therapeutic Abortion in Early Adolescence." *Archives of General Psychiatry* 28(1973):20–26.

Pohlman, Edward. *The Psychology of Birth Planning*. Cambridge: Mass: Schenkman Publishing Co., 1968.

Polak, O., and A.S. Friedman. *Family Dynamics and Female Sexual Delinquency*. Palo Alto: Science Behavior, 1969.

Pool, Janet E. "Female Reproduction Behavior, Part 1." Department of Epidemiology and Community Medicine, University of Ottawa, February, 1975.

Pool, Janet S., and Ian D. Pool. *Contraception and Health Care Among Young Canadian Women*. Ottawa: Carleton University, Department of Sociology, 1978.

Rader Gordon E., D.L. Bekker, L. Brown, and C. Richardt. "Psychological Correlates of Unwanted Pregnancy." *Journal of Abnormal Psychology*, 87(1978):373–76.

Rains, Prudence M. *Becoming an Unwed Mother*. Chicago: Aldine Atherton, 1971.

Rainwater, Lee. *And the Poor Get Children*. Chicago: Quandrangle Books, 1960.

Regina Family Planning Clinic Study. Mimeographed, 1973.

Reichelt, Paul and H. Werley. "Contraception, Abortion and Venereal Disease: Teenagers' Knowledge and the Effect of Education." *Family Planning Perspective* 7(1975):83–88.

Reiss, Ira, Albert Banwart, and Harry Foreman. "Premarital Contraceptive Usage: A Study and Some Theoretical Explorations." *Journal of Marriage and the Family* (August 1975):619–30.

Roberts, Robert W. *The Unwed Mother*. New York: Harper and Row, 1966.

Ryan, George M. and Patrick J. Sweeny. "Attitudes of Adolescents Toward Pregnancy and Contraception." *American Journal of Obstetrics and Gynecology* 137(1980):358–66.

Sachdev, Paul. *Abortion and After: The Unmarried Woman's Personal and Emotional Experience*. Toronto: Butterworths, forthcoming.

Sandberg, Eugene C., Ralph I. Jacobs, "Psychology of Misuse and Rejection of Contraception." *American Journal of Obstetrics and Gynecology* 110(1971):227–42.

Sarrel, Philip M. "Teenage Pregnancy." *Pediatric Clinics of North America* 16(1969):347–52.

Scales, P. "How We Guarantee the Ineffectiveness of Sex Education." *SIECUS Report* 5(1978):1–16.

Schewenger C. "The Need for Family Planning and Population Control in

Canada," in *Family Planning in Canada*, edited by Benjamin Schlesinger. Toronto: University of Toronto Press, 1974.

Scott, K.E., and Stone, S.H. "The Unwanted Pregnancy: Inevitable, Burdensome, the Cause of Overpopulation." *Annals of Royal College of Physicians and Surgeon, Canada* 6(1973):5–8.

Settledge, D., S. Baroff, and D. Cooper, "Sexual Experience of Young Teenage Girls Seeking Contraceptive Assistance for the First Time." *Family Planning Perspectives* 8(1973):233.

Shah, F., M. Zelnik, and J. Kantner. "Unprotected Intercourse among Unwed Teenagers." *Family Planning Perspectives* 7(1975):39–44.

Smith, Elizabeth M. "A Follow-up Study of Women Who Request Abortion." *American Journal of Orthopsychiatry* 43(1973):574–85.

Smith, Elizabeth Mary. "Psycho-social Correlates of Regular Contraceptive Use in Young Unmarried Women." Unpublished doctoral dissertation, Washington University, 1978.

Sorensen, Robert C. *Adolescent Sexuality in Contemporary America*. New York: World Publishing, 1973.

Spanier, G.B. "Perceived Sex Knowledge, Exposure to Eroticism, and Premarital-Sexual Behavior: The Impact of Dating." *Sociological Quarterly* 17(1976):247–61.

Statistics Canada. *Therapeutic Abortions*. Catalogue 82–211, 1978.

Statistics Canada. *Canada's Population: Demographic Perspectives*, Catalogue 98–802E, September, 1979.

Statistics Canada. *Estimates of Population by Marital Status, Age and Sex: Canada and Provinces*. Catalogue 91–203, June 1, 1977 and 1978.

Steinlauf, Barbara. "Problem-solving Skills, Locus of Control, and the Contraceptive Effectiveness of Young Women." *Child Development* 50(1979):268–71.

Sullivan, Gail and Susan Watt. "Legalized Abortion: Myth and Misconception." *The Social Worker* 43(1975):78–86.

Thomas, William I. *The Unadjusted Girl*. New York: Harper and Row, 1967.

Thompson, Linda. "Influence of Parents, Peers, and Partners on the Contraceptive Use of College Men and Women." *Journal of Marriage and the Family* (August 1978):481–92.

Tietze, Christopher. "Repeat Abortions — Why More"? *Family Planning Perspectives* 10(1978):286–88.

Tietze, Christopher. "Repat Abortions — Why More"? *Family Planning Perspectives* 10(1978):286–88.

Treffers, P. "Family Size, Contraception, and Birth Rate before and after the Introduction of a New Method of Family Planning." *Journal of Marriage and the Family* 30(1968):338–45.

United Community Services of the Greater Vancouver Area. *Babies By Choice, Not By Chance*. A Demonstration Project. Vol. 1, 1972.

U.S. Department of Health, Education and Welfare. "Improving Family Planning Services for Teenagers." Office of Assistant Secretary for Planning and Evaluation / Health, 1976.

17

Future Directions for Abortion Morality and Policy

Hyman Rodman

Introduction

There are pervasive moral ambiguities and fundamental moral conflicts about abortion that make it difficult to adopt a clear and satisfactory abortion policy. The laws on abortion in many countries throughout the world represent an attempt at compromise between opposing moral viewpoints, but the compromises do not please the partisans on either side of the abortion fence. The controversy therefore continues in the media, in the legislatures, in the courts, and sometimes in the streets.

Partisans feel so strongly about their moral positions that debate is seldom possible. Research and clinical findings are often shaped to conform to preconceived beliefs. One psychiatrist tells us that guilt never accompanies abortion and another that it always does (Sarvis and Rodman, 1974:106). Reading Watters (1976), it is absolutely clear that a pro-choice position is the only moral position to take — otherwise we are sanctioning compulsory pregnancy. But reading the selections in Kremer and Synan (1974) it is equally clear that a pro-life position is the only moral position to take — otherwise we are sanctioning the killing of human life. It is widely acknowledged that the dark, choppy waters of abortion morality make for difficult sailing. But I believe that in recent years a glimmer of light has appeared and that the future of abortion morality and policy will lead us to calmer waters.

Underlying Moral Differences

Each side in the abortion controversy has adopted a term that aptly summarizes its moral identity and the irresolvable essence of the moral controversy. One side is pro-choice. They insist they are not pro-abortion. They often make it clear that they are against abortion and would like to reduce the number of abortions through improved sex education and family-planning programs. But since they recognize that there will still be unwanted pregnancies, they accept abortion as a last resort, and they deplore any attempt to eliminate that choice from a pregnant women.

The other side is pro-life. They recognize the difficulty of the woman with an unwanted pregnancy. Although they are ambivalent in their support of improved sex education and family-planning programs, they want to prevent unwanted pregnancies or to help women with unwanted pregnancies. But they are not prepared to accept abortion because they believe that it is the killing of human life. It is only when the pregnant woman's life is endangered that they are willing to accept abortion.

While the above attempt to summarize opposing positions is over-simplified, it is a reasonable account of the principal arguments made by each side. The pro-choice groups understandably pay less attention to the technology of the abortion procedure, and get upset at enlarged pictures of human fetuses that pro-lifers sometimes show. And the pro-life groups understandably pay less attention to the trials and tribulations of women with unwanted pregnancies, and get upset at pictures of women who have died at the hands of illegal abortionists.

Until recently, restrictive abortion laws forced many women into illegal abortion and its attendant dangers. As a result, there were dramatic appeals to change the laws, including exaggerated estimates of the number of illegal abortions and deaths resulting from them. This led to revised laws that made abortion legal, at least under some conditions.

Currently, the more permissive abortion laws make possible a growing number of abortions and lead to occasional cases of an aborted fetus that lives for a while and that may have been viable (Tunkel, 1979). As a result, there are now dramatic appeals to restrict abortions, including exaggerated accounts of the human characteristics of the embryo and fetus.

The Canadian abortion law, revised in 1969, is a compromise between opposing moral viewpoints. A therapeutic abortion committee must certify in writing "that in its opinion the continuation of the pregnancy of such female person would or would be likely to endanger her life or health. . . ." There are concurrent pressures for greater liberalization and greater restriction in the federal law. These pressures are also felt at the local level, and many hospitals have not established therapeutic abortion committees and do not perform any abortions. Even in hospitals that have therapeutic abortion committees, there are vast differences in how they interpret the law. Some approve virtually all requests for abortion, and some approve very few. Such variation creates inequities in access to abortion, which is itself a moral issue that is getting attention in Canada (Badgley Report, 1977).

Law and Private Morality

The question about whether the fetus is a human being is the primary moral question, because a positive answer makes other moral issues moot.* And some argue that other moral issues are moot even if our answer to the primary question is "maybe," because we must resolve the doubt in favour of preserving human life.

Other moral issues, however, do enter the discussion. One issue, stemming from the women's liberation movement and from recent United States Supreme Court interpretations of the U.S. Constitution, has to do with a woman's right to privacy — including her right to control her own body and to make her decisions about childbearing free from state coercion. As the U.S. Supreme Court put it, "This right of privacy, whether it be founded in the Fourteenth Amendment's concept of personal liberty and restrictions upon state action, as we feel it is, or, as the District Court determined, in the Ninth Amendment's reservation of rights to the people, is broad enough to encompass a woman's decision whether or not to terminate her pregnancy" (*Roe* v. *Wade*, 1973:37–38).

While the privacy argument is handled somewhat differently in a Canadian context, the issue of the privacy of certain moral decisions, free of civil law, is basically the same argument. The Wolfenden report of 1957, which dealt with homosexuality in Britain, strongly urged the separation of law and private morality: "There must remain a realm of private morality and immorality which is . . . not the law's business" (Wolfenden Report, 1957). This argument, of ancient vintage, produced major changes in British law in 1967, including a liberalization of the abortion law. The argument was also influential in bringing about passage of the revised Canadian abortion law in 1969. Although the percentage of Roman Catholics in Canada is much higher than in the United States, the voice of the Catholic hierarchy in Canada has been muted, and has paid somewhat more attention to the idea of the separation of law and private morality (de Valk, 1974).

If we could clearly distinguish universal values from group-specific values, or public morality from private morality, we might have a route toward a resolution of the abortion controversy. Thus, the 1957 Wolfenden report accepted the idea that homosexuality was in the domain of private rather than public morality. Similar ideas influenced proposed legal changes in Canada for birth control and divorce, and the Roman Catholic Church in Canada generally accepted the distinction between moral law and civil law (de Valk, 1974:29–32). There has been a general movement in the Western world to sever the tie between traditional religious morality and the law on sexual behaviour. As a result, we commonly hear that "the state has no business in the bedrooms of the nation" (Pierre E. Trudeau, quoted in de Valk, 1974:57), and there is a growing acceptance of sexual behaviour as private morality.

---

*Many other moral and philosophical arguments have been made, including some that reject this question as the primary moral issue. For several different viewpoints from works not elsewhere cited in this paper, see Callahan (1970), Bok (1974), Cohen et al. (1974), Hare (1975), and the several articles on abortion in Humber and Almeder (1976).

When we come to abortion, however, it is much more difficult to get a moral consensus. The Roman Catholic hierarchy in Canada was not prepared to deal with abortion in the same way that it dealt with birth control and divorce. Similarly, in the United States, birth control and divorce clearly are in the realm of private morality, but there is no such moral consensus on abortion. This is obviously due to a fundamental difference. For the pro-life partisans, human life is at stake when we deal with abortion. Thus a pro-choice statement that abortion reduces maternal mortality or morbidity, or reduces the suffering of unwanted children, has a hollow sound when it strikes against the idea that each abortion represents the killing of an innocent human life. The abortion controversy therefore persists, and the separation of law and private morality does not seem to be a route that is available to resolve the controversy.

Attempted Compromises

Given the absolute position that abortion is the killing of a human being and the absolute position that a woman has a right to control her own body and her own childbearing, there can be no compromise and no debate — only opposing partisans who talk past each other. But although the moral debate is irresolvable, the legal and judicial worlds have had to prepare written decisions about abortion.

Some have suggested that the best way out of the legal and moral difficulty is to write no law regarding abortion, and to deal with it like any other medical procedure. In that way no legal justifications (such as health or eugenic indications) which might be objectionable to Roman Catholics or others are specifically acknowledged. This is, of course, the same solution as designating abortion to be in the realm of private morality, and separating private morality from the law. It would effectively create a situation in which abortion is treated in a permissive fashion, without any need for special justifications or special procedures. In consequence, this approach is not acceptable to pro-life partisans and it does not readily resolve the legal and moral difficulties.

There have been two kinds of compromises that legislatures and courts have used in deciding difficult abortion questions: (a) permitting abortion for certain reasons only and forbidding all other abortions, and (b) permitting abortions up to a certain gestation time and forbidding later abortions. We shall briefly discuss each of these compromise solutions, and indicate how they point the way towards future directions in abortion morality and policy.

Justifications for Abortion

Under this compromise, abortion is forbidden unless there are certain reasons (indications, justifications) for it. The moral principle that underlies this compromise is that the embryo and fetus have rights, but not the right to life in the same sense that a human being has. As a result, abortion is not available unless it can be justified for certain stated reasons, including at least one reason in addition to the preservation of the pregnant woman's life. According to British law, passed in 1967, the justifications for abortion include danger to the woman's life or health, pregnancy due to criminal assault, a threat of fetal deformity, and socio-economic reasons. According to proposals made by the American Law Institute (1962:189–190), justifications include, danger to the woman's physical or mental health, the threat of severe fetal deformity, and pregnancy due to rape, incest, or other felonious intercourse. Several states in the United States adopted these legal justifications between 1967 and 1970. The law in Canada, passed in 1969, is an excellent example of the "justifications" compromise. It bans abortions unless justified on the grounds of protecting the woman's life or health. There is no time limit in the gestation period after which abortion is forbidden, and thus the Canadian law is a pure case of a "justifications" approach.

Gestation Time

Another compromise is to permit abortion up to a particular time in the gestation process and to forbid abortion after that time. The moral principle that underlies this compromise is that the embryo and fetus represent developing human life. Up to a certain point the embryo or fetus is judged not to be sufficiently developed to warrant protection, and no justification for abortion is needed. Beyond that point, however, the embryo or fetus is judged to have developed sufficiently to be worthy of protection, and abortions are not permitted after that time (except to save the pregnant woman's life).

Alphonse de Valk (1974:102) points out that the United Church of Canada, in 1968, referred to "the accruing value of life" as the fetus develops. The United States Supreme Court referred to "potential life" (*Roe* v. *Wade*, 1973:48), and to viability as the critical point in the gestation process. But this decision, which principally takes a "gestation time" approach, also includes elements of the "justifications" approach. During the first trimester the state cannot interfere in the abortion decision in any way. During the second trimester, the state can become involved only to enact regulations that will make the abortion safer. During the final trimester states may promote potential human life by prohibiting abortions, but they may not ban abortions that are intended to preserve the life or health of the woman.

Future Directions

Although the abortion debate continues unabated, with the moral partisans as far apart as ever, there are some early signs that a resolution of the conflict will eventually be worked out. First I will predict the general shape of the resolution, and then I will point out why I think we are heading in that direction.

I predict that we are going to resolve the moral and legal controversy as a result of two simultaneous developments, one of which involves a more permissive approach to abortion and the other a more restrictive approach.

1. We are moving in a more permissive direction, and I predict that in the

future most nations will permit abortion without the need to justify it.

2. We are moving in a more restrictive direction, and I predict that in the future most nations will prohibit abortion beyond a relatively early stage in the gestation process.

Both trends will be incorporated into future social policy on abortion. Let us first look at my permissive prediction, using the Canadian situation as an example where appropriate. There are several reasons for making this prediction. First, there is the burdensome bureaucratic machinery that must be maintained under the present system to decide whether a particular case is justified. It is generally recognized that the therapeutic abortion committees in Canada are not working very well (Badgley Report, 1977). The members of therapeutic abortion committees do not see the woman whose abortion is at issue; they rely strictly upon the written record. Thus, depending upon the willingness of the woman's physician to tailor the record to the justifications permitted by law, and the willingness of the therapeutic abortion committee to interpret the law broadly, the woman may or may not be approved for an abortion. As a result of this bureaucratic procedure, there are great inequities in how the law is implemented from province to province, from locality to locality, and from hospital to hospital (Badgley Report, 1977).

The "justifications" approach in Canada, and the need for approval from a hospital committee, contribute to unconscionable delays in carrying out abortions. As the Badgley Report (1977:18–19) points out, "the major factor contributing to the delay by most women obtaining abortions in Canadian hospitals occurred after an initial consultation had been made with a physician. An average interval of eight weeks between the initial medical consultation and the performance of the abortion procedure not only extended considerably the length of gestation, but it increased the risk of associated health complications."

Even though the problems associated with therapeutic abortion committees in Canada have been known for a long time (Smith and Wineberg, 1969/1970), no change has yet been effected. But the accumulation of inefficiency, inequity, and (health-threatening) delay will, I predict, eventually bring about a change.

Another reason for predicting change stems from the extreme difficulty of making medical or psychiatric decisions to justify abortions (Sarvis and Rodman, 1974:29–46, 114–118). Physicians may therefore play the role of "a legally authorized bootlegger [who can] grant permission for otherwise prohibited acts" (Szasz, 1962:347); or, as stated by Levene and Rigney (1970:54), the physician "is able to grant dispensation from the law's restrictive consequences." But this medical role, to provide an avenue "around" the law, is not a comfortable role to play. While it provides some communities that would prefer a more permissive law with justifications for abortion, it does not serve all women equitably. It is also demeaning to patients and to physicians to go through the charade of qualifying for, and approving, an abortion. One route by which to circumvent the legal requirements to justify an abortion in Canada and to obtain committee approval is to list an abortion as "spontaneous" or as "Code 644" (a catch-all category of abortions not listed as induced or spontaneous). The Badgley Report (1977:58–64) provides illuminating information on the high and variable rates of these abortions, and in moderate and measured tones suggests they stem "from the different definitions which were used in the classification of abortions." A more strident report might suggest that they represent medical evasions of burdensome legal requirements.

Now let us look at my prediction of movement in a more restrictive direction. The major reason for making this prediction is due to the technological advances in medicine that are taking place (Dellapenna, 1979). First, these advances are making it possible to sustain a fetus outside the mother's body at earlier stages in the gestation process. Second, we will eventually have a contraceptive net, both pre-coital and post-coital, that will reduce the number of unwanted pregnancies. Some of these post-coital methods may turn out to be the abortion methods of choice in the future, regardless of whether they will be referred to in terms of abortion or contraception. Finally, advances in embryology and fetology will not only make it possible to keep the fetus alive earlier, independent of the pregnant woman, but will also provide additional information about the growth and development of the embryo and fetus that will lead to pressure for much earlier abortions.

The future directions I am predicting for abortion morality and policy are already becoming evident. In Canada, for example, despite the legal requirement to justify abortions, some therapeutic abortion committees have finessed the requirement by assuming that a refusal to honour a woman's request for abortion would be detrimental to her health. As a result, all requests for an abortion are approved. Further, some physicians and hospitals have finessed the requirement by relabelling induced abortions as "spontaneous" or "Code 644" abortions.

In both Canada and the United States there is also evidence that abortions are being restricted to earlier stages of gestation. Although the law in both countries permits third trimester abortions, they are now very rarely done. Second-trimester abortions, as a percentage of all induced abortions, are also becoming less frequent — in 1977, down to 9 per cent in the United States (Benditt, 1979) and 16 per cent in Canada (Statistics Canada, 1978). They are more frequent in Canada, the Scandinavian countries, and Britain, because the "justifications" approach causes delays in obtaining permission for an abortion, but even in these countries they are declining in frequency.

Whether through legal changes or through medical practices,* abortion policy is heading in a new direction. The technological advances, the inequities, and the bureaucratic delays will also affect the moral climate, so that abortions will eventually become more widely acceptable as long as they are carried out early. Even though legal changes may lag behind, medical practice will increasingly

---

*In some countries the threat of prosecution for performing abortions in the later stages of pregnancy has discouraged hospitals and physicians from performing such abortions (*Family Planning /Population Reporter*, 1975; Tunkel, 1979).

shift its orientation from a "justifications" to a "gestation time" approach. Virtually all abortions will eventually be carried out during the first trimester, and perhaps during the first eight weeks of gestation. It will indeed be ironic if the future brings about an eight-week gestation approach to abortion, since the present Canadian situation, on average, produces eight weeks of delay. In fifteen years the current justification system will seem archaic. We will then look back at the present Canadian legal compromise as one which may have served its purpose, but which consisted of the worst elements of the "justifications" and the "gestation time" approaches. It required cumbersome, inequitable, and unnecessary justifications that often produced dangerous and unconscionable delays in performing abortions.

In summary, future policies on abortion will synthesize elements from two opposing views. The cumbersome bureaucratic procedures that stem from a "justifications" approach will be shed and justifications will no longer be required for abortion. A "gestation time" approach will be increasingly emphasized and abortions will be prohibited after much earlier times in the gestation period.

References

Badgley Report. *Report of the Committee on the Operation of the Abortion Law* (Robin F. Badgley, Chairman). Ottawa: Minister of Supply and Services, 1977.

Benditt, John. "Second-Trimester Abortion in the United States." *Family Planning Perspectives* 11:358–361.

Bok, Sissela. "Ethical Problems of Abortion," in *Raising Children in Modern America*, edited by Nathan B. Talbot. Boston: Little, Brown, 1974.

Callahan, Daniel. *Abortion: Law, Choice and Morality*. London: Collier-Macmillan, 1970.

Cohen, Marshall, Thomas Nagel, and Thomas Scanlon, eds. *The Rights and Wrongs of Abortion*. Princeton: Princeton University Press.

de Valk, Alphonse. *Morality and Law in Canadian Politics: The Abortion Controversy*. Montreal: Palm Publishers, 1974.

Dellapenna, Joseph W. "The History of Abortion: Technology, Morality, and Law." *University of Pittsburgh Law Review* 40(1979):359–427.

Family Planning/Population Reporter. "Prosecution Fears Justify Physicians' Refusal to Perform Late Abortions." 4(1975):62.

Hare, R.M. "Abortion and the Golden Rule." *Philosophy and Public Affairs* 4(1975):201–22.

Humber, James M. and Robert F. Almeder, eds. *Biomedical Ethics and the Law*. New York: Plenum Press, 1976.

Kramer, Elmar J. and Edward A. Synan, eds. *Death Before Birth: Canada and the Abortion Question*. Toronto: Griffin, 1974.

Levene, Howard I. and Francis J. Rigney. "Law, Preventive Psychiatry, and

Therapeutic Abortion.'' *Journal of Nervous and Mental Disease* 151(1970):51–59.

Roe v. *Wade*, 410 U.S. 113 (1973).

Sarvis, Betty and Hyman Rodman. *The Abortion Controversy*, 2nd edition, New York: Columbia University Press, 1974.

Smith, Kenneth D. and Harris S. Wineberg. ''A Survey of Therapeutic Abortion Committees.'' *Criminal Law Quarterly* 12(1969/70):279–306.

Statistics Canada. *Therapeutic Abortions, Canada, 1977*. 1978.

Szasz, Thomas S. ''Bootlegging Humanistic Values Through Psychiatry.'' *Antioch Review* 22(1962):341–49.

Tunkel, Victor. ''Abortion: How Early, How Late, and How Legal?'' *British Medical Journal* 28(1979):253–56.

Watters, Wendell W. *Compulsory Parenthood: The Truth About Abortion.* Toronto: McClelland and Stewart, 1976.

Wolfenden Report. *Report of the Committee on Homosexual Offences and Prostitution* (Sir John Wolfenden, Chairman). London: Her Majesty's Stationery Office, 1957.